Terrorism Resistance & Islam

(A Study of 7/7 London Bombings)

Terrorism Resistance & Islam

(A Study of 7/7 London Bombings)

Dr. Obaidullah Fahad
Department of Islamic Studies,
Aligarh Muslim University, Aligarh,
India.

SERIALS PUBLICATIONS
NEW DELHI (INDIA)

First Published - 2007

ISBN: 978-81-8387-119-8

Published by

SERIALS PUBLICATIONS
4830/24, Ansari Road, Darya Ganj
New Delhi-110002 (India)
Phone : 91-11-23245225
Fax : 91-11-23272135
E-mail : serials@satyam.net.in,
serialspublications@vsnl.net
Web : www.seriealspub.com

N. Ram
Editor-in-Chief, *The Hindu*

CONTENTS

Acknowledgements i-ii
Table of Contents iii-v

CHAPTER 1
7/7 London Blasts and the After **1-36**
- The Mayor Reacted 2
- World Leaders Condemned 4
- The Arab Leaders Denounced 5
- Battle to win Muslim Hearts 8
- British Muslims Criticised 9
- Backlash against Muslims 11
- Links with Cairo 12
- Pakistan's Involvement 13
- Menezes Shot Dead 16
- Blaming Blair Policies 18
- Jihad against Extremism 19
- July 21 The Motivated 22
- Poisoning Young Minds 24
- Contradictions about 7/21 25
- Bomber Was Brainwashed 32
- Tough Stand against Terrorism 33

CHAPTER 2
Western and American Response **37-86**
- Seumas Milne 37
- Robin Cook 39
- Madeleine Bunting 42
- William Dalrymple 43
- Richard Norton Taylor 47
- Sidney Blumenthal 49
- Adam Crutis 51
- The Americans 54
- Don Van Natta Jr. 56
- Gary Younge 58
- Jonathan Glover 61
- Ian Henshall 64
- Steve Watson 66

- Paul Joseph Watson 69
- Charley Reese 72
- William Blum 74
- Thomas Friedman 77

CHAPTER 3

Indian Reaction **87-128**

- Globalising Democracy 88
- Colour of Terror 91
- Enemy from Within 93
- Fighting through Surrogates 95
- Sustained Insurgency 97
- Imaginary Homelands 99
- Continental Drift 101
- No Double Standards 105
- Coinciding with G-8 Summit 110
- Sweeping Judgements about Islam 111
- Lexicon of Terror 113
- Pakistan – A Repeat of the Post – 9/11 115
- Al-Qaeda or Al-Fāyda 117
- Justice Not more Terror 120

CHAPTER 4

Muslim Apologists **129-161**

- Join the Mainstream 129
- The Price of Occupation 131
- Terror Links 132
- Bombs with Lessons 133
- Can Islam Change? 138
- Fatwa on Fanatics 143
- Terror Roots in Islam 145
- Defining a Moderate Muslim 149
- Muslims Need a Gandhi 152

CHAPTER 5

Islamists' Arguments **162-209**

- Barbaric but not Unexpected 162
- Wahhabism-Synonymous with all Evil? 165
- Struggle for Survival 172
- New McCarthyism 175

- Facing Islamophobic Witch Hunt 180
- Terrorism is Double-Edged 185
- Weaving Terror 189
- Occupational Terror 191
- Why WOT Counter-Productive? 197
- The Present-day Crusaders 200

CHAPTER 6
Islamic Justifications Examined **210-247**

- Official Otherworldliness 210
- The Only Method Survived 212
- Sacrificing One for the Faith 216
- Qaradhawi Cites the Exegesists 218
- The Classical Stand 223
- Deterrence Theory 226
- Ghazwa's Call for Jihad 238
- Jihadist Islamic History 231
- A Shia Legacy 236

CHAPTER 7
Ressistance Vs. Terrorism **248-287**

- Godfather of Resistance 248
- Modern Jāhiliyah 252
- Americanised Islam 255
- Islamic Vanguard 258
- No Forced Islamization 260
- How to Establish the Religion 262
- Islamism Not Terrorism 264
- Voice of Resistance and Liberation 265
- Yousuf al-Qaradhawi 267
- Religious Extremism 268
- Flexible Fatāwa 275
- Lawfulness of Singing and Music 277
- Moderate Islamic Culture 278
- No Violent Jihad 280

Glossary **288-299**
Index **300-315**

*****

1

7/7 BLASTS AND THE AFTER

Britain was in a state of shock on July 7, 2005 after a series of blasts ripped through London's underground train network, claiming the fifty five lives and causing mayhem in a city which only hours before witnessed scenes of jubilation after winning the bid to host the 2012 Olympics.

In what was described as the "stuff of night-mare, atleast seven explosions took place within the space of less than an hour, triggering panic as thousands of shocked commuters – many bleeding, their faces covered with soot-streamed out of tube stations.

The first blast was reported shortly before 9 a.m. at Aldgate station in East London. Within minutes, another explosion took place at Liverpool Street station in the heart of London's business centre followed by blasts at Edgware, King's cross, Old Street and Russell Square stations.

The another incident at Tavistock Square, a device exploded in a double-decker tourist bus, ripping off its roof. One eye witness said the bus was "ripped open like a car of sardines and bodies were everywhere".

By mid-morning the entire public transport system was shut down and the police advised people to stay where they were and remain calm. London remained without trains and buses throughout the day, leaving people stranded across the city and at airports, adding to the sense of panic and confusion.

Prime Minister Tony Blair, who was chairing a summit of world leaders in Gleneagles, Scotland, rushed to London to review the situation even as the summit continued. In a TV address, a visibly shaken Mr. Blair said it was "reasonably clear" 'that the explosions were a 'terrorists attack ... designed and meant to coincide with G8" summit. He said terrorists would not be able to destroy "our values and our way of life". "Whatever they do, it is our determination that they will never succeed in destroying what we hold clear in this country and in other civilized nations throughout the world", he said and that each of the leaders at the summit had "some experience of the effects of terrorism and all the leaders... share our complete resolution to defeat this terrorism".[1].

The Mayor reacted

I don't think now is the time for me to say anything about today's events. And, possibly, I may not ever say anything in this blog (and the one thing I am sure of is that it matters very little what I say here). But, from here is what Ken Livingstone, the Mayor of London, had to say:[2]

This was a cowardly attack, which has resulted in injury and loss of life. Our thoughts are with everyone who has been injured, or lost loved ones. I want to thank the emergency services for the way hey have responded.

Following the *Al-Qaeda* attacks on September 11th in America we conducted a series of exercises in London in order to be prepared for just such an attack. One of the exercises undertaken by the government, my office and the emergency and security services was based on the possibility of multiple explosions on the transport system during the Friday rush hour. The plan that came out of that exercise is being executed today, with remarkable efficiency and courage, and I praise those staff who are involved.

I'd like to thank Londoners for the calm way in which they have responded to this cowardly attack and echo the advice of the Metropolitan Police Commissioner Sir Ian Blair – do everything possible to assist the police and take the advice of the police about getting home today.

I have no doubt whatsoever that this is a terrorist attack. We did hope in the first few minutes after hearing about the events on the underground that it might simply be a maintenance tragedy. That was not the case. I have been able to stay in touch through the very excellent communications that were established for the eventuality that I might be out of the city at the time of a terrorist attack and they have worked with remarkable effectiveness. I will be in continual contact until I am back in London.

I want to say one thing specifically to the world today. This was not a terrorist attack against the mighty and the powerful. It was not aimed at Presidents or Prime Ministers. It was aimed at ordinary, working-class Londoners, black and white, Muslim and Christian, Hindu and Jew, young and old. It was an indiscriminate attempt to slaughter, irrespective of any considerations for age, for class, for religion, or whatever.

That isn't an ideology, it isn't even a perverted faith – it is just an indiscriminate attempt at mass-murder and we know what the objective is. They seek to divide Londoners. They seek to turn Londoners against each other. I said yesterday to the International Olympic Committee, that the city of London is the greatest in the world, because everybody lives side by side in harmony. Londoners will not be divided by this cowardly attack. They will stand together in solidarity alongside those who have been injured and those who have been bereaved and that is why I'm proud to be the mayor of that city.

Finally, I wish to speak directly to those who came to London today to take life.

I know that you personally do not fear giving up your own life in order to take others – that is why you are so dangerous. But I know you fear that you may fail in your long-term objective to destroy our free society and I can show you why you will fail.

In the days that follow look at our airports, look at our sea ports and look at our railway stations and, even after your cowardly attack, you will see that people from the rest of Britain, people from around the world will arrive in London to become Londoners and to fulfil their dreams and achieve their potential.

They choose to come to London, as so many have come before because they come to be free, they come to live the life they choose, they come to be able to be themselves. They flee you because you tell them how they should live. They don't want that and nothing you do, however many of us you kill, will stop that flight to our city where freedom is strong and where people can live in harmony with one another. Whatever you do, however many you kill, you will fail.

And I think that is more than sufficient, for now.

World Leaders Condemned

The world's most powerful leaders assembled in Gleneagles united on the same day Thursday to condemn the wave of bombings in London, saying they would not bow to terrorists – but the attacks clearly side tracked the ambitious Group Eight Summit agenda for easing poverty in Africa and lacking climate change. Britain Prime Minister, summit host, insisted talks would continue despite what he described as "barbaric attacks". Nevertheless he left Gleneagles resort by helicopter for London to be briefed by police chiefs and government officials – and eagerly awaited declarations on climate change and the global economy were postponed until the next day.

The leaders in a show of solidarity, stood shoulder-to-shoulder with Mr. Blair as he read a joint statement from the G-8 summit. They were joined by U.N. Secretary General Kofi Annan, European Commission President Jose – Manuel Barroso and the leaders of Mexico, Indian, China, South Africa and Brazil. "The terrorists will not succeed," Mr. Blair said. "Today's bombings will not weaken in any way our resolve to uphold the most deeply held principles of our societies and to defeat those who would impose their fanaticism and extremism on all of us. We shall prevail, and they shall not".

U.S. President George W. Bush said "the war on terror goes on". German Chancellor Gerhard Schroeder condemned the "perfidious attacks" and stressed the importance of fighting terrorism "with all the means at our disposal". French President Jacques Chirac said "the great nations of the world" must unite to fight terrorism. "All of our countries have suffered from the impact of terrorism", a G-8 statement said. "Those responsible have no respect for human life. We are united in our resolve to confront and defeat this terrorism that is not an attack on one nation but on all nations and on civilized people every where."

Mr. Blair said earlier that it was "reasonably clear" that the attacks were "designed and aimed to coincide" with the G-8 meeting. "It is particularly barbaric that this has happened on a day when people are meeting to Jack Straw chairing the talks in Mr. Blair absence, British officials said. "We will not allow violence to change our societies or our values, nor will we allow it to stop the work of this summit. We will continue our deliberations in the interests of a better world. Here at this summit, the leaders are striving to combat poverty and improve human life. The perpetrators of today's attacks are intent on destroying human life." Mr. Blair said.[3]

The Arab Leaders Denounced

The Arab leaders[4] deplored the series of explosions which targeted London on Thursday, stressing the rejection of the Arab states for such aggressions and voiced solidarity with Britain in its crisis.

The Syrian President Bashar al-Asad extended a cable of "condemnation and denunciation" to the British Prime Minister in which he said "In my own name and the name of the Syrian people we condemn and strongly deplore these hated acts."

The Moroccan King stressed "that terrorism which does not know a religion not a homeland aims at violating human rights and the right to live".

The secretary general of the Arab League (AL) Amr Moussa announced "AL rejection of these acts taking place in London or in any European or Arab Capital or in any place in the world".

The Egyptian Foreign Minister Ahmad Abu al-Ghait expressed in a telephone call with the British ambassador in Cairo "Egypt's solidarity with Britain in its crisis".

An official source in Saudi Arabia stressed Riyadh's position "on the importance of the international community intensification of the efforts to fight terrorism, which threatens our security and the security of all our people and that of the world as a whole".

The Secretary General of the Gulf Cooperation Council GCC Abdul Rahman bin Hamad al-Ateyah stressed the "rejection of the GCC to terrorism regardless to its source," calling for "fighting it in all its forms and pictures".

The Iraqi President Jalal al-Talibani considered that "terrorism is an international crisis, showing that what is taking place in Iraq might also happen in any other country." He warned "I am saying it to our Arab brothers, should terrorism take place in Iraq today, then it will be tomorrow in other Arab countries."

The Minister of State for Foreign Affairs in the United Arab Emirates Sheikh Hamdan Bin Zayed al-Nahyan expressed UAE solidarity with the British Government and its support for measures taken to withstand them".

The Jordanian King Abdullah II underlined the "importance of intensifying efforts of all sides concerned to fight all form of terrorism and forces standing behind it."

The Libyan Foreign Ministry stressed cooperation with all countries in "fighting terrorism so as this epidemic which threatens world peace and security will be eliminated".

Chief Palestinian negotiator Saeb Oreikat said "we strongly condemn these aggressions and offer our condolences to the British government and people, hoping quick recovery for the wounded".

Meantime, the Deputy Chairman of the Political Bureau of the Hamas Movement Mousa Abu Marzouq considered that targeting of civilians in their transportation means "is a rejected matter and should be deplored". One official source at the Yemeni Foreign Ministry considered "criminal acts once again disclosed the ugly face of terrorism which pursues a policy rejected by all divine and humanitarian principles".

Egyptian citizen being interrogated about London explosions.[5]

An Egyptian report said that an official Egyptian Ministry of Interior source stated today that in regards to an alleged connection of an Egyptian citizen to the bombings that had taken place in London.

The aforementioned Egyptian citizen was arrested and is a resident of Egypt in the Basateen area (Cairo) with his family. He holds a Bachelors of Science degree from the University of Cairo (1994) and is currently employed at the National Center for Research. He travelled to the United Kingdom to study at the University of Leeds setting there from year 2000 to the present and earned a Doctorate degree earlier this year. He departed from the UK for a month and half study break and plans to return to Britain to continue his studies. He denied any connection to the aforementioned occurrences in London and noted that all his personal property was still in his apartment in Britain. Questioning of the aforementioned individual continues.

Al-Azhar Grand Imam regrets linking *jihad* to terrorism.[6]

The Grand Imam of Al-Azhar Mohamad Sayyed Tantawi affirmed that peace was one of Islam's principles, pointing out that Islam considered any attack on a human being as an attack on all humanity.

The Grand Imam regretted attempts aiming at mixing *Jihad* with terrorism, saying that *Jihad* was enacted in Islam for self-defence and "helping" the wronged.

During a meeting on Wednesday with a US Church delegation, the Grand Imam condemned all forms of terrorism either against Muslims or non-Muslims.

On his part, Bishop Thomas Hewitt, the Head of the delegation expressed appreciation of Al-Azhar's role in presenting the true image of Islam.

He said that the National Council for Churches in the United States was working hard to achieve peace in the Middle East, especially between the Palestinians and Israel.

The Grand Imam of Al-Azhar Sheikh Mohamed Sayyed Tantawi on Tuesday denied foreign pressures while setting down curricula offered by the institutions of the world's highest religious Sunni authority.

At a meeting with an American delegation, Sheikh Tantawi said the syllabuses are laid down by he scholars of Al-Azhar with no influences whatsoever from inside or outside parties. He told the delegation, which included congressmen, of the difference between *Jihad* in Islam and terrorism.

Islam considers that attack on one person an aggression on the whole of humanity, as it is a religion reaching out to all those seeking peace, the Grand Imam of Al-Azhar added.

He noted that Azhar had led world religious institutions that condemned that September 11 attacks on Washington and New York.

Battle to Win Muslim Hearts

British Prime Minister on 09.07.2005 called for a "battle" to win the hearts and minds" of Muslims in the campaign against terrorism as Britain's top Muslims in a joint statement condemned last week's London bombings as "utterly criminal and absolutely un-Islamic". Denouncing terrorism as an "evil ideology", Mr. Blair said it had to be pulled up "by the roots" and dismissed suggestions that the July 7 attacks were a "revenge" for the British-US invasion of Iraq. "If it is Iraq that motivates them, why is the same ideology killing Iraqis by terror in defiance of an elected Iraqi government? Why, if it is the cause of Muslims that concerns them, do they kill so many with such callous indifference?" He said speaking at Labour Party's National Policy Forum. He said the battle against terrorism meant "confronting" the fanatics "head on". "It is a battle of ideas and hearts and minds both within Islam and outside it... A battle not just about terrorist methods, but their views... It can not be beaten, in my view, except by confronting its symptoms and causes, head on," he said adding: "we must pull this up by the roots. Within Britain we must join up our, with our Muslim community to take on the extremists. Worldwide we should confront it everywhere it exists."[7]

After the July 7 carnage, it was amazing to experience with no such organized backlash in London as was witnessed in Britain against the Muslim community after 9/11, 2001. In a large measure, this was because Britain's Muslim community has learnt a few lessons in the past four years. This is not to ignore the incidents of intimidation and stone-throwing or deny that a climate of fear existed. Worshippers at a north London mosque were reportedly abused by passers by as news of the blasts spread, and the Muslim Council of Britain reported receiving some 30,000 abusive and threatening e-mail within hours of the explosions. There have also been reports of incidents at mosque outside London, and mysterious fire broke out at *gurduwara* in Kent after being apparently mistaken for a place of Muslim worship. But this was minor stuff, isolated acts of individual fanatics.

British Muslims Criticised

It is significant how quickly and sharply Muslim leaders and ordinary Muslims reacted to the July 7 attacks. Within hours they were on television looking reactionary and sounding angry at what had happened. Statements from Muslim organizations started pouring into newspaper offices offering help in tracking down those behind the bombings. Refreshingly there was no reference to any Muslim-related issue in any of the reactions and the revulsion seemed genuinely felt and expressed. As *The Guardian* noted even in places like Luton, regarded as a hot-bed of Islamic extremism, the anger was palpable – and denunciation unambiguous. In a sign of how much the mood was changed, activists of the radical *Hizb al-Tahrir* group were seen handing out leaflets outside a mosque declaring that Islam did "not allow the harming of innocent civilians".

Not only have leading Muslim scholars and religious figures made common cause with other faith communities in denouncing terrorists, some *fatwas* were issued, against those who kill the ordinary citizens in the name of Islam.[8]

On July 9, 2005 the British Security Forces warned that the terrorists behind Thursday's (July, 7) serial bomb blasts in London could strike again as they were still at large. The British police still had no idea who the perpetrators might have been, though suspicion continued to be centred around a group or groups with links to *Al-Qaeda*, especially after another extremist website on Saturday claimed that terrorists of the outfit carried out the bombings.

The claim was made in a statement pasted in the name of European division of *Al-Qaeda's Abu Hafs al-Masri Brigades*. "A group of *Mujahidin* from a division of the *Abu Hafs al-Masri Brigades* piled blow after blow on the infidel capital, the British capital, leaving dead and injured" it said. As London started returning to a semblance of normality, the police warned that the threat persisted. Security sources were quoted as saying that the people responsible for the atrocity were "still out there, and could do it again".

A key line of police inquiry focussed on the possibility that terrorists behind bombings might have been "home-grown" British citizens radicalized by religious extremists in the wake of Afghanistan and Iraq wars. Prime Minister Tony Blair said no amount of security was a guarantee against a terrorist attack. "Probably with this type of terrorism the solution can not only be the security measures... If people are actually prepared to go on to the Tube or a bus and blow up wholly innocent people... you can have all the surveillance in the world and you could not stop that happening", he told the BBC. He praised the "great inner resilience" of Londoners and said their response to the tragedy was "extraordinary". He welcomed the strong condemnation of the attacks by Britain's Muslim community. He said the important thing was to "pull together and to make sure that people can not divide us".[9]

Backlash against Muslims

On the very next day to London bombings, the first indications of a possible backlash against British Muslims came on Friday with reports of suspicious fires at a mosque in the city of Leeds and a Sikh Temple in the country of Kent, south-east of London, as police confirmed that tension around the country was increasing. Meetings were being held across Britain as the authorities and communities moved to limit any backlash. Police said about 70 incidents against minorities had been recorded. They ranged from the suspicious fires to two possible assaults, verbal abuse and threatening calls. Community tensions were discussed on Friday at the Cobra meeting, the Government's Crisis Command group. Imams used Friday sermons to condemn the bombings and to tell Muslims they "have no reason to feel shamed" and should go about their daily lives. Home Secretary Charles Clarke after meeting faith leaders including Sir Iqbal Sacraine of the Muslim Council of Britain (MCB) said, there were only "very, very minor" indications of a backlash.

A wave of shock, anxiety and embarrassment swept through Britain's Asian Muslim Community on 13.07.2005 after the police announced three of the four alleged "suicide bombers" were young men of Pakistani origin, all born and brought up in Britain. They were identified as Shehzad Tanweer (22), Hasib Husain (19) and Mohammad Siddique Khan (30) – sons of respectable and hard-working immigrant families from Pakistan settled in the predominantly Asian area of Leeds in West Yorkshire. The identity of fourth man has also been established but details are not immediately known except that he too belonged to Leeds. Police were reported to be looking for a fifth man. The four allegedly blew themselves up while carrying out what the police called Western Europe's first terrorist attack involving a British "suicide" squad. They were described as "clean skins" – men who do not appear on the "security radar" because they had no previous record of having been involved in any terrorist activity.

Prime Minister Tony Blair said there would be "a sense of profound shock and anxiety" that the suspected terrorists were British. He called for efforts to "mobilise the moderate and true voice of Islam". He met Muslim MPs to discuss ways to tackle "this evil within the Muslim community", the vast majority of which, he said, was law-abiding and peaceful. Amid fears of an anti-Muslim backlash, leaders from across the political divide appealed for peace and sought to unite behind the message that what happened last week was the work of "evil men", motivated by what Mr. Blair described as a "perverted" reading of Islam. A prominent Labour M.P., Shahid Malik urged the Muslim community to play its "role" in combating terrorism. He said the situation represented the 'most profound challenge yet faced by the Muslim community" – a view echoed by Muslim leaders.[10]

The fourth alleged suspect was also identified as a Briton of Jamaican origin who converted to Islam, but police were still looking for a man who, they believed, masterminded the London attacks. Media reports speculated that he was "understood" to have flown out London on the eve of the bombings. The BBC claimed that a suspected *Al-Qaeda* member entered Britain two weeks before the attacks but was not kept under watch by intelligence agencies even though he was on a security watch list. It said he was not considered high enough on the list to "merit surveillance". It was not clear whether he was the same man as mentioned in other media reports or some one else.

Meanwhile the fourth alleged suicide bomber was variously described as Lindsey Germail or Jamal, because of confusion over his surname after his conversion to Islam. He was believed to be in his twenties and married to a white woman who also converted to Islam. Jamal lived with his wife and a child in a quiet suburb of Buckinghamshire, far removed from the Leeds area of Yorkshire, which had been home to the other three alleged suspects, all of Pakistani origin.[11]

Links with Cairo

It was claimed that the alleged maker of bombs in the July 7 London terror attacks was arrested in Cairo, and was being interrogated. ABC News reported on Friday July 15, 2005, citing sources including the FBI. "ABC News has exclusive information that the worldwide manhunt for the man that police think has built those bombs has … been caught in Cairo and is being interrogated right now", ABC television said. "The FBI in North Carolina joined the search" it said. "Authorities in Egypt tell ABC News he was tracked down and taken into custody overnight in suburban Cairo. British authorities had initiated a worldwide manhunt for 33-year-old Magdy Elnashar, who left England two weeks before the bombings. The police said it was he who helped the bombers set up their bomb factory". While the man under custody claimed he was innocent, an official at Egypt's Interior Ministry said on Friday.

"He has denied any involvement in the London bombings", said a statement from the official, referring to Magdy Elnashar (33). Mr. Elnashar "is being investigated to find out whether he was involved in the bombings", said the source. "He said he had gone to Britain to study at Leeds University and has resided in Britain since 2000 until now to obtain his doctorate, which he did earlier this year. "He said he had come back to Egypt for a month and a half holiday and was planning to go back to Britain to resume his studies and that all his belongings are still in his flat in Leeds", the source said, adding that "the investigation would go on." British police said they were "aware" of an arrest in Egypt in connection with the investigation into last week's London bombings. "We are aware of an arrest made in Cairo but are not prepared to discuss if we may or may not wish to interview (the person) in connection with this investigation", a spokesman for London police said.

Pakistan's Involvement

Pakistan President Gen. Parvez Musharraf on the same day (July 15, 2005) was very quick to launch a new campaign against extremism in his country following the London attacks whose perpetrators included three ethnic Pakistani Britons. The President told an unprecedented gathering of some 200 senior police officers from all over Pakistan that they must remove hate material including booklets, pamphlets and computer disks from local markets. "You must ensure that this material is not available in the markets, at the latest by December this year", he said, according to an official statement. He also asked the police to crack down on militant outfits which were trying to resurface under new names after he banned most of them since the September 11, 2001 attacks on the United States. The new measures should not be seen as anti-religion but were meant to curb the 'extremist minority' harming Pakistan's interest and tarnishing the image of Islam, he said. Thursday's bombings in London have thrown the terror spotlight back on Pakistan, where Islamist militants continue to thrive despite a crack down on Osama bin Laden's *Al-Qaeda* network.

According to AFP, PTI Pakistan was the principal backer of the hardline Taliban movement, which ruled Afghanistan from 1994 until their ouster by US-led forces in late 2001 for harbouring *Al-Qaeda.* Pakistan, a key US ally in the war on terror, arrested around 700 *Al-Qaeda* militants and handed over some key figures. As the probe into the London bombings pointed to the involvement of Pakistani origin, Gen. Musharraf assured British Prime Minister of his country's full cooperation in the investigation. Gen. Musharraf who spoke to Mr. Blair over phone on Thursday night, offered Pakistan's support and assistance in the investigation of the terrorist acts, an official release from Islamabad said. The Pakistani leader also expressed shock and condolences on behalf of the people and the Government of Pakistan over the bombings. Mr. Blair thanked the President for his unequivocal support. He appreciated the crucial role Islamabad played in the international fight against terror.[12]

On July 22, 2005 Muttahidah Majlis-e-Amal (MMA), the alliance of six religious parties of Pakistan observed a protest day against the alleged indiscriminate raids on Islamic seminaries as part of the campaign on crackdown of hardliners. The protest day, held a day after Musharraf's address to the people, evoked a low-key response in most parts of the country. The MMA usually chooses Friday for its protests and mobilisation programmes. Observers see it as a tactic that makes it easy for the religious parties to reach out to people who gather for the weekly prayers. In his speech on Thursday night Gen. Musharraf prescribed hate sermons from mosques and warned of stringent action against those violating it. The MMA leaders alleged that Gen. Musharraf resumed the crackdown on seminaries and arrests of Islamic scholars and students in order to please Washington and London. They claimed that the latest crackdown being launched under the special directives of British Prime Minister, who at a press conference along with Afghan President Hamid Karzai, asked Gen. Musharaf to take strict action against seminaries, accusing them of promoting sectarianism and extremism. The MMA leaders accused Gen. Musharraf of putting the whole nation and country at stake only to save his rule.

Meanwhile, security forces arrested nearly 100 more suspected Muslim militants overnight. "During raids overnight in all the four provinces of Pakistan, around 90 more suspected militants were rounded up and the number of people in preventive detention was more than 300 now" said an Interior Ministry official monitoring the campaign.

Raids targeted shops selling "hate material" in print, audio and video form, and both police and intelligence services were instructed to arrest anyone inciting violence during sermons at Friday prayers, the official said. "It is the firm resolve of the Government and we will not spare anyone found to be breaching the law," he said. In his national address, Gen. Musharraf, who had been waging an often unpopular campaign against extremists and had survived atleast two assassination attempts by suspected extremists, said there could be no letup on terrorism. He appealed to moderates to pray for "Pakistan's deliverance from the menace of extremism" and said his nation would stand together with Britain "to the end, until we emerge victorious". He named two groups, the *Hizbul Tahreer* and *Al-Muhajiroon*, which he said were responsible for spreading a message of hate and violence. Pakistan has also arrested over 700 suspects linked to *Al-Qaeda* sicne the September 11 attacks including the group's number three Khalid Sheikh Mohammad.[13]

Menezes shot dead

On another dramatic day in London, police shot dead a suspected suicide bomber on July 22, 2005 as he tried to board a train in Stockwell Underground Station near Oval in South London – the scene of one of the four explosions which rocked the city less than 24 hours before. This man was later on identified as a 27-year-old unmarried electrician from Brazil, Jean Charles de Menezes who had been living and working there for upto four years. He was on his way to work when three undercover policemen started following him from the moment he left his home in Tulse Hill, South London which had been under surveillance after July 7 bombings. At Stockwell tube station, hey said they "challenged" him but when he did not respond they chased and killed him before he could get on to a waiting train – pumping at least five bullets him.

Police would have known immediately that they have killed an innocent man but it took them more than 24 hours to publicly acknowledge it – and more to give out his name and nationality. The Brazilian Foreign Minister said it was "shocked and perplexed" and wanted the British Government to explain the circumstances that "led to this tragedy". In a statement it said Brazilian Foreign Minister Celso Amorin expected on a visit to London for a conference, would seek "clarifications" from British Foreign Secretary Jack Straw.

Sir Ian Blair, Chief of Metropolitan Police, after insisting that the victim was "directly linked" to Thursday's incident, apologised to the victim's family who expressed their anger and disbelief saying that there was "no reason to think that he was a terrorist."

There had been widespread condemnation of the police action and Sir Ian was under pressure to review tactics which human rights groups said amounted to a "shoot to kill" policy. There were also calls for a public inquiry into the murder amid fears that such incidents could undermine police efforts to public cooperation in fighting terror. Alex Alves Pereira, a cousin of Menezes who lived in London and identified his body, said he could not believe that "they shot him because he was not a terrorist". "He was an honest man... I am sure he did not do anything wrong. It was not right for the police to do it" he said. He denied that the reason why Menezes did not stop when "challenged" by the police was because he had something to hide. He was obviously sacred and that's why he ran. It's normal for someone to run when they are being chased," Mr. Pereira said. Family members of the victim, who came from a small town, north of the Brazilian capital Rio de Janeiro, scotched speculation that he had illegal immigrant and that is why he might have panicked when stopped by the police. "He spoke English very well and was legal. He had permission to study and work in Britain", one family member said.[14]

A news report published in *Guardian* on July 24, 2005 discovered that links had been uncovered between the two teams of bombers who brought terror to the streets of London over the past two week's, said security sources. Police now believed that some of the men they were pursuing for last week's abortive attacks – on Shepherd's Bush, Oval and Warren Street underground stations and a No. 26 bus in Hackney – attended a whitewater rafting trip at the same centre as two of the 7 July bombers Mohammad Siddique Khan and Shehzad Tanweer.

The news raised the distinct possibility that the two operations were connected as part of a larger plan to bring carnage to the capital. Evidence discovered in the rucksacks left behind by the failed bombers led police to three addresses in London. When investigators cross-referenced them with the electoral register they discovered names that tallied with individuals who had attended the outdoor adventure course in Snowdonia last summer.

Scotland Yard had already confirmed that the explosive used in the 21 July bombings bore a similarity to that used in the earlier attacks. Investigators were examining the possibility that the trip to Bala in North Wales was used a bombing experience for the cell. The Bala centre is one of the Britain's most popular canoeing and rafting centres, attracting 80,000 visitors a year. One line of inquiry being pursued was whether a cleric was responsible for organizing the trip to bring the two cells together. Armed police stormed an address in Scotia Road, Tulse Hill, South of Stockwell, on Saturday afternoon. It was thought that they were looking for the man seen running away from Oval station in a distinctive "New York" top. The house had been under surveillance since last Thursday and the man shot on Stockwell station on Friday morning was believed to have left the same premises. In a separate development, police were investigating an East African link to last week bombers. Scientists were also examining the explosives connected to both attacks to try to establish if there was a strong forensic link between the cells.[15]

Blaming Blair Policies

Relations between Britain and Pakistan in the aftermath of the London bombings were put to the test on July 17, 2005 when one of Islamabad's most senior diplomats advised against trying to shift responsibility to his country, and blamed British Prime Minister Tony Blair's policies in West Asia. As investigations intensified into possible links between the British bombers and extremists in Pakistan, its UN ambassador, Munir Akram, insisted that the London bombings were a British internal problem. As well as blaming Mr. Blair's foreign policy, he also cited a failure by British society to integrate its Muslims. He said: "It is important not to pin blame on somebody else when the problem lies internally. Your policies in the Middle East, your policies in the Islamic World, that is the problem with your society and that is where the problem lies as far as this incident is concerned. It would be a grave mistake to point fingers at Pakistan or anybody outside your country".

Such outspokenness is unusual in diplomatic circles, particularly at such a sensitive time. Mr. Akram's comments came as British and Pakistan investigators were examining a possible role played in the bombings by Osama Nazir, a top Pakistani militant leader with alleged links to *Al-Qaeda*, who is being held over attacks in Pakistan. Reports claim that he admitted from jail to having met with Shehzad Tanweer. One source close to the investigation also said that calls placed by Tanweer from his Leeds home appeared to lead to *Muridke*, a *madrasah* near Lahore, which Tanweer might have visited during the Pakistan trips. Although British authorities were making much of the visits by the bombers to Pakistan, the Pakistan Government and security services were playing down the significance of the short time they spent there.

In an interview on the *BBC's The World This Weekend*, Mr. Akram said: "Brain-washing is a long process. You can not brain-wash somebody instantly, unless he is inclined to be brain washed. Rather, it was the years spent in Britain that transformed them into the UK's first suicide bombers. It is not because their blood was from Pakistan. Whatever anger they had was a result of living in Britain". He said: "You have to look at ... what you are doing to the Muslim community and why the Muslim community is not integrating in British society". Hilary Benn, the British International Development Secretary, rejected the idea that all of the bombers had not been integrated into society. He pointed out that Mohammad Siddique Khan had been a popular teacher.[16]

Jihad against Extremism

Addressing the National Youth Convention at Islamabad on July 18, 2005 Pakistan President appealed to the youth to launch a *Jihad* against extremism for peace, brotherhood and unity in society. "I appeal to you to stand up and launch a *jihad* against extremism for peace, brotherhood and unity in the society and for knowledge, progress and poverty alleviation. You should discard those who can not deliver on these objectives." Describing extremism as the main hurdle in the way of Pakistan's "fast paced" development, he urged the youth to launch a movement against ignorance, parochialism, and intolerance to achieve poverty reduction and progress for all. "The entire nation has to reject extremism particularly the youth, who are the future leaders, should stand up against the malaise and support the Government's campaign in ridding the society of the malaise. Therefore you should launch a movement, a *jihad* against it". He asked the youth to reject extremists, as the Pakistan was tolerant, progressive and moderate as envisioned by its founders, the Quaid-e-Azam and Allama Iqbal, Pakistan, he said, had to confront terrorism, religious and sectarian extremism and violence and therefore, the nation should reject proponents of retrogressive thinking.

"Pakistan undoubtedly is an ideological state and an Islamic republic where the overwhelming majority is Muslim but where the minorities also enjoy full rights. But we have to understand true values of Islam and clearly differentiate as to who wants to push us backward and those who want to steer us forward in the light of Islamic teachings, which clearly emphasise the importance of moderation, learning and tolerance" he clearly urged the message.

Gen. Musharraf urged the world to join hands in addressing the state of mind called "*Al-Qaeda* phenomenon" through just resolution of the underlying causes of terror-political disputes. Asserting there was no network of *Al-Qaeda* in Pakistan, he told a news conference in Lahore that the "*Al-Qaeda* phenomenon" meant an individual who has followers and carries out violent action claiming that he is a member of *Al-Qaeda* or is a branch of *Al-Qaeda*. The world must understand that this *Al-Qaeda* has become a phenomenon – it has no command structure originating from Pakistan and conveying messages to the whole world to do this act under total coordination of some commander. It is a phenomenon where everyone has started calling himself *Al-Qaeda*, whether he had done it in London or Sharm el-Shaikh. Now we have to deal with this phenomenon and phenomenon is a state of mind – it is in the mind of people – so to deal with the phenomenon you have to change the state of mind."

Gen. Musharraf said military action alone would not lead to ultimate success in the fight against terror as they only gain time for other instruments to be used to change this phenomenon. "The other instrument is resolution of political disputes. I have been calling for this during the last few years – resolve political disputes because that leads a person to extreme acts since he is feeling deprived and hopeless," he said, addressing extremism in the long term also involved the issues of poverty and education. "It may be a long-term strategy but what I am saying is to kill this phenomenon, which is a state of mind, we act with the military to gain time by hitting and curbing terrorists and Pakistan will remain in the lead role. But to attack the phenomenon in the mind, the whole world has to act to resolve political disputes and social issues. The sooner it is understood, the better for the entire world", he said. He claimed that as a result of Pakistan's sustained and effective campaign against terrorism, *Al-Qaeda* is unable to operate from the country.[17]

Pakistan President then announced on July 29, 2005 that 1400-odd foreign students at the religious educational institutions (*madrasas*) in the country have been told to pack up and leave and insisted that unlike 2002, he was ready to "rock the boat" in his battle with extremists and fundamentalists. In an interaction with foreign correspondents on the challenges faced by Pakistan in tackling fundamentalism, Gen. Musharraf was at pains to emphasise that unlike 2002, today he was in total command of the situation in the country and the world has to take his latest crackdown on militancy seriously.

In his hour-long introductory remarks prior to the interaction, Gen. Musharraf said when he learnt that a record number of foreign correspondents were roaming in the streets of Islamabad to understand the phenomenon of extremism in the country, he decided to meet them in a bid to explain them the efforts by his Government to take on the fundamentalist forces. In response to specific questions on the difference between the crackdown he had ordered in 2002 and now. Gen. Musharraf said the world and media should not judge the performance of his Government through the eyes of the past. "Today it is a totally different environment", he equipped.

Elaborating on the point, Gen. Musharraf said three years ago, the economic situation of Pakistan was not stable. Besides, he did not enjoy the confidence of the world as a military ruler and his country was engaged in a 10-month military stand off with India "If I had operated strongly (against fundamentalists) the boat would have capsized". When a western journalist asked why he was not serious in his earlier attempt to curb militancy Gen. Musharraf retorted, "You have to be realistic and take cognisance of the ground situation. By taking stringent action against fundamentalists I would have risked the prospect of a million Talibans on the streets of Pakistan". He ticked off another journalist who wanted to know why he was not in favour of strengthening democratic institutions and democracy: "I think you are referring to my uniform that is the only issue. But two-thirds majority in Parliament has sanctioned it. If this is not democracy what else is it? You want me to dissolve the National and Provincial Assemblies. Is this your definition of democracy? Please understand that Pakistan has a certain environment and we have democracy."

The President said, in the next few days, he would promulgate an ordinance to regulate the functioning of the religious schools and it would be mandatory for them to register with the Government by December 31. "At the same time I urge you to be realistic. If 5000-odd seminaries refuse to register, I am not going to close them down. We would like to adopt a strategy for persuasion". He said the *Al-Qaeda* has become an "international phenomenon" and urged the world to join hands in addressing the state of mind called "*Al-Qaeda* phenomenon" through just resolution of underlying causes of terror – political disputes. Asserting there was no network of *Al-Qaeda* in Pakistan, he said "The world must understand that this *Al-Qaeda* has become a phenomenon – it has no command structure originating from Pakistan and conveying messages to the whole world to do this act and do that act under total coordination of some commander. It is a phenomenon where everyone has started calling himself *Al-Qaeda*, whether he has done it in London or *Sharm al-Shaikh*" he urged.[18]

July 21 the Motivated

The abortive bomb attacks in London on July 21, 2005 were a reaction to the Iraq war, had nothing to do with religion and were not meant to kill people, one of the suspects was reported to have claimed denying links with *Al-Qaeda* or with the July 7 attacks.

Osama Hussain (27), who was arrested in Rome on July 30 in connection with a failed attempt to trigger an explosive at Shepherd's Bush tube station, reportedly told an Italian court: "Religion had nothing to do with this. We watched films. We were shown videos with images of the war in Iraq. We were told we must do something big. That's why we met. I didn't want to kill, ours was supposed to be a demonstrative act. We didn't want to kill, only to spread terror."

La Republica newspaper quoted Hussain, also known as Issac Hamdi, as telling the court: "Rather than praying we discussed work, politics, the war in Iraq… we always had new films of the war in Iraq… those in which you could see Iraqi women and children who had been killed by US and UK soldiers". The court would decide whether he should be extradited to Britain to face trial as demanded by British authorities. His lawyer Antonietta Sonnessa said the client would fight extradition and the process could take months.

During the hearing Hussain reportedly said that after seeing the footage of the Iraq war, there was a "feeling of hatred and a conviction that it was necessary to give a signal – to do something." Denying accusations of alleged links with *Al-Qaeda*, the Ethiopian – born Briton reportedly said: "we never had contacts with the bin Laden organization, we knew that they existed. We had access to their platforms through the Internet, but nothing direct". He was among the four, police claimed, who were behind the July 21 bungled explosions in three underground stations in London and one on a bus. The other three were in police custody. Two were arrested in London on Friday July 30 and one in Birmingham earlier last week. A fifth man, not directly linked with the attacks, was also arrested on Friday. According to Italian news agency, ANSA, a man believed to be Hussain's brother was arrested in Brescia in northern Italy on Sunday. He was named as Fati Isaac.

According to PTI reports, Hussain claimed that the bombers were led by Mukhtar Said Ibrahim, the bus bomber, who was arrested in London on Friday. Milan's *Corriere della Sera* newspaper said Hussain first told authorities he did not know what was in the backpack he took on the London underground, then changed his version, saying he was told the attackers were only supposed to carry out "demonstrative" attacks. But the Rome daily II *Messaggero* said the suspect told investigators "we were supposed to blow ourselves up".

The revelations come as police in the UK began hunting an *Al-Qaeda* mastermind believed to be behind the recruitment and training of both sets of London bombers. The prospect of a UK mastermind controlling the cells raises fear that other units may be active in Britain. Despite the arrest of all five men wanted in connection with the failed attacks, the Metropolitan Police Commissioner, Sir Ian Blair warned on Saturday night of the risk of further bomb attacks. "Our boss taught us to make explosives out of fertilisers", Hussain is reported to have said, claiming the men put them into rucksacks and used timers.[19]

Poisoning young Minds

Muslim scholars started a tour of their communities in Britain to underline their unequivocal horror at suicide bombings and terror attacks. Using texts from both the Qur'ān and Islamic jurisprudence, they would speak in Bradford, Birmingham, Sheffield and London after an initial meeting in Leeds where three of the July 7 bombers lived. Seven lecturers were addressing open meetings in English, Arabic and Somali in a programme entitled 'Islam's war on Terror", backed by posters and leaflets which described suicide bombers as "perpetrators of evil". "We have been arguing this case for many years, with regard to such bombings overseas, including in Muslim countries such as Saudi Arabia and Egypt", said Asaf Choudhary, one of the organizers of the opening meeting in Leeds. "But now there is all the more need for the voice of truth to be heard".

More than 150 persons listened to 90 minutes of closely argued reasoning at the Pakistan community centre in Harehills, Leeds, where the attacks were condemned as contrary to every principle of Islam. Abu Khadeejah Abdul Wahid, a scholar from Birmingham, accused radical clerics such as Abu Hamza, former Imam of the Finsbury Park Mosque in London, of "poisoning young minds" with an entirely false version of the religion. He deplored the combination of human rights laws and constant media attention which gave exiled radicals in Britain a platform to "preach evil" for more than a decade and commit acts absolutely abhorrent to Islam such as circulating videos of terrorist beheadings and other atrocities. Twisting of the concept of *Jihad* had led to grandiose visions of "Islamic empires" and the right to kill so-called "apostates" (disloyal Muslims) which were nowhere supported in the Qur'ān. "I become a target. You become a target", he said. " The terrorists make no distinctions and are absolutely indiscriminate. It is the most disgraceful of crimes".

A simplistic anti-American feeling had also led people to claim sectarian terrorists in Iraq, or even Saddam Hussain, as Muslim or Arab heroes when they did nothing of the sort. He also called on Mosques and communities to address the problem of disaffected Muslim youth in Britain. He told the meeting: "They have a burden of personal baggage – confusion about their culture, identity and religion – and we must make it clear that we understand this and care about it. We must get out on to the streets and speak to them on their level. Because if we do not, Hamza and bin Laden will".

The meeting also discussed the issue of raising the level of understanding of Islam in British mosques and the effects of a lack of intellectual training – and also experience of the West – among some Imams recruited from overseas. Abu Khadeejah said that it was a cause for concern that of 105 mosques in Birmingham, only one conducts Friday sermons in English. "Our mosques should have more contact with all communities and that is handicap," he said. "There is a danger that we spend too much discussing foreign politics insteadc of addressing the problems of Muslims here." The message was well received but organizers who admitted that it was not a forum likely to attract disaffected youth. "There were very few here", said one, "and they left early".[20]

Contradictions about the 7/21 Incident

In the following pages the details about the second attack in London are provided in the form of the news items even on line. If a man goes through these clippings he would find so much conflicts and contradictions and would be doubtful about the authenticity and accuracy of these news. The full text may be read as follows:

London – This time, the real victim may have been Londoners' peace of mind.

The four nearly simultaneous attacks today on three subway trains and a double decker bus didn't kill anyone, and the only reported injury turned out to be an asthma attack.

But the attacks were hauntingly, unnervingly similar to deadly explosions set off by four suicide bombers exactly two weeks before – and an inescapable message that life in London now means living with the threat of terror.

"We can't minimize incidents such as this," Prime Minister Tony Blair said. "They're done to scare people, to frighten them and make them worried."

They did that.

Although the explosive devices were either faulty or too small to cause bloodshed, Thursday's lunch-hour blasts rattled a capital already on edge after the July 7 explosions, which killed 52 people and four suicide bombers.

Police said two men were arrested and were being questioned. One man was detained near Downing Street, site of the Prime Minister's residence; the other was picked up near Tottenham Court Road, close to the Warren Street subway station where one attack took place.

Authorities said it was too early to determine whether the attacks were carried out by the same organization as the July 7 blasts – or whether they were linked to *Al-Qaeda.*

"Clearly, the intention must have been to kill," Police Commissioner Ian Blair told reporters. "You don't do this with any other intention. And I think the important point is that the intention of the terrorists has not been fulfilled."

Londoners fled the three underground stations at midday, some sprinting barefoot after leaving their shoes behind in the scramble.

Witnesses on the underground heard a pop like a bursting champagne cork. Others smelled an odor like burning rubber. At least one reported a minor explosion in a man's backpack, and then the man muttering that something had gone wrong.

Bus passengers reported a bang on the upper level, where windows were blown out. But some witnesses said that blast wasn't loud. Witnesses first saw the police running up the road, followed soon after by news cameramen lugging tripods.

The Prime Minister appealed for calm, and a Buckingham Palace garden party for 8,000 people, hosted by Queen Elizabeth II, went ahead.

But even among the famously stoic British, nerves were on edge.

"when I got home, my hands were shaking," said 24-year-old Lisa Chilley, who uses the targeted Oval station. "I'm panicking like hell. It's just too close to home."

Firefighters and police with bomb-sniffing dogs sealed off city blocks and evacuated rows of restaurants, pubs and offices.

Britain's Press Association news agency reported detectives were working on the belief that the bombs were not properly primed – which could help explain the limited damage.

Although authorities did not say how many devices exploded, Paul Beaver, an independent defence expert, said an official told him it appeared that two bombs detonated and two others did not. Detonators are often faulty on commercial and military explosives, he said.

"These attacks don't look like they were a hallmark of any one group," Beaver said. "They don't fit into any clear patterns that we know of except they were timed."

One of the greatest police fears is that an audacious attack will inspire similar attacks, said Rachel Bronson, director of Middle East Studies at the New York-based Council on Foreign Relations. "It's all done to sow terror, and there's nothing more terrifying than bombs followed by bombs," she said.

Alarmingly, it appears the group was able to attack in the midst of an intense investigation of the previous bus and train bombings. Often such follow-up attacks are uncovered and thwarted, Bronson said.

"what is very worrisome, London intelligence, which is among the best in the world, was not only surprised two weeks ago, but they're surprised by this," she said.

Emergency teams were sent to the three Underground stations after the attacks, and the police commissioner said forensic evidence collected could provide a "significant break".

In one closely watched development, an armed police unit entered University College hospital shortly after the blasts. Sky News TV reported that police were searching for a man with a blue shirt with wires protruding from his pocket. Officers asked employees to look for a black or South Asian man about 6-foot-2.

By late today, the hospital said police had searched the facility but that three small rooms in an unoccupied part of the complex were cordoned off.

The attacks paralleled the July 7 blasts, which involved explosions at three Underground stations simultaneously starting at 8:50 a.m., followed about an hour later by a bomb going off on a bus. Those bombings took place in the center of London.

Today's attacks were more spread out and occurred during the lunch hour – beginning at about 12:38 p.m.

The bombs, which targeted trains near the Warren Street, Oval and Shepherd's Bush stations, did not shut down the subway system, only three of its lines. The bus was hit while on Hackney Road in East London.

With fear spreading to other capitals, New York City Mayor Michael Bloomberg said authorities would begin conducting randon searches of packages and backpacks carried by people entering the subway.

But Transport for London, which runs the British capital's bus and transport network, rejected such measures. Spokesman Steve Taylor said it would be impractical to check bags or install airport-style metal detectors and X-ray machines. London buses and subways carry 9 million passengers a day.

"We are running a massive transport infrastructure," he said. "Would people accept an additional 30 to 40 minutes on their journey every morning and afternoon? It would bring the network to a standstill."

Dozens of people living near the attacks were unable to return home by late this evening, and police set up reception areas to help them.

Panicked and screaming commuters fled the three affected Underground stations, sometimes leaving behind their shoes.

Stagecoach, the company which operates the stricken bus, said the driver heard a bang and went upstairs, where he found the windows blown out. The company said the bus was structurally intact and there were no injuries.

The incidents paralleled the July 7 blasts, which involved explosions at three Underground stations simultaneously starting at 8:51 a.m., followed quickly by a bomb going off on a bus. Those bombings, during the morning rush hour, also occurred in the center of London, hitting the Underground from various directions.

Thursday's incidents, however, were more spread out.

Emergency teams were sent to all three stations after the incidents, which began at 12:38 p.m.

"People were panicking. But very fortunately the train was only 15 seconds from the station," witness Ivan McCracken told Sky news.

McCracken said another passenger at Warren Street told him he saw a backpack explode. The July 7 bombs were carried in backpacks, police said.

McCracken said he smelled smoke, and people were panicking and coming into his carriage. He said he spoke to an Italian man who was comforting a woman after the evacuation.

"He said that a man was carrying a rucksack and the rucksack suddenly exploded. It was a minor explosion but enough to blow open the rucksack," McCracken said. "The man then made an exclamation as if something had gone wrong. At that point everyone rushed from the carriage."

Losiane Mohellavi, 35, who was evacuated at Warren Street, said, "I was in the carriage and we smelled smoke – it was like something was burning. Everyone was panicked and people were screaming. We had to pull the alarm. I am still shaking."

The explosions came as Pakistani intelligence officials said authorities are seeking the former aide of a radical cleric in Britain in connection with the July 7 bombings.

The officials said British investigators asked Pakistani authorities to search for Haroon Rashid Aswat, who reportedly had been in close contact with the suicide bombers just before the July 7 attacks.

Aswat, 31, was of Indian origin and may not be in Pakistan, according to two intelligence officials in Islamabad and one in Lahore, all speaking on condition of anonymity because they are not authorized to talk to the media and because of the sensitivity of the investigation.

Aswat reportedly was an associate of Abu Hamza al-Masri, the radical Imam who is awaiting trial in Britain on charges of incitement to murder. Al-Masri also is wanted in the United States on charges of trying to establish a terrorists training camp in Bly, Ore.; involvement in hostage-taking in Yemen; and funding terror training in Afghanistan.

Quoting unidentified intelligence sources, *The Times of London* said Aswat visited the hometowns of all four London bombers and selected their targets. It also reported there had been up to 20 phone calls between Aswat and two of the bombers in the days before the attacks.

Aswat's relatives in Batley, near the northern English town of Leeds, which was home to two of the July 7 suicide bombers, said they had not heard from him for many years.

"He has not lived at this house and we have no contact with him for many years," said his father, Rashid, who asked for his family to be left in peace. "There is no story that we can provide."

Authorities are investigating whether the London bombing suspects, three of whom were of Pakistani origin and travelled to Pakistan last year, received training or other assistance from militants in that country.

One of the July 7 bombers, Shehzad Tanweer, 22, is suspected of visiting a *madrasa* linked with militants in Lahore which has become a focus of the inquiry.

According to a report in a Pakistani newspaper, Tanweer revered Osama bin Laden. The English-language *Dawn* newspaper said Tanweer visited relatives in November in a farming village near Faisalabad in eastern Pakistan. During his weeks long stay, he was visited by another suicide bombing suspect, Mohammed Siddique Khan, 30, Tanweer's uncle told the newspaper.

Pakistan has pledged to curb religious extremism amid international concerns that Islamic schools, or *madrasas*, are promoting extremism.

Associated Press reporters Thin Lei Win and Kate Bouey in London and Christopher Torchia in Islamabad, Pakistan, contributed to this report.

According to The Associated Press reporter "A police officer rushes with cordon tape as cordons are setup around Shepherd's Bush underground station in London, following an incident at the station, London, Thursday July 21, 2005. Explosions struck London's transport system Thursday, shutting down three underground train stations and blowing out the windows of a double-decker bus, authorities said, two weeks after four deadly suicide bombings.[21]

Bomber was brain-washed

In an emotional outburst, the wife of one of the July 7 bombers said extremist elements, operating out of mosques, were responsible for "brainwashing" her husband and turning a "naïve and innocent" man into a terrorist. Germaine Lindsay, who blew himself up on a train near King's Cross station killing 26 persons, became a "changed person after he came under the influence of a group of people from mosques in Luton and London, his wife Samantha Lewthwaite said denouncing his actions as "totally abhorrent."

In an interview with *The Sun* Ms. Lewthwaite (21), who like her husband converted to Islam, said his life began to change in October-November last year after he got "involved in mosques" controlled by radical groups. "His behaviour gradually began to change. He turned from the man I married... He became a man I did not recognise. I have no doubt his mind was twisted in there" said the mother of a 15-day-old baby. She insisted that he was an "innocent, naïve and simple person" whose mind was "poisoned" by people he got to know in the mosques. The Jamaica-born Lindsay, who changed his name to Jamal after converting to Islam, was a "Peaceful man who loved people." "How these people could have turned him and poisoned his mind is dreadful," she said adding that she would have to tell her children "what he did."

Ms. Lewthwaite, who first met him during an anti-war rally in Hyde Park, said he wanted to become a human rights lawyer and make a difference to the world through peaceful means. They married in 2002. She was pregnant with a second child when he left on his suicide mission. Earlier, she had "ordered" him to leave the house because he had got into the habit of "vanishing" for days and she suspected that he was having an affair. "He left with a holdall and a bunch of door keys... He kissed our child goodbye and then crept off to blow up King's Cross" she said.[22]

Tough Stand against Terrorism

Mr. Tony Blair the Prime Minister before introducing some new legislative measures against terrorism in the parliament spoke about his plan. He declared that his proposals directed against terrorism and extremism only whatever form it takes, and whichever faith it claims. They were not aimed at decent law-abiding British Muslims – or Britons of any other faith. The full text of the speech is quoted here:

Britain is proud of its global and deserved reputation as a tolerant, multi-cultural society where people of all nationalities, backgrounds and faiths live in peace and friendship.

The unified and calm response of the British people to the terrorist attacks in London last month – in which the victims were of all faiths and none – underlined the tolerance and strength of our society. While there have been isolated and completely unacceptable acts of religious and racial hatred, the overwhelming response of our population was that these attacks were the work of a few fanatics, not of any section of our society. If a goal of these attacks was to turn our citizens against each other, they failed.

But there is also an almost universal agreement – among the two-million strong British Muslim community as much as any other group – that we can't continue to allow extremists to abuse our freedoms and the tolerance of our society to support encourage, condone or glorify terrorism. Indeed it is the Muslim community who understand more than most what a menace these fringe fanatics are to good relations and to cohesiveness of our country.

So we are bringing forward a package of measures aimed at closing the loopholes in our law which these extremists have been exploiting. But these are not crude measures. Part of our long-held and valued traditions of freedom and tolerance is a commitment by any government to consult widely across the breadth of society before bringing forward any new legislation.

I am determined to maintain these proud traditions – and the reputation which goes with them. None of the new measures will threaten these. But equally, the rules of the game have changed, and we need to respond. Young men, born in Britain, have been brainwashed by extremists to the point where they blow themselves up and murder innocent people.

The new measures I am proposing are directed against extremism and extremism only – whatever form it takes, and whichever faith it claims to represent. In some cases I suspect there will be surprise abroad that they are not already in place. So we will seek new powers to deport or exclude foreign nationals who foster hatred, advocate violence or justify such violence. This will include clerics associated with extremism.

There has, for some time, been a call for action from within the Muslim community against such clerics. With the help of the community, we will now draw up a list of foreign-born clerics who will not be allowed to preach in the U.K. and who can be excluded. For British citizens, we will bring in a new offence of condoning or glorifying terrorism in the U.K. and abroad.

These measures are not aimed at decent law-abiding British Muslims – or Britons of any other faith. We know that this fringe of extremism does not truly represent Islam. British Muslims have made abundantly clear how they abhor the actions of the extremists and how they fear that the good name of the community will be contaminated by the words and actions of these fanatics.

Many, after all, made their homes in the U.K. exactly because they enjoy in the U.K., like all other faiths, the complete freedom to worship and to make a better life for their families.

Their children have been born here. British Muslims make a huge and welcome contribution to our national life.

We will continue to welcome as well those, of all backgrounds, who visit our country from abroad in peace and who understand that the respect and tolerance towards others in which we believe is the surest guarantee of freedom and progress for people of all religious faiths.

But coming to Britain is not a right, and even when people have come here, staying here carries with it a duty. That duty is to share and support the values of freedom and tolerance that sustain our shared way of life. Those that break that duty and try to incite hatred or engage in violence against our country and its people have no place here. On this principle, people of all faiths in Britain are agreed. And it is my job to act on it.[23]

*****

NOTES AND REFERENCES

1. *The Hindu*, July 8, 2005
2. *http://www.livejournal.com/userinfo.bml?user=srk1srkI*
3. *The Hindu*, July 8, 2005
4. *http://www.arabicnews.com/ansub/Daily/Day/050715/2005071524/ html.Regional UK, Politics, 7 August 2005.*
5. Egypt-UK, Local, July 15, 2005.
6. Egypt-Regional, Religion 1/27/ 2005.
7. *The Hindu*, July 17, 2005.
8. *The Hindu*, July 13, 2005.
9. *The Hindu*, July 10, 2005.
10. *Ibid.*
11. *The Hindu*, July 19, 2005.
12. *The Hindu*, July 16, 2005.
13. *The Hindu*, July 16, 2005.
14. *The Hindu*, July 23, 2005.
15. *The Hindu*, July 25, 2005.
16. *The Hindu*, July 25, 2005.
17. *The Hindu*, July 19, 2005.
18. *The Hindu*, July 26, 2005.
19. *The Hindu*, July 30, 2005.
20. *The Hindu*, August 01, 2005.
21. *The Hindu*, July 31, 2005.
22. http://www.officialconfusion.com/Audio/Shayler 060805. mp 3 Homepage: http://www.nineeleven.co.uk./board/viewforum.phb?f=9.
23. *The Hindu*, September 24, 2005.

2

WESTERN AND AMERICAN RESPONSE

Seumas Milne

The British columnist Seumas Milne while criticizing the British foreign policy in Muslim affairs has declared an 'insult to deny Iraq link to London attacks'. He was surprised to see that when the newly elected respect (anti-Iraq war) MP, George Galloway – who might be thought to have some locus on the subject, having overturned a substantial Labour majority over Iraq in a London constituency with a large Muslim population – declared that Londoners had paid the price of a "despicable act" for the Government's failure to heed those warnings, he was accused by Defence Minister Adam Ingram of 'dipping his poisonous tongue in a pool of blood". On Wednesday, just one day before 7/7 attacks, Liberal Democrat leader Charles Kennedy was in the dock for a far more tentative attempt to question this suffocating consensus. Even Ken Livingstone, who had himself warned of the danger posed to London by an invasion of Iraq, now claimed the bombings were nothing to do with the war something he clearly does not believe.

Mr. Milne has called this British policy as "official otherworldliness" that is not ready to take the ground realities in to account and only blames this trend as an "evil ideology". But it is an insult to the dead to mislead people about the crucial factors fuelling this deadly rage in Muslim communities across the world, Mr Milne explains: The first piece of disinformation long peddled by champions of the occupations of Iraq and Afghanistan is that Al-Qaeda and its supporters have no demands that could possibly be met or negotiated over; that they are really motivated by a hatred of western freedom and way of life and that their Islamist ideology aims at global domination. The reality was neatly summed up this week in a radio exchange between the BBC's political editor Andrew Marr and its security correspondent Frank Gardner, who was left disabled by an Al-Qaeda attack in Saudi last year. Was it the "very diversity, that melting pot aspect of London" that Islamist extremists found so offensive that they wanted to kill innocent civilians in Britain's capital, Mr. Marr wondered. "No, it is not that", replied Mr. Gardner briskly, who is better acquainted with Al-Qaeda thinking than most. "What they find offensive are the policies of western governments and specifically the presence of western troops in Muslim lands, notably Iraq and Afghanistan".

The second disinformation line peddled by government supporters, according to Milne is that the London attacks had nothing to do with Iraq. Labour MP Tony Wright insisted that such an idea was "not only nonsense, but dangerous non-sense". Mr. Blair has argued that, since the 9/11 attacks pre-dated the Iraq war, outrage at the aggression could not have been the trigger. It is perfectly true, the writer analyses, that Muslim anger over Palestine, Western-backed dictatorships and the aftermath of 1991 war against Iraq-US troops in Arabia and a murderours sanctions regime against Iraq – was already intense before 2001 and fuelled Al-Qaeda's campaign in the 1990s. But that was aimed at the US not Britain, which only became a target when Mr. Blair backed Mr. Bush's war on terror. Afghanistan made a terror attack on Britain a likelihood; Iraq it a certainty.

Mr. Milne finally concluded:

"We can't of course be sure of the exact balance of motivations that drove four young suicide bombers to strike last Thursday, but we can be certain that the blood-bath unleashed by Mr. Bush and Mr. Blair in Iraq – where a 7/7 takes place every day was at the very least one of them.

"The London bombers were to blame for attacks on civilians that are neither morally nor politically defensible. But the Prime Minister – who was warned by British intelligence of the risks in the run-up to the war- is also responsible for knowing putting his own people at risk in the service of a foreign power. The security crackdowns and campaign to uproot an "evil ideology" the government announced on Wednesday will not extinguish the threat. Only a British commitment to end its role in bloody occupations of Iraq and Afghanistan is likely to do that".[1]

Robin Cook

MP and former U.K. Foreign Secretary Robin Cook needed rethinking on fighting. To him a war on world poverty may well do more for the West's security than a war on terror. The Prime Minister had declared the London bombings an attack on our values as a society. But "we should remember that among those values are tolerance and mutual respect for those from different cultural and ethnic backgrounds. Only the day before, London was celebrating its coup in winning the Olympic Games, partly through demonstrating to the world the success of our multicultural credentials. Nothing would please better those who planted Thursday's bombings than for the atrocity to breed suspicion and hostility to minorities in our own community. Defeating the terrorists also means defeating their poisonous belief that people of different faiths and ethnic origins cannot coexist", he reminded.

Mr. Cook further says that in the days to come they would be subjected to a spate of articles analyzing the threat of militant Islam. Ironically they would fall in the same week that they would recall the tenth anniversary of the massacre of Srebrenica, when the powerful nations of Europe failed to protect 8,000 Muslims from being annihilated in the worst terrorist act in Europe of past generation. He adds that Osama bin Laden is no more a true representative of Islam than General Mladic, who commanded the Serbian forces, could be held up as an example of Christianity. After all it is written in the Quran that we are made into different peoples not that we might despise each other, but that we might understand each other, as Mr. Robin Cook well analysed.

The learned champion of anti Iraq war in the West discussed in detail about bin Laden, a product of monumental miscalculation by western security agencies. Throughout the 1980s he was armed by the CIA against the Russian occupation of Afghanistan and thousands of *mujahidin* were recruited and trained to defeat the Russians. In explicably, and with disastrous consequences, it never appears to have occurred to Washington that once Russia was out of the way, bin Laden's organization would turn its attention to the West. The danger now is that the West's current response to the terrorist threat compounds that original errors. So long as the struggle against terrorism is conceived as a war that can be won by military means, it is doomed to fail. The more the West emphasizes confrontation, the more it silences moderate voices in the Muslim world who want to speak up for cooperation, Mr. Cook cautions his people honestly.

He further suggests that success will only come from isolating the terrorists and denying them support, funds and recruits, which means focussing more on our common ground with the Muslim world than on what divides us .... We are not going to address the sense of marginalization among Muslim countries, if we do not make more of an effort to be inclusive of them in the architecture of global governance. But the G8 should try its best to seize the opportunity to address the wider issues at the root of terrorism.

Among these wider issues of common concern eliminating poverty ranks the first, as Mr. Cook concludes. "It would be perverse if the focus of the G8 on making poverty history was now obscured by the bombings. The breeding grounds of terrorism are to be found in the poverty of back streets, where fundamentalism offers a false, easy sense of pride and identity to young men who feel denied of any hope or any economic opportunity for themselves,"[2] he finally presented his remarks.

London's Mayor Ken Livingstone described publicly these attacks as "a reaction to decades of misguided Western policies motivated by a need for oil". He criticized U.S. and British foreign policy in the Arab world and called the Israeli-Palestinian conflict a "running rose" that alienated Muslims and sincited extremists. He condemned U.S. and British actions since early in the 20th century. He offered a sweeping indictment of western policy from the world war-I through the treatment of prisoners at the U.S. naval station at Guantanamo Bay, Cuba "I think you have just had 80 years of western intervention into predominantly Arab lands because of the western need for oil", he said on BBC Radio 4's Today programme. "We have propped up unsavoury governments; we have overthrown ones we did not consider sympathetic". He said he had no sympathy for the mbombers, and he condemned all violence. But he contended that fear of losing oil supplies motivated Western governments to intervene in West Asia time and again.[3]

Madeleine Bunting

Mr. Bunting analyses the 7/7 agonising attacks alongwith the heartfelt self-criticism. He admits that "it is an agonizing moment to be a British; this has been their worst nightmare come true: British-born young men from families that were well-established in this country allegedly have carrying out a suicide bomb attack. From what we know of their lives, one was at university, another might have had a small child, another's father had a fish and chips business; they did not live in ghettos but in ethnically mixed suburbs – the like of which surrounded many British towns. In other words they were unexceptional; until July 7, they seemed to illustrate with thousands of other Muslims, Britain's pragmatic multiculturalism. But the actions of these men have thrown British Muslims into the biggest crisis of their community's history". The narrative of this is in contrast to those of Madrid or New York. "The enemy is in our midst"; it puts the British model of multiculturalism under unprecedented scrutiny. Its hallmark, a kind of British indifference, often distinguishable from tolerance, that leaves people to get on with things in their own way, will be questioned. It was always obvious that British multiculturalism had major inadequacies – particularly pertinent right now are facts such as 70 per cent of Pakistani and Bangladeshi children grow up in poverty – but never before have we had to ask ourselves if the model had a basic design fault.

Mr. Bunting has described the two charges against the Muslim community of Britain, that are repeated time and again in the western media but are false and are categorized 'near impossible tasks" to be performed. Firstly Muslims are called to account for how their own children would have taken this path of terrorism – and without anyone tipping off the police. People are asking each other: "Some one must have known, why did not they tell anyone?" The second painful process that the Muslim community has already embarked on is desperate soul-searching. According to

Bunting the self-criticising process is very painful but an emergent need of the time.

The analyst emphasizes on the British foreign policy and its role in creating a world of terror. He calls it a "cancer in our community, corroding trust in the British political system and poisoning our youth". The honesty and new thinking required by us, say Muslims, must be mirrored by the government; it can not pretend Iraq and Palestine are irrelevant. He further suggests that there is no point alienating another generation of Muslim men with an intrusive, aggressive state; that will only push more of those poised on the margins into secretive extremism. The writer advises "to be very careful to pick the right targets" – since much of the talk about radical *imams* is misplaced; most British mosques are cautious and have lost touch with their younger populations, who look to the internet for inspiration, not the *imam*, as he evaluates.

Mr. Bunting gives his concluding remarks in the following words: "one of the most extraordinary side effects of 9/11 and of Iraq war has been the energizing of the Muslim community in this country; thousands of groups and local initiatives have spring up. Some have campaigned alongside non-Muslims against British foreign policy; some have built up dialogue in their communities. One of the most hopeful possibilities is that 7/7 will have the same impact in mobilizing people to make more effort to understand each other better and find common cause".[4]

William Dalrymple

According to western media three of the bombers Mohammad Siddique Khan, Shehzad Tanweer and Hasib Hussain suspected to be behind the London blasts, visited Pakistan in the year preceding the attack and learned the militant teachings of the religion in the *madrasa* and were trained therein. The British press quickly followed the United States line: last weekend the *Sunday Telegraph* was helpfully translating the Arabic word *madrasa* as terrorist training school", while Tuesday's *Daily Mirror* confidently asserted over a double-page spread that three of the bombers had all enrolled at Pakistani "terror schools".[5] This thinking was initially led by the U.S. policy makers. Colin Powell and Donald Rumsfeld were not known for their close agreement on matters of foreign policy, but one thing that they were united upon was the threat posed by Pakistan's *madrasa*. In 2002 Mr. Rumsfeld posed the question" "Are we capturing, killing or deterring and dissuading more terrorists every day than the *madrasas*... are recruiting training and deploying against us?" "A year later, Mr. Powell described *madrasas* as a breeding ground" for fundamentalists and terrorists".[6]

Tony Blair on July 19, 2005 urged Pakistan to take crack down on *madrasas* which contributed to the rise of religious extremism. At a joint press conference with the visiting Afghan President Hamid Karzai in Downing Street London, Mr. Blair said Pakistan suffers from terrorism and it was in its own interest to take steps to root it out.[7]

The British writer William Dalrymple describing all such allegations invalid out-rightly rejects any *madrasa* link to London attacks. To him it is now becoming very clear that "producing common-fodder for the Taliban and graduating local sectarian thugs is not at all the same as producing the kind of technically literate Al-Qaeda terrorists who carried out the horrifyingly sophisticated attacks on the World Trade Centre." The writer differenciates between *madrasa* graduates – "who tend to be pious villagers from impoverished economic backgrounds possessing little technical sophistication" – and the sort of middle class, politically literate, global *Salafi jihadis* who plan Al-Qaeda operations around the world. "Most of these turn out to have secular scientific or technical backgrounds and very few actually turn out to be *madrasa* graduates".

Mr. Dalrymple categorically declares that those who planned and carried out the attacks on America were confused, but highly educated, middle class professionals. Mohammad Ata was a town planning expert; Ayman al-Zawahiri, Osama bin Laden's chief of staff, is a paediatric surgeon; Omar Sheikh, the kidnapper of Daniel Pearl, is the product of the same British public school that produced film-maker Peter Greenaway. The learned writer quotes Peter Bergen of Johns Hopkins University who has recently published the conclusions of his indepth study of 75 Muslim terrorists who had carried out four major anti-western attacks. According to this study "53 per cent of the terrorists had either attended college or had received a college degree. As a point of reference, only 52 per cent of Americans have been to college". Against this, the background of British bombers should not come as a surprise, Dalrymple says. He also refers the French "authority" on Islamists, Mr. Gilles Kepel who has arrived at a similar conclusion. The new breed of global jihadis, Kepel writes, are not the urban poor of the third world – as Tony Blair still claims – so much as "the privileged children of an unlikely marriage between Wahhabism and Silicon Valley". Islamic terrorism, like its Christian predecessor, remains a largely bourgeois endeavour, he concludes.

Dalrymple offers some exceptions to the above thesis. He like the American theorists describes "the terrifyingly ultra-conservative Taliban regime – unquestionably a product of Pakistan's *madrasas* a fundamentalist in its approach to the scriptures subscribing to the most hardline strains of Islamic thought that preach violent jihad. He applies the Taliban case unhesitatingly to some radical *madrasa* graduates who have become "involved with Al-Qaeda". He refers in this case to "Maulana Masud Azhar, leader of the banned Islamist militant group *Jaish-e-Muhammad*, who originally studied in the ultra-militant Binnori Town *madrasa* in Karachi".

The exception from the thesis of Kepel may be true to some extent but its application upon Binoori Town *madrasa* is categorically wrong. This *madrasa* like others teach the

Nizami curricula based upon the subjects of classical Islamic sciences and rational philosophy along with some essential modern subjects like English, Unani medicine and history introduced during the Mughal period. If this system of education did not ever create and promote terrorist mentality in the past, how is it blamed to do so in the contemporary world?

Mr. Dalrymple, however admits that "by and large" *madrasa* students "do not have the technical expertise or conceptual imagination necessary to carry out the sort of attacks we have seen Al-Qaeda pull off in the past few years. Their focus, in other words, is not on opposing the West – the central concern of the *Salafi* jihadis – so much as fostering what they see as proper Islamic behaviour at home".

All this highlights, Dalrymple further argues, how depressingly unsophisticated the debate about the British bombers is in this country. Again and again we are told that terrorism is associated with poverty and the basic Quranic education provided by *madrasas*. We are told that the men who carry out this work are evil madmen with whom no debate is possible and who, according to Frank Field on last weeks' Question Time, "aim to wipe us out". All links with Iraq and Afghanistan are vehemently denied, he criticises.

In actual fact, Al-Qaeda operatives,, Dalrymple argues, tend to be highly educated and their aims clearly and explicitly political. Osama bin Laden, in his numerous communiqués, has always been completely clear about this. In his first public statement "A declaration of war against the Americans" issued in 1996, he announced he was fighting U.S. foreign policy in the Middle East and, in particular, American support for the House of Saud and the state of Israel. His aim, he stated, was to unleash a clash of civilizations between Islam and the "Zionist crusaders" of the West, and so provoke an American backlash strong enough to radicalize the Muslim world and topple pro-western government. George W. Bush has nullified Osama bin Laden's every hope. Through the invasion of secular Bathist Iraq, the abuses in Abu Gharib, the mass murders in Falluja, America with Britain's obedient assistance – has turned Iraq into a jihadist playground while alienating all moderate Muslim opinion in the Islamic heartlands and, crucially in the West.

Mr. Dalrymple advises his countrymen to take the issue seriously. The condemnation of horrific atrocities is not enough. Unless we attempt to understand the jihadis, read their statements and honestly analyse what has led these men to blow themselves up, we can never defeat them or even begin to drain the swamp of the grievances in which they continue to flourish.[8]

Richard Norton Taylor

Mr. Taylor, the security affairs editor of the London-based *Guardian* newspaper is vocal about the reality of the 'war on terror' and is explicit that it is too much to hope Blair and his foreign policy makers will learn from the limitations of intelligence amply demonstrated in London on July 7. On Feburary 10,2003, a month before the onslaught on Iraq, Whitehall's (UK civil service officials') joint intelligence committee told Tony Blair that "Al-Qaeda and associated groups continued to represent by far the greatest terrorist threat to western interests, and that threat would be heightened by military action against Iraq". It added that the collapse of the Iraqi regime would increase the risk of chemical and biological warfare agents technology finding their way into the hands of terrorists. On Monday the Royal Institute of International Affairs published a paper co-written by Paul Wilkinson, a professor at the University of St. Andrews, U.K. He is no radical polemicist, rather an epitome of conventional wisdom. "The U.K. is at particular risk" warns the paper, "because it is the closest ally of the United States" and joined the U.S. led military action in Afghanistan and Iraq. It says a key problem facing the government is that it "has been conducting counter – terrorism policy 'shoulder to shoulder' with the U.S., not in the sense of being an equal decision – maker, but rather as a pillion passenger compelled to leave to the steering to the ally in the driving seat". Iraq has imposed particular difficulties for Britain, the authors continue, since "it gave a boost to Al-Qaeda network's propaganda, recruitment and fund raising, caused a major split in the coalition, provided an ideal targeting and training area for Al-Qaeda-linked terrorists, and deflected resources and assistance that could have been deployed to assist the Hamid Karzai Government and to bring Osama bin Laden to justice".

Mr. Taylor continues, Al-Qaeda is now as much of a concept as an organisation or network. It blossomed in Afghanistan, and the U.S. soon became a target, partly because of its military presence in West Asia. In what sound like a perverse justification of the invasion, Mr. Blair and George W. Bush say, Iraq has become a magnet for terrorists. Britain and the U.S. must ensure that the insurgents and foreign fighters are defeated and not allowed a victory in the 'war on terror" – a phrase that makes security and intelligence agencies and military commanders cringe, for it suggests that the fight against terrorism can be won by force of arms. It is the causes, they say, that matter. And these include the Government's foreign policy. The security and intelligence agencies, along with most among the senior ranks of Whitehall, opposed the invasion of Iraq on the grounds that it could not be justified. They knew the Bush administration was not telling the truths when it claimed there was a link between Al-Qaeda and Baghdad. Officials who expressed concern about the claims were slapped down by Foreign Office diplomats – though they also, privately opposed the war because of the damage such honesty might do to U.S.-U.K. relations. If Whitehall opposed the war, it was horrified at Washington's failure to consider the consequences and its dismissal of British suggestions. The security and intelligence agencies had their own specific concerns. Britain's alliance with the U.S. did not help their attempts to recruit agents or informants where they most needed them, in the mosques and the souks. They were angry at the way the Pentagon paraded pictures of prisoners at Guantanamo Bay, Taylor argues.

"Intelligence and facts were being fixed around the policy", Sir Richard Dearlove, then head of M16 (British intelligence), told in a meeting chaired by Blair on July 23, 2002, the minutes of which were leaked to the (London) *Sunday Times* and are now making waves on websites in the U.S. (but not in the U.K.). Taylor further says that "the limitations of intelligence were amply demonstrated in London on July 7. The security and intelligence agencies have said they will learn lessons. Is it too much to hope that Mr. Blair and his foreign policy makers will too", he concludes.[9]

Sidney Blumenthal

Sidney Blumenthal, the former senior advisor to President Bill Clinton and the author of *The Clinton Wars* expressed categorically that the situation in Afghanistan, where the U.S. is in charge, is one of the barely managed chaos. On the day of the London bombings, President George W. Bush proclaimed: "The war on terror goes on". Through the 2004 campaign, his wining theme was terror. He achieved the logic of a unified field theory connecting Iraq to Afghanistan by threading terror through both, despite the absence of evidence. He insisted that if we did not fight the terrorists there, we would be fighting them at home. In January, the Central Intelligence Agency's thinktank, the National Intelligence Council, issued a report describing Iraq as the magnet and training and recruiting ground for terrorism. The false rationale for the invasion had become a self-fulfilling prophecy. With his popularity flagging, Mr. Bush returned to the formulations that succeeded in his campaign.

In Mr. Bush's "global war on terror" (GWOT), Iraq and Afghanistan present one extended battlefield against a common enemy – and the strategy is and must be the same. So far as Mr. Bush is concerned, it is always either the day after 9/11 or the day before the Iraq invasion. Time stands still at two ideal political moments. But his consequences since are barely managed chaos. "I was horrified by the President's last speech (on the war on terror), so much unsaid, so much disingenuous, so many half-truths", said James Dobbins, Mr. Bush's first envoy to Afghanistan, now director of international programmes at the Rand Corporation. Afghanistan is now the scene of a Taliban revival chronic Pashtun violence' dominance by U.S. supported war lords who have become narco-lords and a human rights black hole.

From the start, Mr. Dobbins said, the effort in Afghanistan was "grossly underfunded and undermanned". The military doctrine was the first error. "The U.S. focus on force protection and substitution of firepower for manpower creates significant collateral damage." But the faith in firepower sustained the illusion that the mission could be "quicker, cheaper, easier". And that justification fitted with Afghanistan being relegated into a sideshow to Iraq. According to him, there was also "a generally negative appreciation of peace keeping and nation building as components of U.S. policy, a disinclination to learn any thing from Bosnia and Kosovo". Lack of accountability began at the top and filtered down, Blumenthal argues.

Democracy was an afterthought for the White House, which believed it had little application to Afghans. At the Bonn Conference establishing international legitimacy for the Kabul government, "the word democracy was introduced at the insistence of Iranian delegation", Mr. Dobbins points out. However, democracy – now the overriding rationale for the GWOT – does not include support for human rights. "In terms of the human rights situation in Afghanistan, Mr. Karzai is well-meaning and moderate and thoroughly honourable", said Mr. Dobbins, "but he's overwhelmed".

Donald Rumsfeld's Pentagon and the White House removed restraints on torture. "These were command failures, not just isolated incidents ... You did not have the checks and balances. They have, had consequences in terms of public image". In April, the U.S. succeeded in abolishing the office of the U.N. Rapporteur on Human Rights for Afghanistan. Mr. Dobbins believes that the operation in Afghanistan has improved, but that the administration "has not readily acknowledged its mistakes and corrected them only after losing a good deal of ground, recoverable ground... most of the violence is not Al-Qaeda type, but Pashtun sectarian violence. It is not international terrorism".

Facts on the ground can not alter Mr. Bush's stentorian summons to the GWOT. "This is a campaign conducted primarily, and should be by law enforcement, diplomatic and intelligence means", Mr. Dobbins said. "The militarisation of the concept is a theme that mobilizes the American public effectively, but it is not a theme that resonates well in the Middle East or with our allies elsewhere in the world". "We are taking the fight to the terrorists abroad, so we do not have to face them here at home". Mr. Bush declared in June – and repeated endlessly-finally appearing vindicating with the London attacks. London like Iraq and Afghanistan, is "there", not "here", Blumenthal concluded.[10]

Adam Crutis

Adam Crutis, the author of *The Power of Nightmares, the Rise of the Politics of Fear* (which was broadcast on BBC television in October 2004) has described the post 7/7 situation as that of creating the "Islamist phantoms". He concluded his discussion as we dreamed up "Al-Qaeda". Let us not do it again with "evil ideology". Rules that would guide the deportation of alleged terrorist sympathizers were published by the British government. It is a key part of its attempt to deal with the "evil ideology" of Islamism and its role in inspiring terrorist attacks on Britain. But there is growing unease about whether this response is right or will be effective in stopping future attacks. There is an even more serious fear that we might be making the situation worse. Mr. Crutis warns.

This is exactly what happened in the reaction to the attacks on America in 2001, the writer argues. For years after 9/11 "we were told that we faced a powerful, well-organized enemy, who had established a centrally coordinated command structure that needed to be sought out and crushed. We went storming into Iraq to prevent a rogue state from supplying weapons of mass destruction (WMD) to this organization. This would make the world a safer place. But the enemy was not an organized network, and going into Iraq has done the opposite of what we intended. Our actions have inspired resentment throughout the Middle East and Iraq is now the world centre of terrorist activity".

Mr. Crutis refers to the series of documentaries made by himself for the BBC. *The Power of Nightmares*, which showed how a fantasy image of the Al-Qaeda organization was created. The films told how the response to the shocking events of September 11, 2001 swing out of control, and the threat became exaggerated to a dangerous level. Although there was a serious terrorist threat, the films criticized the apocalyptic vision of what lay behind it – the "nightmare" of a uniquely powerful network, unlike any previous terrorist danger and capable of overwhelming our society and our democracy, the writer criticizes.

The Power of Nightmares said bluntly that this was a fantasy. The real threat came not from a network, but from individuals and groups linked only by an idea. U.S energies were going into fighting a phantom enemy. We were looking for a network that did not exist when we should have been dealing with an idea that does.

The evidence we have what lies behind the London bombings, says Adam Crutis, confirms that this was the real nature of the threat. It is fascinating to see how suddenly all the terror "experts" have changed their time. For three years they told us breathlessly about a terrifying global network. Now, suddenly, it has gone away and been replaced by "an evil ideology" that inspires young, angry Muslim men in our own society. It is good that we now all agree on the nature of the threat, but there remains a danger that the "idea" will be simplified, exaggerated and distorted just as the "network" was, and that in this mood of fear the government will bring in policies that will alienate young Muslims further and drive them towards dangerous extremism, the writer cautions.

Modern Islamism, according to Crutis' statement, "is a complex political movement with a history that goes back more than 50 years. Its most influential ideologist was an Egyptian school inspector, Sayyid Qutb. In the 1950s he wrote a series of book that put forward a powerful critique of modern western culture and democracy, and called for a new type of utopian society in Muslim lands in which Islam would play a central political role." Out of this has come a movement for revolutionary change in the Islamic world that includes an extraordinary range of grouping and variations on Qutb's original arguments.

As per the analysis made by this writer, it is only a tiny minority in the Islamist movement who have developed these ideas into a politics that advocates terrorism against the West. Historians of Islamism have shown that this minority, grouped initially around Osama bin Laden and Ayman Zawahiri in the late 1990s turned to attacking the West only because of the failure of the wider movement to achieve its revolutionary aims in the Muslim world. " We must be aware of this distinction so as to avoid a witch-hunt against the whole Islamist movement", Mr. Crutis suggests. He further explains that "We may not agree with its reactionary vision of the political use of Islam and the pessimistic, anti-progressive beliefs that lie at the heart of Qutb's teachings, but it is essential to realize that there is no inherent link between these ideas and terrorism. There are varying signs that journalists are confusing the murderous beliefs of a genuinely destructive minority with the political ideas of a much wider movement. By lumping Islamism into a frightening, violent, anti-western movement led by the "preachers of hate", they risk exaggerating and distorting the threat yet again".

The real danger in the words of Adam Crutis, is that, "by suppressing Islamism, we will make its ideas more attractive to already marginalized young men. In the process we may inadvertently drive them further towards the extreme militant wings of the movement, and prove yet again the old adage that the real threat to democracy from terrorism is not the action but the reaction", he concludes.[11]

The Americans

Sunday Times has published a special report on the terrorism and how the political analysts and media men explain the 9/11 and 7/7 attacks in America and London. This report talks especially of the American response to Osama bin Laden the "Ghost who stalks'. The 25 million dollars question: where is Osama bin Laden? Despite the bounty dubious forces are no closer to smoking him out. This report finds out why the Osama puszzle still has *'em foxed.* According to terrorism expert Peter Bergen, as the report discovers, bin Laden and his deputy (or his 'teacher', according to some) Ayman al-Zawahiri have released 29 messages since the September 11 attacks on the U.S. in 2001. In one of the last ones, bin Laden spewed a 70 minute invective soon after a terrorist attack in Jeddah, mentioning the incident only 10 days after it occurred. The ten-day turn-around time between the attack and the release of the tape, said Bergen, is the fastest he could recall between a terrorist event and a communication from bin Laden, suggesting that he feels secure enough to send his message. The more recent tape about the London bombings by suicide bomber Siddique Khan, spliced with footage of Zawahiri endorsing the attack, bears this out. Bin Laden and his companion are well on the top of the situation.

For many Americans, Washington's inability to focus on bin Laden and capture him dead or alive has become a national embrassment. "Bush is very fortunate his political opposition was not able to capitalize on his failure to get bin Laden in 2004", writes commentator Joseph Farah in a 9/11 anniversary purview. "If he (Bush) cares about his country, his party, justice and winning this titanic global conflict with pure, unadulterated evil, he's got to finish the little matter of bin Laden... and if that means attacking him in Pakistan or Iran or any other nation, we do it. If we have to use bunker-buster bombs or tactical nuclear weapons, we do it".

Easier said than done, because for all its efforts, which do not seem to be much, Washington does not appear to have a clue about bin Laden's whereabouts and doest not seem to even care, now that it is overwhelmed by the situation in Iraq. According to some accounts, there were now less people and resources devoted to the 'bin Laden desk' created at the CIA's counter-terrorism Centre than before or in the immediate aftermath of 9/11. This desk, code named "Alec Station", came closest to mailing bin Laden at an Afghan terrorist camp in 1999, but was held up by higher-ups in the political chain of command because, as one member of the desk put it, "there were some Arab princes eating goat with bin Laden". That member, CIA operative Michael Scheuer, who subsequently went public with the blunders that enabled bin Laden to escape today believes the war in Iraq has completely side tracked the hunt for the Saudi terrorist. "The war in Iraq – if Osama was a Christian – it's the Christmas present he never would have expected", Scheuer told CBS *60 Minutes* recently. But U.S. officials insist that the hunt for bin Laden continues, amid signs of greater momentum in recent months with the reported introduction of more commandos from the elite Delta Force and Navy Seals in to the border region between Afghanistan and Pakistan.

These American units are also believed to have the go ahead to infiltrate into Pakistan to get bin Laden if the need arises, not-withstanding Islamabad's insistence that its borders not be violated. In Washington, Pakistan's protestations carry little value, and there is increasing skepticism about the role of the Paksitani military and intelligence in the whole bin Laden affair, especially after Pakistan's military ruler Pervez Musharraf said last month that he would not allow U.S. forces to come inside Pakistan to capture bin Laden and insisted his own men were capable of doing the job. In fact, CIA Director Porter Goss recently stunned the intelligence community by saying he had an "excellent idea" where bin Laden was, but that the Al-Qaeda Chief would not be captured "until the weak links in the war on terrorism are strengthened". Many analysts saw this as a transparent reference to Pakistan and its dodgy role in the whole business. But Goss's remarks also suggested as the reporter concludes, the US may be panting down the Osama trial much more than is publicly acknowledged. There are elements in the U.S. intelligence for whom "We will not forget" is more than just a policitial statement. In a country that has more TV shows dedicated to cracking crime (*Cold Case, Law and Order, CSI* etc.). than any other, and where long-forgotten murders and mysteries are resolved years and decades after they have occurred, the hunt for the mastermind of 9/11 is far from no matter what seems like to the rest of the world, Chidanand Rajghatta reaches at the decision.[12]

Don Van Natta Jr.

New York Times news reporter Don Van Natta Jr. provides the information the police investigating the terrorist bombings in London have begun a worldwide hunt for a former aide to one of the Britain's most militant Islamic clerics who they believe may have played a key role in the July 7 attacks, according to British, European and American intelligence and law enforcement officials. The man, identified as Haroon Rashid Aswat, 31, originally from

Dewsbury in north-central England, was a senior aide to Abu Hamza al-Masri, the blind, one-armed militant cleric who preached at the Finsbury Park Mosque in north London until his arrest in April 2004. Masri, who urged young men to wage jihad in Afghanistan, Iraq and beyond, is now facing extradition to the U.S. to face terrorism-related charges.

Several intelligence and law enforcement officials said, as reported by Don Van Natta Jr., they belived that Aswat was also involved in plan to set up a training camp for Al-Qaeda in Oregon six years ago. A theory now being pursued by Scotland Yard is that Aswat provided the four British bombers with support for the coordinated attacks in London's public transportation system, killing 56 people and wounding 700, several senior intelligence and law enforcement officials said. Those officials declined to say what especially made them believe that Aswat was linked to the bombers, all of whom died in the attacks. One official noted that Aswat was raised in Dewsbury, the same area where Mohammad Siddique Khan, 30, one of the four bombers, lived. On Wednesday. Aswat's family said he had not lived at the family's home near Dewsbury for two years. Aswat's whereabouts are unknown, but several senior investigators said they were almost certain that he was not in Britain now. Officials say he is of Pakistani descent, like three of the four bombers, but his family's neighbours said the family was from Gujrat. "No body's trying him in or making him the mastermind yet," a senior American official said. "There is no real substantiation yet. But people are looking at some of his confederates and connections, and saying that it is a possibility."

An American official and two European officials said Aswat spent several weeks in Bly, Oregon in late 1999 and early 2000, trying to help several associates establish Al-Qaeda training camp there. Although he was not identified by name in court papers in the Oregon case, several American officials said he was an unindicated co-conspirator in the indictment of James Ujaama, who pleaded guilty to aiding the Taliban. Ujaama, 39, is now the leading witness in the U.S. terrorism indictment of Masri, American officials said. Two American officials cautioned it was not fully confirmed that Aswat being sought was the same man implicated in the Oregon case. Aswat is believed to have met Osama bin Laden sometime in the late 1990s senior investigators said.[13]

Gary Younge

The bombers look like every body else. They are not super natural. Mr. Gary Younge, therefore, suggests if the security services are going to have any chance of infiltrating the bombers they must first humanize those involved. In the movie *Adams Family*, Wednesday Adams heads off to a fancy dress Halloween party in her regular clothes. "I am a homicidal maniac" she explains when questioned by Morticia about her attire. "They look like everybody else." Just over two weeks ago Jean Charles de Menezes "looked like everybody else" in London, but on Friday morning, in the eveys of the traveling public and the police, he was transformed into a potential "homicidal maniac", Mr. Younge criticizes.

In a clear indication of how terrorism not only destroys bodies but also contaminates perceptions, fellow travelers say they saw an "Asian man" with "a bomb belt and wires coming out". What they actually saw was a young Brazilian in puffa jacket. The police saw a threat. To them De Menezes looked like another " clean skin" (a perpetrator with no history of previous terrorist involvement or affiliation) on the run and possibly about to act. Having cornered him and pinned him to the fround they pumped five bullets into his head at close range.

In a world where every brown skin is little more than a "clear skin" waiting to happen. Younge bitterly argues, stop and search will inevitably become stop and shoot. "The dominant mood that we are better safe than sorry is understandable, but after Friday's incident we are left with one man dead, no body safe and everybody sorry". If there is one thing the West has learned over the past two years, it is that a pre-emptive strike with no evidence causes more problems than it solves, the writer comments.

DeMenezes' killing came the day after the police presented Prime Minister Tony Blair with a shopping list of new measures they say they need to tackle terrorism.. As though the plea not to allow terrorists to change our way of lige, Younge further says, does not apply to the authorities, they want to increase the amount of time they can detain a suspect without charge from 14 days to three months. Given that they already have the option of shooting unarmed, innocent people dead in the underground, the police clearly have more power than they can responsibly handle. But De Menezes' death does not make the case against giving police extra anti-terrorist powers-it simply illustrates it.

Anti-terrorist legislation, Gary Younge suggests, has a proven record of catching just about anyone apart from those for whom it was originally designed. We knew this way before September 11. According to Home Office statistics, 97 percent of those arrested under the Prevention of Terrorism Act- a series of draconian measures supposed to thwart the IRA- between 1974 and 1988 were released without charge. Only one percent were convicted and imprisoned. The strike rate since the declaration of the war on terror has not been particularly in pressive either. More than 700 people have been arrested under the Terrorism Act since September 11, but half have been released without charge and only 17 convicted. Only three of the convictions relate to allegations of extremism related to militant Islamic groups.

As the hunt continues for those involved in the last two terrorist incidents, the author continues, the authorities appear so closer to devising a strategy for working out where the next one might come from. They have proven their skill to gather evidence to reconstruct what has happened after the fact; but are as yet unable to fathom the admittedly far more difficult task of how to gather the kind of intelligence that might prevent the fact itself. For political and emotional reasons it has been necessary for some to dehumanize the bombers-to eviscerate them of all discernible purpose, cause and motivation. Stripped to their immoral minimum, they are simply "evil masters". For those who wish to vent as need to grieve, such a response is understandable.

Those looking for tails and tridents on the CCTV footage of the bombers will be disappointed. In the words of Wednesday Adams, they look everybody else, says, Gary Younge, "If the security services are going to have any chance of infiltrating the bombers they must first humanize those involved. They need to find out what would motivate young men who apparently have so much to live for to die-and kill-in such a manner. Only then can they discover how to stop the determined and stop them in their tracks, and how to catch those vulnerable to their message before they fall into the clutches of the terrorists."

The author emphasises upon the mobilization and persuasion needed necessarily in the war on terror. The police requires "the ability to gain the confidence of the Muslim community by convincing them that the aim is to catch terrorists, not to criminalize their community." In February 2005, after Sajid Badat, a 25-year old exgrammer school boy from Gloucester, admitted planning to blow up a flight between Amsterdam and the U.S., the head of the Metropolitan police's anti-terrorist branch, Deputy Assistant Commissioner Peter Clarke, said: "We must ask how a young British man was transformed from an intelligent, articulate person who was respected, into a person who pleaded guilty to one of the most serious crimes that you can think of." A policy that lets police shoot first and ask questions later will have a drastic effect on the kind of answer they are likely to get, the writer concludes.[14]

Jonathan Glover

The London bombings pose a dilemma. It is hard to believe that the right response to terrorism is to make concessions. But the terrorism also seems part of cycle of violence in which both the parties envolved. Mr. Jonathan Glover warns of "a cycle of potential war between Islam and the West that threatens to spin out of control. The author questions: Should we do nothing, leaving the violence to accelerate ?

The terrorist attacks appal us because of the loss of lives, the writer evaluates, but even more because the killing is deliberate to make a political point. It is this that arouses the resentful backlash. In the climate after 9/11, with 3000 murdered in the symbolic heart of America, any President might have found retaliation imperative. Some of the bombs dropped on Afghanistan carried the initials of the New York Police Department. But the 20,000 killed in Afghanistan fed Islamic resentment in turn. So too did the attack on Iraq. (Some rightly say Iraq was not the cause of the London bombings. But surely it was a cause?)

The writer asserts that the Al-Qaeda response to Iraq, in Madrid and now in London, propels the war on terror. And so it all goes on. "We have seen these cycles before, "the analysis goes on, "The Israeli and Palestinian responses to each other's violence are pilot study in entrapment. Each killing is depended as retaliation for the last. Now the West and the Islamic world may repeat the same cycle on a huge scale. The response to it triggered the 20th century world wars, the analysis continues, so 9/11 and the response to it could ruin our century. So much depends on whether we can break out the cycle of violence. This requires a serious dialogue between the overlapping worlds of the West and Islam before irreversible mutual hatred sets in.

Dialogue, according to Glover, may sound vacuous, but that is misleading. In Britain we do not need just any old talk, but some quite deep and sustained discussion of particular issues. It could be one of the great projects of mutual education of our time. Two topics would be central. One would be the different systems of belief on each side. The other would be our different narratives of recent history.

The author then talks of the psychology of conflict which involves persuading groups to listen to each other's stories and to look for the possibility of a narrative that does justice to the truths in both. Some times this happens after conflicts, with truth and reconciliation commissions. The urgent need is for it to happen before further conflict between the Islamic and "Western" views in Britain.

What is needed, the analysis goes on, is not a one-sided dialogue in which "we" undermine "their" fanaticism. There are indeed questions to ask about setting political issues by murder or about setting moral issues by appeals to the supposed authority texts claimed to be the word of God. But there are also questions about "our" morality, the write up continues. And there are questions about the supposed moral difference between bombs in the underground and cluster-bombing civilians in an alleged war.

In genuine dialogue, Jonathan Glover puts the concluding remarks, both sides have positions at risk. Paradoxically, this can start a virtuous circle. One side admitting intellectual vulnerability may make the other side less defensive too. "We should not reward terrorists by capitulating to their demands. We do not know exactly what they want. And some alleged demands are unacceptable, such as forcing Israelis or Spaniards to live in some totally Islamic caliphate. But the alternative is not passivity. It is talk. "Never talk to Terrorists "is a bad slogan. Talk will not stop the killing tomorrow. But we need long-term thinking too. The right kind of talk opens chinks that let in doubts. And in religion and politics doubts about beliefs save lives."[15]

How surprisingly unaware of the demands, challenges and ideas of bombers or extremists is a scholar who is a teacher of human values in one of the London colleges of worldwide repute! If he does not know[16] "exactly "What the bombers and the like want" then how these demands are treated "unacceptable"? Then how are those suicide attackers "forcing Israelis or Spaniards to live in some totally Islamic caliphate"? Bin Laden, Ayman Zawahiri, Abu Musab Zarqawi, Abu Hamza Masri? What did they demand? They are struggling what for? Their statements, videotapes, speeches and announcements are known to every body. They are sacrificing all their belongings in order to revive the glory and dignity of the Muslim world. They are talking repeatedly of the U.S. and allied forces' withdrawal from Iraq. They demand the just implementation of equality in the Muslim world. Suppose, they claim for an Islamic caliphate" in their home land what do they wrong? In a democratic set up if the majority of Muslim population in a country expresses their voices in favour of caliphate what is the bothering point for the West? Why the West is determined to oppose the "Islamic caliphate "? Does the Islamic caliphate inherit dictatorship, theocracy and clergy domination? Did Islam oppose the democracy, freedom equality and progress? Does the holy Quran negate the scientific advancement and material prosperity? If not-and positively not-then why so much oppositions? Let the Muslim world establish their society and state according to their decrees and teachings and let the world experience with the noble objectives of Islam.

And whether Israelis are being forced to live in "Islamic caliphate"? or Palestinians from the last 50 years are struggling to survive ? What is the reality in the history ? Why the Israelis are hated by the Arabs or the Muslims ? Let me quote Abdur Raziq Abu al-Hayyah, the Palestinian Administrator for the Jenin refugee camp who expressed to Ramzy Baroud, the veteran Arab-American journalist and the editoar-in- chief of *Palestine Chronicle. com.* He said to the journalist clearly : "If they will destroy the camp many times the people of Jenin will rebuild it, because with every time the people's courage and determination intensify. The more Israel brutalizes palestinans, the stronger their resistance shall be. Israel can not resolve its prolems by force. They have to understand that Palestinians' quest for freedom can not be stopped. It is only human nature for people to resist, to regain their freedom.

"The people of Jenin do not hate Israelis because their names are different, or because their language is different. Nor do they hate them because they have anything against the jewish religion, but because they are occupiers, the resistance will go on. The Palestinian resistance will go on. The Palestinian resistance shall live as long as the occupation lives."[17]

Ian Henshall

After the Madrid attacks blamed first on ETA then on "Al-Qaeda" network, the media in Spain discovered that the alleged bombers had intimate links with key members of the Spainish bomb squad. Mr. Ian Henshall has already detailed the evidence for this in his book *9/11 revealed.*

48% of New Yorkers now believe, Henshall says, the 9/11 attacks were consciously allowed to happen by elements in the U.S. government (Zogby). The anthrax attacks were traced to a U.S. military strain of anthrax and, contrary to the neo-con claims at the time, had no connection with Iraq. The timing of the London attacks is a political god-sent for Tony Blair, coming only one day after the decision to award the 2012 Olympics to London, and while he is facing a public revolt over plans to introduce identity cards. Already the authorities are fostering an atmosphere of panic, with the likely intention of strengthening their political hand in Westminster.

On past experience it is like that the authorities will rapidly arrest a group by of alleged "terrorists" who, they will say, are linked to Al-Qaeda, Mr. Henshall forecasts. The mainstream media, the author further suggests, should ask the following questions:

1. Why did a senior police officer tell the BBC less than 24 hours before the London attacks that the London Police felt that they were on top of the terrorist threat?

2. Were the alleged bombers under surveillance before the attacks and if not how were they apprehended?

3. To what extent were the bombers motivated by rage at the failure of the U.K. media to report truthfully on the war on Iraq where torture and death squad killings by the U.S./U.K. puppet regime have reached a similar scale to the Saddam Hussein regime ?

4. Does the Blair government now admit that the illegal invasion of Iraq has aided terrorism?

5. Blair boasted to the *Jewish Chronicle* that he has given more support to Israel than any other U.K. premier, will Blair now reconsider his support for Ariel Sharon and his decision to breach his own arms guidelines to supply the occupation forces there with the means to kill Palestinian children?

6. Why did initial reports say the Underground was disrupted by a power surge?

The official story of the Madrid attacks collapsed when the authorities squabbled over whether the attacks were carried out by Basque separatists or Al-Qaeda. An event that looked certain to ensure the re-election of Bush/Blair ally Premier Aznar backfired.

History shows, says Ian Henshall, that U.K. penetration of the IRA was for greater than the authorities admitted at the time. After swallowing all the Blair lies about weapons of mass destruction it would be outrageous if the media now let themselves be panicked by the Blair government into believing whatever they say about the current attacks. The British people will hold media figures who give aid and comfort to Blair's lies to be responsible along with Blair for the continuing carnage that the Blair/Bush/Sharon so called war on terror has unleashed.

I support the call, by U.K. 9/11 skeptic and by reopen 9/11 org., for a fully independent investigation conducted by people from outside Washington in to the official story of the 9/11 attacks," Henshall demands. Recently a senior Republican was quoted in the *Washington Times* as stating that the official story-that the Twin Towers collapsed at almost the speed of free fall, defying the law of conservation of momentum-is highly unlikely. "In our book," says the author," we quote other senior Republicans who have stated that the 9/11 attacks were the Reichstag Fire of the Bush regime, intended to launch an endless war and kill of the U.S. constitution." The author concludes :" I call on broadcasters to follow their legal obligation to exercise due impartiality. They must balance their credulous acceptance of the official 9/11 story as established fact with a fair-minded discussion of the alternative theories.[18]

Steve Watson

The Dud Bombers of 21/7, the patsies, have all been rounded up along with 18 others currently under questioning, yet the so-called "mastermind" is allowed to go free and is protected time and again by M15, M16, FBI and CIA, says Steve Watson in the latest writeup on the London episode. The same thing happened in93 with the WTC bombing, 95 with the OKC bombing, 01 with 9/11 and its happening again, it's the same type of operation every time, the author further argues.

The July 29 edition of FOX News Channel's Day Side programme revealed that the so called mastermind of the7/7 London bombings, Haroon Rashid Aswat, is a British intelligence asset. Former Justice Dept. prosecutor and

Terror expert John Loftus reveled that the so-called al-Muhajirun group, based in London had formed during the Kosovo crisis, during which fundamentalist Muslim leaders (or what is now referred to as Al-Qaeda) were recruited by M16 to fight in Kosovo. Loftus stated that" ... back in the late 1990_s the leaders all worked for British intelligence in Kosovo. Believe it or not, British intelligence actually hired some Al-Qaeda guys to help defend the Muslim rights in Albania and Kosovo. That's when Al-Muhajirun got started."

We have previously revealed how former M15 officer David Shayler has alleged, and French intelligence sources have corroborated, that the M16 paid a Libyan Al-Qaeda cell £ 100,000 in 1995 to assassinate Colonel Qaddafi. The use of the group that has come to be known as "Al-Qaeda" as assets by intelligence services the world over is well documented.

The *London Independent* also reported 2 days before the London bombings how M15 has previously used so-called Al-Qaeda operatives as informants, allowing them to be left alone as a trade off. This only came to light when Bisher al-Rawi was captured by the CIA and taken to the detention centre at Guantanamo Bay. The original independent link has now mysteriously been removed.

John Loftus went on to spell out that British intelligence and the U.S. Department of Justice had protected Haroon Rashid Aswat : "Back in 1999 he came to America. The Justice Department wanted to indict him in Seattle because he and his buddy were trying to set up a terrorist training school in Oregon[19]......we have just learned that the headquarters of the U.S. Justice Department ordered the Seattle prosecutors not to touch Aswat....... Apparently Aswat was working for British intelligence."

Haroon Aswat, the so-called mastermind of the London bombing with radical cleric Abu Hamza al-Masri in a

London cab on Jan, 20, 1999. This information is startling and again highlights how Al-Qaeda exists as an organized body only where the intelligence services have created, funded and employed it, says Steve Watson. Loftus points out that several weeks before the London bombings; Aswat was again allowed to slip away, this time to London:

"He was a British intelligence plant. So all of a sudden he disappears. He is in South Africa. We think he's dead; we do not know he is down there. Last month the South African Secret Service come across the guy. He is alive.... The Brits know that the CIA wants to get a hold of Haroon. So what happens? He takes off again, goes right to London. He is not arrested when he lands, he is not arrested when he leaves.... He is not on the watch list. The only reason he could get away with that was if he was working for British intelligence. He was a wanted man."

Loftus' information is backed up by the *New York Times* and CNN who reported on this incident also: "We have seen this many times before and continued to expose this kind of activity. Mr. Aswat is not the only "Al-Qaeda operative" who has been protected while in the U.S.-the 199/11 hijackers and their associate Zaccharias Moussaoi seem to have been as well. FBI agent Robert Wright blew the whistle on obstruction of counter terrorism investigations targeting Hamas and Al-Qaeda before 9/11.[20] The sabotage by the highest levels in the FBI of Coleen Rowley's desperate attempt to investigate Moussaoui,[21] for instance, is striking parallel to the "hands-off" order regarding Aswat, and its far from being the only one. The CIA met with bin Laden in July 2001[22] in a Dubai hospital where he was being treated for kidney problems. They gleaned detained information regarding possible massive terror attacks on the U.S. yet Bin Laden was allowed to slip away (either that or he passed away). Bin Laden is or was a known CIA asset.[23]

Khalid Sheikh Mohammad, mysteriously arrested[24] as the alleged mastermind behind the September 11 plot, was granted a visa[25] to enter the U.S. just six weeks before the terrorist attacks in Washington and New York. The American Al-Qaeda operative, Iyman Faris, who planned to bring down the Brooklyn Bridge was also revealed to be an FBI operative.[26] We also have several other reports[27] stating how the men used as hijackers on the planes on 9/11 were monitored before the event and allowed to enter the U.S. They were even trained at U.S. flight schools.

After 9/11 these so-called terrorists, says further Mr. Steve Watson, have been allowed to go on with business as usual[28], despite the war on terror and in many instances have been protected. It seems that the authorities find it more useful to restrict the liberties of law abiding citizens by introducing draconian restrictive laws such as the Patriot Act and Free Speech Zoning, whilst allowing those they label as terrorists to go undetected.

Haroon Rashid Aswat, Steve Watson concludes, allegedly left London for Pakistan on July 6, one day before the London bombings. He was then arrested in Pakistan, but released again within 24 hours. He reportedly traveled to Zimbabwe and then Zambia, where he may have been arrested again.[29] Why does the so-called mastermind of 7/7 keep being released and allowed to slip away in the same type of operation over and over again.[30]

Paul Joseph Watson

In his interesting article Paul Joseph Watson describes in detail how the government staged the London bombings in the ten easy steps. He suggests the ten methods to stage any terrorist attack:

1. Hire a Crisis Management firm to set up an exercise that parallels the terrorist attack you are going to carry out. Have them run the exercise at the precise locations and at the very same time as the attack. If at any stage of the

attack your Arabs get caught, tell the police it was part of an exercise.

2. Hire four Arabs and tell them they are taking part in an important exercise to help defend London from terrorist attacks. Strap them with rucksacks filled with deadly explosives. Tell the Arabs the rucksacks are dummy explosives and would not harm a fly.

3. Tell four Arabs to meet up at London Underground and disperse, each getting on a different train. Make sure Arabs meet in a location where you can get a good mug shot of them all on CCTV which you can later endlessly repeat to drooling masses on television.

4. While four Arabs are in London, plant explosives in their houses in Leeds. Plant some explosives in one of their cars in Luton for the police to later discover. Remember that Quran and flight manual in the hijackers' car? Ha ha, they fell for that one hook, line and sinker. No need to change tactics on this one.

5. Before the bombings take place, make sure you warn any of your buddies who are scheduled to be any where near where the bombs go off. If this gets leaked to the press, just deny it.

6. 4th Arab goes out partying in London night before and ends up getting out of bed late. No worries, the 9/11 'hijackers' did the same thing but that did not cause us a big problem. 4th Arab catches bus to see if other Arabs are waiting for him. 4th Arab starts hearing bout explosions in the London Underground. 4th Arab comes to the realization that this he is being set up and freaks out. 4th Arab starts fiddling in his suck sack. 4th Arab sets bomb off and is blown up.

If you hired any additional Arabs and they also got wind of the set up, make sure there are GPS locators in the rucksacks so you can have police snipers ready to kill them before they can blow the whistle.

7. After the bombs go off, put out a story for over an hour that the explosions are a simple electrical fault. This gives you cover time to make sure the lazy bus Arab is dead and any other hired Arabs who reneged are also dead. Make sure any CCTVfootage that does not support your official story is either seized or destroyed.

8. A few hours after the bombings, have one of your boys post an 'Al-Qaeda statement claiming responsibility. Don't worry about the whole 'misreferencing the Quran' thing, these idiots do not have the attention spans to figure it out.

9. After you have made sure that all the Arabs are dead and you are managing the story accordingly, wait for your days until the police piece together the story and find the explosives you planted in Leeds and in the car in Luton. Remember that Quran and flight manual in the hijackers' car? Ha ha they fell or that one hook, line sinker. No need to change tactics this time either. The time delay will convince the gullible public that a real investigation is taking place. Create a background of the hired Arabs being militant Muslims. The drooling masses, as was the case with the '9/11 hijackers', will ignore stories of neighbours saying they were the quiet, educated types who liked children and playing sports.

   BBC excerpt: One local resident described him as "a nice lad". "He liked to play football, he liked to play cricket. I am shocked". Another resident said he was just a "normal kid" who played basket ball and kicked a ball around.

10. Sit back and enjoy as Blair and his minions grandstand in front of television cameras about staying the course in the war on terror. The pay raise, extra agency funding, and power to strip more freedoms and liberties made the

> ten easy steps to staging a terrorist attack a worthwhile venture. The dozens of dead people were necessary collateral damage. This is a dirty war, we need to be less moral than the terrorists to defeat them.

After suggesting the ten easy steps Paul Joseph Watson says, "And that is how the Government staged the bombings in these ten steps. Granted, you can interchange different pieces of the puzzle. The bombers could be real terrorists that knew exactly what they were doing. All you would need to do is control the 'mastermind' behind the attack and make sure his boys carried out the job in the way you wanted, Viola.[31]

Charley Reese

He has been a journalist for 49 years, reporting on everything from sports to politics. He served two years active duty in the U.S. army as tank gunner. He is of the firm view that no terrorist attacks any civilization. British Prime Minister and the U.S. President went into their standard routine after the London bombings. This was an attack against civilization and all civilized nations, they said.

That's bosh and hokum, and it does a disservice to the people. The first step always in solving any problem is to define the problem correctly. There are no terrorists in the world, argues Mr. Reese, whose goal is the destruction of civilization, western or otherwise. The terrorist attacks against the U.S., Great Britain and Spain are motivated exclusively by western policies toward the Palestinian – Israeli conflict and the presence of western military forces in Islamic countries. Al-Qaeda, the ideological source of these attacks has always been crystal-clear and specific about its reasons for declaring war against the United States.

You can not win a war, says the author, unless you know who your enemy is, know why he is your enemy and know what his objectives are. Only then can you properly direct your military and political forces to combat him successfully. Unfortunately, very early on, President Bush decided to create a mythical enemy of vague and ambiguous proportions and irrational motives. This was done to the government to pursue policies that really had nothing to do with fighting Al-Qaeda e.g. invading Iraq, putting North Korea and Iran in the "axis of evil" including groups on the enemies list that were in fact not our enemies.

The confusion this causes, the author further explains, was illustrated by television coverage of the London attacks. Several commentators limped together the terrorist attacks against public transport in Moscow, Madrid and London. However, the Moscow attack had nothing to do with the attacks in Madrid and London or with U.S. Moscow is fighting Chechen rebels who want independence for Chechnya. Chechen attacks against Russia like Palestinian attacks against Israel, are not directed at U.S; they are motivated by specific political objectives. Chechens and Palestinians have no desire to destroy civilization; they simply wish to take their place in the family of nations as independent countries.

You can not have a war against terrorist because, as many people have pointed out, terrorism is a tactic employed by people who have no real military power. It is not an entity. There is no worldwide terrorist organization, Reese argues strongly. Terrorist tactics work because we live in a wired world. Ten or twelve people can set off a few bombs in London, and the world turns its electronic eyes on the story and chats, discusses and shows video clips until some other event distracts it. The media attention and the inflated rhetoric of politicians magnify the terrorist act for beyond its actual import.

These attacks, pinpricks really in terms of any damage they do to national power, can not be completely stopped, the writer ecplains. A few malcontents inspired by some ones rhetoric can get together and set off a bomb or two or shoot some people. Terrorists should be considered criminals, and their acts as ordinary crimes. Physically dealing with terrorists is properly ordinary police work. There is no war involved. What the United States should be doing instead of invading and occupying countries re-examining its foreign policy vis-à-vis the Islamic world, Charley Reese suggests wisely. There is no natural conflict between the West and Islam, the author claims. The followers and true believers of Osama bin Laden are a tiny minority. The best way to cut the ground out from under him is to develope and pursue policies that treat all of the Islamic countries with fairness and respect.[32]

William Blum

William Blum has counted London another casualty of the war on terror. He has criticized the British government and declared its foreign policy responsible for the London attacks. In the period leading up to the U.S invasion of Iraq from many quarters came the warnings of the great chaos and violence this would lead to in various parts of the world, the many new anti-American-terrorists and otherwise who would be produced. But it can be said now that the consequences have been even worse than predicted. Indonesia, for example, more than once. Turkey more than once Pakistan repeatedly Saudi Arabia Morocco, Madrid. And now the people of London have just experienced what the people of Baghdad, Falluja and many other Iraqi cities have been experiencing almost daily for more than two years. This is but to name some of most serious attacks amongst the thousands of terrorist acts against American targets and Washington's allies since the United States imposed its so-called war on terror upon the world. Contrary to the lie machine, the world has not been made safer, Mr. Blum has criticized.

Then the author asks: Do we need any more evidence that there is no security solution to terrorism? No military solution. How can you stop subway and bus bombs? Check every passenger throughout the day, every day, forever? X-ray all bags and backpacks at Times Square during the rush hour? Whether we like it or not we must admit that terror is a message and we better learn to listen to it with as unindoctrinated a mind as we can summon from our depths.

Mr. Blum further analyses that there are the violent messages and there are the verbal messages. A group calling itself the organization of Al-Qaeda Jihad in Europe claimed credit for the attacks in London in an internet posting. The group said the attacks were in response to the massacres carried out by Britain in Iraq and Afghanistan....we continue to warn the governments of Denmark, Italy and all the Crusaders that they will meet the same punishment if they do not withdraw their troops from Iraq and Afghanistan. Notice that, as usual, there was no reference to Western values, wealth, freedom, democracy or any of the other thins George W. Bush never tires of telling us the terrorists, hate and the reasons they attack the West, the write up goes on.

It does not particularly matter if this statement is or is not an official statement from the office of Al-Qaeda group (if such a group still exists or over existed), or if the group had any direct connection to the fourmen from Leeds named as the perpetrators. The offsprings and the sympathizers of Al-Qaeda are out there and are increasing in number and anger with each passing day that the United Sates and its allies remain in Iraq and Afghanistan. If cricket-playing British-born Muslims can be inspired to become suicide bomber, then the United States and the United Kingdom have only two options to choose from: Remove the source of the inspiration by changing their foreign policy, or continue in politically convenient denial, the author suggests.

Mr. William Blum explains his suggestion. Exit strategy.... That's the buzz word on the Sunday morning talk shows and from members of Congress, Conservatives and Liberals like, calling upon the White House to announce a timetable for withdrawal from Iraq. For many it serves as their criticism of the administration's Iraq policy; its about as tough as their criticism gets (along with demands for more troops, more armored vehicles, and more body armor). But even if we were to take such talk seriously, what does it actually mean? Mr. Blum puts the question. He then immediately responds: I suggest that to evaluate these demands we have to know that what the speaker believes is the reason for the U.S. presence in Iraq. If one believes that the basic motivation behind Washington's invasion and occupation was altruistic-overthrowing a dictatorship and establishing a truly free, independent, democratic, secular and prosperous society-then of course, one could argue that the U.S should not leave in as much as the present situation is light years removed from such a noble goal. However, if one is not actually suffering from this advanced stage of dementia and knows, or at least seriously suspects, that things like oil, Israel, the dollar vs. the euro, the empire, and US corporations were, and remain, the *raison d'etre* of the American presence, then that would be the purpose of calling for a time table for withdrawal? The oil, et al. are continuing considerations for the White House. There was no exit strategy because there was no strategy to exit. Thus the only demand to be made must be to get out now, starting packing up tomorrow, if not to night.

Every day the occupation continues, concludes Mr. Blum, adds to the terrible suffering of the Iraqi peoplě. The daily bombings and murders may well end as soon as the US leaves; the end of the occupation has certainly received more than passing attention in the communiqués from insurgents. The fact that the US is creating more anti-American "Jihadists" each day – which the CIA has recently confirmed – is reason enough all by itself for leaving. A question some one should ask Bush or Rumsfeld: "If you knew for certain that the bombings, kidnappings and assassinations in Iraq would cease immediately upon the US leaving, would you leave immediately":[33]

Thomas Friedman

Thomas Friedman sees all the suicide bombings as reaping what was sowed by the Arab/Muslim rulers in their homelands. Way too many Arab intellectuals and religious and political leaders were ready to extol suicide bombing when it was directed against Israelis. Now they are seeing how this weapon of nihilism - once sanctified and glorified - can be used against their own societies. "It was wrong when it was used against Jews and it is wrong when it is used against Muslims. Yon can not build decent society on the graves of suicide bombers and their victims", Friedman issues the verdict. The columnist is of the conviction that these bombings in Iraq Egypt and Saudi Arabia are also sign of the deeper struggle that the U.S. attempt to erect democracy in Iraq has touched off".

Friedman quotes in his favour his friend Raymond Stock, the biographer and translator of Naguib Mahfouz and a longtime resident of Cairo. The columnist quickly forgets the controversy among the Muslim world over the novels of Naguib Mahfouz and that how he was treated as an agent of the West in Egypt and the rest of the Arab countries and those who highlighted this novelist were politically motivated as the Arabs viewed. Such kind of experts on Islam and Muslims are now exposed to the Muslim world as less-reliable.

Raymond Stock, as claimed by Friedman, has argued that he was seeing in Baghdad, Cairo and Riyadh the modern incarnation of several deeply-rooted and interlocking wars. These are, he said, "the war within Islam between traditionalists and rationalists, which dates back to Baghdad in the ninth century; the struggle between ardent Sunnis and Shiites, which dates back to succession battles in early Islam; and the confrontation between Islam and the West, which dates back to the Arab conquests of the seventh century and the crusades." How unrealistic and even unhonest is this analysis and predating of terrorism!

"The Iraqi election was a total shock to the militant jihadist forces in the Arab-Muslim world". Stock noted. "They warned Iraqis that 'you vote-you die', and instead milions of Iraqis said back to them, 'we vote-we decide". And the thing they are deciding on, Friedman comments, is not "to be pro-American, to be pro-western, but to try to build their own Arab society in a way that will be open to modernism and interpretations of Islam that encourage innovation, adaptation and progress".

Can anyone ask Friedman which brand of Islam he has experienced with? Has he studied any variety of Islam that is opposed to modernization and scientific advancement? Do the holy verses of the Quran not persuade to march towards thinking, reflection, enquiry and acuqisition of scientific knowledge? and which are those Islamic interpretations that discourage the progress and prosperity? Friedman, however, expresses his views saying: "The jihadist forces hate this (modern) notion. They see the struggle for democracy in Iraq as anathema to every thing they stand for: a literalist interpretation of Islam, unsullied by modernity, adaptation, women's rights or political and religious pluralism".

He quotes Abu Musab al-Zarqawi, the Jordanian-born Jihadist behind much of the Iraqi violence, who spelled it his declaration last January. Democracy must be opposed, he said all out in because it based "on the right to choose your religion" and that is "against the rule of God". He added "Oh people of Iraq, where is your honour? Have you accepted oppression of the Crusader harlots?" Zarqawi and his Saudi and Egyptian allies, Friedman further says; are trying to defeat America and its allies in the heart of the Arab Muslim world, but Zarqawi and Co. are losing – and they know it. Having lost the argument with their own community, and unable to offer any programme, the Sunni-traditionalist-jihadists seem to have become totally unhinged, with people becoming suicide bombers at the rate of three and four a day. The jihadists "know that if democracy comes to this part of the world, the Zarqawis and their ilk are done", Stock said. "Because the majority of people do not buy their methods or most of their message. They do no want to live like the Taliban. If democracy manages to spread in the Arab world, it will not necessarily be pro-American, but it will definitely be pro-living, not pro-suicide. It will not be a cult of death, but a cult of life". A recent cover of a popular Egyptian magzine *Rose el-Youssef*, Stock noted, shows two well-known female Arab pop singers under the head line: "stronger than Extremism".

Friedman rejoices the growing tendency of socalled modernity and welcomes the forced liberalism, democracy and sponsored election process. He continues: "Yes, this is a big struggle in Iraq. Yes, the forces of decency and pluralism are slowly wining. But it is not over – not by a long shot. The U.S. army and the first freely Iraqi elected government still do not control all the terrain there. Unless we can help the Iraqis create a secure environment in their country, and unless their new government can find a way to integrate the more pragmatic Sunni Bhathists, and even dejected jihadists, who want to be part of a better future for Iraq, that nation will not see self-sustaining democracy. The bad guys wo'nt win, but neither will the good guys, and all we will have produced is a bloody stalemate", Friedman concludes.[34]

The bombings in London are profoundly disturbing, Friedman explains, because that is a bombing in his mother country and closest ally, England is almost a bombing in his own country; partly because one assault may have involved a suicide bomber, bringing this trouble jihadist weapon in to the heart of a major western capital. That would be deeply troubling because open societies depend on trust – on trusting that the person sitting next to one on the bus or subway is not wearing dynamite. These are disturbing also because when jihadist bombers take their 'madness" into the heart of open societies, these are never again quite as open.

But may be the most important aspect of the London bombings, as Friedman points out, is this: when jihadist-style bombings happen in Riyadh, that is a Muslim – Muslim problem. That is a police problem for Saudi Arabia. But when Al-Qaeda like bombings come to the London Underground, that becomes a "civilizational problem", the columnist goes on. Every Muslim living in a western country suddenly becomes "a suspect, becomes a potential walking bomb". And when that happens, it meant that western countries are going to be tempted to crack down even harder on their own Muslim populations. That portrait too is deeply troubling. The more western socieites – particularly the big western societies, which have much larger Muslim populations than America – look on their own Muslims with suspicion, the more internal tensions this creates, and the more alienated their already alienated Muslim youth become. This is exactly what Osama bin Laden dreamed of with 9/11: to create a great gulf between the Muslim world and the globalising West, the writer further explains. To limit this "civilizational fall out" from the bombings is not so easy. Because unlike 9/11 there is no obvious easy target to retaliate gainst for bombings like those in London. To the writer, the Muslim world should "begin to really restrain, inhibit and denounce its own extremists" or the West is to do it for them. And the West will do it in a rough, crude way – by simply shutting them out, denying them visas and making every Muslim in its midst guilty until proven innocent. And because the writer thinks that would be a disaster, it is essnetial that "the Muslim world wake up to the fact that it has a jihadist death cult in its midst. If it does not fight that death cult, that cancer, within its own body politic, it is going to infect Muslim –western relations every where. Only the Muslim world can root out that death cult. It takes a village".

How darely does the writer involve the entire Muslim society in the bombings and how biasedly he portrays the situation. This type of logic, reasoning and argumentation is basically always responsible for creating uncalled troubles and unexpected disturbances. The writer calls it 'rooting out a cancer' without going into the root causes of this cancer.

He tries his worst to make the Muslim world responsible for the attacks planned in London, and is not ready to write a single line on the terror links with the western exploiting foreign policy. The writer is exposed when he suggests: "What do I mean? I mean that the greatest restraint on human behaviuor is never a policeman or a border guard. The greatest restraint on human behaviour is what a culture and religion deem shameful. It is what the village and its religious and political elders say is wrong or not allowed. Many people said Palestinian suicide bombing was the spontaneous reaction of frustrated Palestinian youth. But when Palestinians decided that it was in their interest to have a seaze-fire with Israel, those bombings stopped cold. The village said enough was enough "Some Muslim leaders have taken up this challenge. This past weeak, king Abdullah II hosted a conference in Amman for moderate Muslim thinkers and clerics who want to take back their faith from those who have tried to hijack it. But this has to go further,:" Friedman concludes.[35]

The writer surprisingly lays all the responsibility on the teachings of Islam. Of course the religion is the greatest restraint, on the how and when? Does he think that the bombers are the champions of the religion? Is there any Islamic movement throughout the world that has encouraged the suicide attacks? Does the author trace any *alim* or *mufti* who might have issued any legal verdict in favour? Did the Britain Muslims themselves not oppose those attacks publicly and on the television channels? Did the huge majority of the Muslims all over the world not nullify these bombings as un-Islamic? If the answer is yes-and of course there may be no other answer – then how and why these suicide attacks are not stopped? why Thomas Friedman does not root out the real factors and actual causes behind these incidents - the causes which are clearly visible? The causes elaborated in detail by most of the unbiased and independent writers and journalists were intentionally or unintentionally ignored by Friedman. Why? Is there any answer to this 'why'?

The analysis provided above by the academicians, journalists, politicians and writers from Britain, America and the West reveals a deep understanding of the tragedy 7/7 and its aftermath, the factors responsible, the power mentality prevailed, and the campaign of war on terror that turned into war on Islam. Not confined to the western countries the third world also especially India and its intellectuals were among the severe critics of the hegemony of the super powers and the West on the crucial issues and their westernized images.

*****

Notes and References

1. **Seumas, Milne, insult to deny Iraq link to London attacks, *The Guardian*, July 14, 2005, also visit: smilne @guardian.co.uk**
2. Robin Cook, Rethink needed on fighting terror. *The Hindu*, July 9, 2005, p. 11.
3. *The Hindu*, July, 22, 2005. for Livingstone's ideas of multiculturalism.
4. Madeleine Bunting, For get the heavy mob. *The Hindu* July 15, 2005 and for the efforts to keep London Open to Change, see Graham Bowcey's feature. *The Hindu* Magazine, September 25, 2005, p. 4
5. *The Hindu*, July 21, 2005.
6. *Ibid.*, This line of thinking against *madrasa* education led by U.S. foreign policy was blindly followed by BJP led-coalition government in India when the champions of *hindutwa*- politicians, diplomats, journalists and intellectuals as well - launched a full fledged campaign throughout the country and propagated the rumour that *madrasas* are den of terrorism wherein militants and ISI agents are recruited. According to a news published in *Hindustan Times*. (Thursday, June 6, 2002, p. 11). "The International Bureau has prepared a Report on unregistered *madrasas* in the country and submitted it to the Home Ministry. It has recommended a central legislation to curb establishment of *masrasas* and regulate construction of *masjids* ... It is also stated to have cited instances of misuse of *madrasas* for subversive purposes eg. storage of arms, ammunition and explosives and recruitment of youth for terrorist outfits". According to *The Hindu* (June, 13, 2002). "the Gujarat chief Minister Mr. Narender Modi indicated that *madrasas* inculcating the *jihad* mentality were responsible for the Godhra incident and the communal mayhem that followed RDX and AK_47s were recovered from some *madrasas* in Gujarat". According to another report, "Terrorist activities in Kerala were centred in some *madrasas*, that *madrasas* posed a danger to the internal security of the country; that a majority of the *madraasas* have shady dealings". *The Hindu*, Apirl 9, 2002.

7. *The Hindu*, July 20, 2005, p. 11.
8. William Dalrymple, No. madrasa link to London attacks, *The Hindu*, July 21, 2005.
9. Richard, Norton Taylor, The reality of the 'war on terror', *The Hindu*, July 20,. 2005.
10. Sidney Blumenthal, War on Terror: Democracy afterthought, *The Hindu*, July 22, 2005.
11. Adam Curtis, The problem with creating Islamist phantoms, *The Hindu*, august 31; 2005.
12. Chidanand Rajghatta, Ghost who tstalks, *Sunday Times of India*, September 11, 2005, p. 8.
13. Don Van Natta Jr., JK hunt on for Islamic cleric's ex-aide, *Times of India*, July 22, 2005.
14. Gary, Younge, Bombers look like every body else. *The Hindu*, July 26, 2005.
15. Jonathan Glover (who teaches human values and contemporary global ethics at King's College, London), Dialogue the way forward, *The Hindu*, July 28, 2005.
16. **Shared Destiny, Shared Defiance, Ramzy Baroud, The Milli Gazatte, 1-15July 2005 p. 22. The essay is a part of his new book entitled *A Force to be Recknoed with : Writings on second pelestinis uprising,* email: ramzibaroud @hotmail.com**
17. http://www.aljazeera.com/cgi-bin/conspiracy_theory/fullstory.asp?id=249
18. http.//www.latimes.com/news/local/la-fq-awsat25jul25, 1, 7530 68.story?coll=la-headlines-california & ctrack=1&cset=true.
19. http://www.prisonplanet.com/911.html # w199i
20. http://www.prisonplanet.com/911.html # w199i
21. http://www.prisonplanet.com/911.html # binladen.
22. http://www.prisonplanet.com/911.html # ciaasset.
23. http://www.prisonplanet.com/mystery_ surrounds convenient arrest of al qaeda_ member.htm.
24. http://www.propagandamatrix.com/260104 granted_visa.html
25. http://www.prisonplanet.com/captured_al-qaeda_man_was-fbi_spy.htm.
26. http://www.prisonplanet.com 911.html# easy.
27. http://www.prisonplanet.com/911.html #protection.

28. For conflicting reports visit: http:www.timesonline.co.uk/article/0,,22989_1716 691,00,html.

29. http://www.infowars.net/Pages/Aug05/ 020805 Awsat.html.

30. For John Loftus' interview about Al-Muhajirun and its leader Osama Hussain and the CIA's game in this regard see, Excerpts from the 29 July 2005 edition of Fox News Channels' "Day Side" programme, *The Milli Gazette,* 16 Aug-15 Sep. 2005, p.27.to read the full interview visit: htt://www.foxnews.com/story/0,2933, 164377,00.html.

31. http://www.prisonplanet.com/artiles/July 2005/130705 teneasysteps.htm.

32. Charley Reese, No body attacks civilization, *The Milli Gazette*, 1-15 Aug. 05, p. 23.

33. Mr. William Blum publicly demounces those who warns of a civil war in Iraq. If the U.S. pulls out, and says that these people are basically the reminiscent of those who warned of a communist blood-bath in Vietnam if American forces left. This warning, according to the author, was repeated in the media to the point of cliché. However, there was never any kind of bloodbath. All that happened was that some of the collaborators with Vietnam's enemies were sent to "re-education" camps, a lot more civilized treatment than in post-world war Two Europe where many of those who had collaborated with the Germans were publicly paraded, shaven bald, humiliated in other ways, and/or hung from the nearest tree. The author is firm that the United States will eventually have to leave Iraq at least partially. But when that happened, watch carefully. The author suggests: observe who has retained control of the oil and other economic entities, and who has retained various privileges. In the early days of the occupation, the coalition Provisional Authority under American official Paul Bremer passed a number of laws which guaranteed American corporations all kinds of benefits within minimal risk. Those laws are still on the books and, as written, will be very difficult to change. And what Iraqi governing body will be able to make the U.S. close its bases, including the new ones currently being built? To

read full article visit: http://informationclearinghouse.info/ article9539.htm.

34. Thomas Friedman, Reaping what it sowed, *The Hindu,* May, 5, 2005.

35. Thomas Friedman, Routing out a Cancer, *The Hindu*, July 9, 2005. It is very interesting to note that most of the Indian essayists and columnists have seen 7/7 attacks in a specific perspective. To them this incident proved India to be used as a terror lab has Western intelligence agencies failure to recognize India as a victim of terrorism and their lack of interest in terrorist *modus operandi.*

3

INDIAN REACTION

India being the champion of independent foreign policy and keeping itself away from power politics of military blocs under the leadership of Pandit Jawaharlal Nehru maintained its non-aligned policy from the very beginning. Nehru, while speaking on India's understanding of the non-alignment said on 9 December 1948: "when we say our policy is one of non-alignment, obviously we mean non-alignment with military blocks... This in itself is not a policy; it is only part of a policy."[1]

Nehru further observed that the policy could only be a policy of acting according to one's best judgement and furthering the objectives and ideals cherished by one's country. He further declared: "Every country's foreign policy, first of all is concerned with its own security and with protecting its own progress... A deliberate policy of friendship with other countries goes further in gaining security than almost anything else. Apart from this, from the larger point of view of the world also, we have laboured to the best of our ability, for world peace... Our foreign policy has thus positive aspect of peace. The other positive aspects are an enlargement of freedom in the world, replacement of colonialism by free and independent countries and a large degree of cooperation among nations."[2]

Prior to the holding of First Non-Aligned Summit at Belgrade in 1961, the concept of neutrality, non-involvement, positive neutralism were prevalent in the country but all these concepts of the pre or post-NAM did never mean an exact objectivity or watertight in partiality.[3] The government and the intellectuals both being neutral in the foreign policy matters were always supportive, within their limitations and keeping their local perspective alert and active, to all the campaigns of freedom, self-reliance and sustenance. The case of Palestine is a bright example in this regard. The London bombings on July 7, 2005 are no exception in this direction. Most of the media people and the political leaders, the intellectuals and the literary men criticized the Western strategy of war on terror and defended a balanced approach in this regard.

Globalising Democracy

The Times of India in its editorial note on July 26, 2005 has highlighted the common feature of the shootings in the UK and India on behalf of the two states and entitled them the "Twin Terror". There is an uncanny congruence among events in the UK, India and Iraq, where overreaction by security forces fuels terrorism they are supposed to combat. London police gunned down a Brazilian youth trying to enter an underground station, under shoot-to-kill orders that came from the top. Many are drawing the conclusion, the editorial note continues, that to look vaguely South Asian in London is to invite suspicion that one is suicide bomber. This can only strain London's much-vaunted multiculturalism and enhance the alienation felt by a British Muslim underclass, which will enable Al-Qaeda to recruit a new crop of Euro-*Jehadis*. In Iraq, the Americans inflict a great deal of what they like to call collateral damage in their anti-insurgent campaign, including the levelling of the city of Fallujah. They reap the whirlwind in the form of renewed insurgent recruitment, so that Iraq is turning into what an analyst has called the *Harvard of Jehad*. And in India, the army guns down four teenage youths, including an eight year-old, in Kupwara in north Kashmir. This is exactly what terrorists want, as it reinforces the US against them mentality that they wish to propagate.

The newspaper further argues that the terrorists are, in effect, challenging the liberal state to prove its credentials, and the liberal state is unable to rise to the challenge. Not to put too fine a point on it, the war against terror is failing. It needs better human rights strategies, precisely what it claims it is fighting to preserve, the editorial writing insists on. In London, shoot-to-kill tactics were adopted reportedly on advice from Israeli experts but it is doubtful whether British democracy can sustain for long draconian Israeli methods of fighting terror. Kashmir is about to turn the corner on its past and the army must revise its rules of engagement to prevent shocking incidents like the shooting of four innocent youths. One must also recognize, however, that security forces on hair-trigger alert to stave off possible suicide bombers do not have an easy task. Better human rights sensitisation is part of the answer, but will not in itself do the trick in the absence of long-term political strategies to combat the insurgent power that terrorists often command. The answer to the globalisation of terrorism is the globalisation of the democracy, not just within countries but also in international institutions where the vital interests of many countries are negotiated, the editorial concludes.[4]

The editorial management in another issue explicitly argues in favour of eliminating the root causes of terrorism through providing employment to youths and changing the political, economic and social conditions in which they live. Isolating a country rarely brings about political change. In Cuba and Iran, countries that have been facing American sanctions for years, there is no sign of regime change. The only way to topple authoritarian regimes is through global integration via free media and trade ties. A free exchange of ideas hastened the dismantling of the Berlin Wall and triggered to velvet revolutions of East Europe. The authoritarian regimes that are the breeding ground for terrorists can be toppled through global integration.

But in the 'counter view' column in the same issue of the newspaper, Anita Sen has opposed the political solutions. "The only way out", she suggests unambiguously, "is to inspire those regimes which back such violent attacks with the threat that they will go the way of Saddam Hussein". She has quoted Libya's Muhammad Gaddafi's case in this regard who gave hp his ways after being threatened with stronger action than just sanctions. "There is nothing that will alarm shadowy rulers like those in Saudi Arabia that they lose their enormous power and privilege and be left to the mercy of a more democratic system as Saddam is now facing",[5] she thus provokes the super power to capture such countries forcefully and implement its goal-serving democracy that would ensure its interests in the region.

The same newspaper in it's another editorial writeup has questioned the seriousness of the West about the war on terrorism. The editor forecasts that Bush would not budge on semantics of the terror. Someone who witnessed the destruction of the Twin Towers at close quarters could be forgiven for thinking that America was at war although even at the time many had wondered whether war was the correct description for the campaign against terror that must follow, the writer says. Despite such reservations the global war on terror, with the ugly acronym GWOT, came into being, and brought in its train considerable re-conservative baggage, such as the idea that only unilateral American supremacy could secure the world from terror. 'War' suggests a predisposition towards using military means rather than a campaign to win hearts and minds. That was precisely the sequence of events that unfolded. American forces, helped by the Northern Alliance, ousted the Taliban from power, which was necessary as the Taliban sheltered Al-Qaeda and Osama bin Laden on its territory. But then the Americans were disinclined to stay and assist in the nation-building efforts needed to make Afghanistan safe for democracy. This has ensured, the analysis goes on, that the Taliban is now resurgent, while Al-Qaeda's top leaders are still holed out somewhere in the region.

Instead, the Americans invaded Iraq. Looking for set piece battles where they could destroy President Saddam Hussein's decrepit military. But in the ruthless war that has exploded since the guerrilla resistance resorted to unconventional tactics, and may have finally buried dreams of unilateral dominance in Iraq's desert sands. Washington has become a victim of its own success precisely because American military power is now unchallenged, the opposition has also evolved, seeking asymmetrical methods to disrupt it. According to this analysis, Al-Qaeda has become, in some ways, like a computer virus – a de-territorialized phenomenon that can rapidly mutate and has no obvious centre that can be attacked. Resistance to GWOT tactics is now coming from the American military itself, and realists within the administration suggested switching to GSAVE or global struggle against violent extremism. This would work, the editor suggests, "if it is accompanied by a change in mind set, which stressed political and diplomatic means that would deny Al-Qaeda the steady stream of supporters it gets. That would have to include pulling out of Iraq, helping Afghanistan get back on its feet, pushing democracy in the Arab world and Pakistan, and loosening up international institutions to accommodate the interests of developing countries. But President Bush is nothing if not dogged, and does not admit to mistakes easily. He has decided, as of now, to stick to GWOT," the editor criticises.[6]

The Colour of Terror

On the page of editorial opinion of *The Times of India* Mr. Jug Suraiya talks about the fear of being brown in post 7/7 Britain. After the London bombings and the subsequent gunning down by the police of a man who "looked like a Pakistani" according to an eyewitness but who turned out in fact to be a Brazilian, the sense of intrusive unease, of being in an environment which implicitly questions one's legitimacy, is likely willy-nilly to be magnified many times over for not only Asians but many other ethnic minorities living in Britain, the writer analyses.

Inspite of all the regrets offered by the British administration and the efforts of minority leaders to appease the growing fears, the inescapable reality, as the analyst marks, is that brown has become the colour of terror in a once-insular society which, till the bombings and the aftermath, seemed to be emerging, haltingly but irreversibly, as a multicultural and multiracial polity.

In her Sunday column, Eurovision, in the same paper, Rashmee Roshan Lal quoted a letter from a reader of Britain's *Daily Telegraph* who wrote that he had quickly got off a train when he saw that one f his co-passengers was a bearded 'Asian Looking' man holding a knapsack on his knees. Brown plus beard plus knapsack equals potential mass murderer. At one stroke a great neo-racist divide has been created... This is racism of deep, visceral fear, inaccessible reason or liberal legislation.

Like jealousy, of which it is the mirror image, paranoia is a disease which feeds on itself and leads to mental ghettoisation "us against them". Jug Suraiya then raises a question: "But who is 'them'? Certainly not us, some sections of the Hindu immigrant population in Britain are already saying, seeking to distance themselves from their Muslim counterparts." Already there is a tacit or articulated admonition of "We told you so. Yet you sided with them on Kashmir, you supported Pakistan. See what that's led to". Can fragile multiculturalism survive in such an atmosphere of many-layered mistrust? Will Muslims in Britain, as many have done elsewhere post 9/11 and after the Gujarat riots, shave their beards so as not to invite suspicion or reprisal? Will Hindus or Buddhists, take to displaying tokens of their faith as prophylactics against xenophobia? He surprisingly questions.

A poll conducted by *The Guardian* in the aftershock of 7/7 shows that almost two-thirds of Britain's 1.6 millions Muslims have thought about what their future will in their adoptive country, with 63% seriously considering whether it is safe to stay on. One out of every five polled said that they or someone in their family had faced verbal or physical assault after the terrorist strikes. Related reports cited police records according to which there have already been some 1200 "Islamophobic incidents" across the country following the bombings. Not a few of these involved violence, leading to a fatality in one case. All this brings the terrorists that much closer to victory, Jug Suraiya goes on saying, for the battlefield of terror is not based on differences of religion or race. "It is based", as the writer concludes, "on the fundamental difference between those who believe in free societies, however imperfect these may be, and those who would impose fear societies on us. 'Us' and 'them' is not about the colour of one's skin or the contours of faith. It is about democracy and demonisation. Trouble is, democracy is not skin deep. Demonisation is".[7]

Enemy from Within

Rashmee Roshan Lal, the columnist in *The Times of India* is not surprised to find the London bombers from within the country. The enemy within UK is not so shocking after all. "It is entirely unsurprising that Britain's own sons have seen fit to make their motherland bleed. The only surprise is that it took this long. "She requests the readers to pay their attention back to the history of Ahmad Omar Sheikh, Richard Reid the newly convert to Islam and others all the West born-and-bred. The first, a Brit with a beard and a burning anger against the injustice meted out by "Hindu India to Kashmiri brothers" played an important role in the kidnapping of a Delhi-based Romanian diplomat in 1996. There was a shoot out. Sheikh wound up in police custody. Later he was to find his way back to Pakistan. Much later, he would lure the young American journalist Daniel Pearl, to a promised "big" interview and behead him. Sheikh was supposedly a posh Anglo-Pakistani from east London. His father was a prosperous clothes merchant, who had clearly made it in the West. He earned enough to send his handsome clever son to an A class fee-paying London school. Sheikh would later enter the London School of Economics. And he would go on to perform that almost routine act of charity common to many young white Britons – getting involved with the demand and dispossessed in other benighted parts of the world. Accordingly Sheikh went off to Bosnia, his heart bleeding for the suffering he first glimpsed on a video screening possibly at the LSE. Till then, it was all pretty standard – the Western do-gooder strutting his stuff. The difference was that Sheikh actually appears to have felt the pains of the people he was there to help far more keenly than the average Briton. The result was Sheikh's radicalisation. He got involved with a radical Islamist group and learnt the "dark arts of hostage-taking and high-end terrorism" that would later make headlines around the world.

Rashmee quotes the Christmas Day 2000 when a wired-up car explodes in Srinagar, blowing up the bomber and ripping through the lives of dozens of innocent passers-by. That act came directly from Birmingham, executed by one Abdullah Bai, *nom de guerre* of an allegedly inoffensive young man, who had hitherto displayed typical young Brit proclivities towards nightclubs and nubile girls.

The rest is better known to the world outside India, Rashmee further says, Richard Ried, Londoner and convert to Islam, who famously became the "shoe-bomber" in December 2001. Ried tried to blow up the plane by setting alight the explosives in his shoes. One of his comrades was Sajid Badaat, a clever, geeky, grammar school boy, who bottled out, at the last miniature, despite preparing hard for the role of "shoe-bomber". Badaat's background was fairly British, middle-class. His father worked for Wall's ice cream. And then there were the two others, with English accents and a fire in their bellies, who went off to bomb a Tel Avive bar.

How surprising is it then, argues Rashmee, that Hasib Hussain, Shahzad Tanweer and Mohammad Siddique Khan have now joined those others on the terrible roll call that leaves in its wake tragedy and terror? "We have it on good authority" she further says, "that Britain and much of the West increasingly needs to recognise the terrorists threat as no longer posed by "the other". She refers to American professor Marc Sageman, who last year carried out a unique study of the individuals who make up *Al-Qaeda*. Most of them, he said, were "global citizens". They had either been despatched to the West to study or work. Or they were at home in the West and thereby, privileged by their passports and prospects. Sageman said more than 70% of 382 members of *Al-Qaeda* or affiliated groups, turned *Jihadi* somewhere abroad while based in the West. To that extent, Rashmee concludes, there is no surprise that bombers are from within Britain itself.[8]

Fighting through Surrogates

Mr. Swagato Ganguly suggests the West to fight terrorism directly. Fighting through surrogates, the West can never win decisively. It is the history of the West that it has mostly used surrogates to fight its wars, that in practice gives rise to an unending cycle. The West needs new surrogates to fight its former surrogates. Something like this happening in the current war against terror. The writer analyses the Second World War in this direction.

Popular Anglo-American accounts produce the overwhelming impression that British and American forces were instrumental in ridding Europe of Nazi tyranny. By way of a reality check, as many as 80% of German military casualties were inflicted not by British and American forces, but by Soviet forces. Hitler's foreign minister, Joachim von Ribentrop, saw three main reasons for Germany's defeat: powerful resistance from the Soviet Union, the end-lease agreement which transferred arms on a large scale from the US to the Soviets and air supremacy achieved by the Western allies. The US and UK are credited only with support roles: providing arms and equipment, and running bombing campaigns from the air. An inevitable payoff for the preponderant Soviet role in winning World War II was that about half of 'liberated" Europe had to be ceded to Stalin, Mr. Ganguly further elaborates. This was, in effect, the understanding arrived at between Roosevelt, Churchill and Stalin at Yalta. But equations changed somewhere between the Yalta and Potsdam conferences with the Anglo-American insistence that Poland, which had been conquered by Soviet troops and was firmly in the Soviet orbit, had to have a freely elected government on the Western model. Stalin, of course, would have none of this, and Truman fired the first rhetorical shots of the Cold War declaring, in January 1946, that he was 'tired of babysitting, the Soviets who understand only an iron fist and strong language.

Mr. Ganguly reminds of 1980s when the same pattern was repeated by the West. The West decided to train and arm the Islamist guerrilla force operating in Afghanistan to bring down its Cold War adversary. Two quotes are opposite in this context. The former is from Zbigniew Brzezinski, national security adviser to President Carter and enthusiastic proponent of such a policy" "which was more important in world history? The Taliban or the fall of the Soviet empire? A few over-excited Islamists or the liberation of Central Europe?" The latter is a secular Afghan's comment on the same policy: "For God's sake, you are financing your own assassins". The Soviet invasion of Afghanistan caused the West to enter into a "strange love affair" with radical *Sunni* Islamist forces, as ABC correspondent John Cooley wrote in his prescient 2000 book *Unholy Wars*. If such a romance seems strange in the backdrop of 9/11, it is no stranger than the earlier courtship of Comrade Stalin, or the current tango with General Musharraf, Mr. Ganguly analyses.

The West, according to this analysis, wanted to bring down the USSR, but it did not want to rub the USSR the wrong way. Operational control of the anti-Soviet *Jehad* was outsourced to Pakistan and the ISI, in the interests of '*plausible deniability*'. The ISI, in turn, challenged billions of dollars in aid and armaments not to those who were effectively conductive the guerrilla resistance inside Afghanistan, such as Ahmad Shah Masood, but to *Sunni* fanatics like Gulbadin Hekmatyar. Under the watchful eyes of the CIA, the ISI and Saudi intelligence, Osama bin Laden set up shop in Peshawar to fight the Soviets, and formed the *Maktab al-Khidmat* (MAK), a Mulim equivalent of the International Brigades. The MAK morphed into the *Al-Qaeda*. Ergo, yesterday's freedom fighters had become today's terrorists.

"If bin Laden is now the enemy", Mr. Ganguly argues in his own way, "questionable friends have once again been recruited to fight the enemy. These are the tyrants of the Muslim world, cordially hated by most of their populace. *Al-Qaeda* is uninhibited about exporting *Jehad*, but the West feels diffident about promoting its ideology, liberal democracy when it comes to the Muslim world. It goes on, instead, for the strategic equivalent of a quickie by consorting with its dictators." The writer is quick in quoting General Musharraf in this context who was "a pariah when he carried out his military coup in 1999.

9/11 captulated him into the front ranks of statesmen battling terror. This gives him, and the military apparatus he represents, strong incentives to pay both sides, as they know that their relevance will be finished one's Pakistan's terror infrastructure is taken down," the analyst evaluates.

"Pushing democracy in the Muslim world", the writer describes the Western fear, "has its risks, as it is possible that a government with Islamist leanings is elected democratically." But within a short time the citizens of that country will discover that a "purer version" of religion is no solution to earthly problems and vote the government out, he forecasts according to his perception and understanding of the religion. And in that stage "if democracy is abrogated by the Islamist rulers, the West could move in with its regimes of containment," he suggests the West unhesitatingly accepting an overall hegemony of the super powers. The writer then puts a question: "But does the West have the gumption to carry through such a policy?" He very objectively admits: "Past history suggests the answer is in the negative".[9]

Sustained Insurgency

The famous writer on terrorism Dilip Hiro, whose 26th book *Secrets and Lies*: *The True Story of the Iraq War* presents before us the other side of the picture and describes in detail the exposure of American selectivity in choosing its targets. He in a conversation with Ziyaus Salam has exposed the 'war on terror' without an end. Responding to the question, why this global conspiracy of silence regarding the US invasion of Iraq, he said that actually much is being said about the Anglo-American invasion of Iraq in the United States itself. According to a Gallup poll in mid-June 2005, six out of ten Americans wanted to see some or all US troops withdrawn from Iraq. And by 4.3 Americans say that the Bush administration made a mistake in sending troops to Iraq. What is more, a USA Today/CNN/Gallup poll showed that for the first time a plurality of Americans (50-47 percent) sees the war in Iraq as separate from the war on terrorism, and say that the war in Iraq has made the US less safe from terrorism.

Asked as the US has known for long that Iraq was using chemical weapons, then why did it need 15 years to act, Hiro was of the view that six weeks after Iraq had used chemical weapons against the Iranians in the 1983 Iran-Iraq war, the then roving US ambassador in the Middle East, Donald Rumsfeld, met Iraqi President Saddam Hussein. They discussed constructing a pipeline to carry oil from southern Iraq to the Jordanian port of Aqba. Saddam continued using chemical weapons against Iran until the end of war in August 1988. During that time Washington actually increased its aid to Iraq-financial, military and intelligence – while maintaining the fiction of being "neutral", he criticised.

Post-9/11 the US has successfully morphed Osama bin Laden and Saddam Hussein. How? Hiro shows us the other aspects of the story while answering this question. He indicates the US foreign policy in this regard. First Bush's efforts to show that Saddam was linked to *Al-Qaeda*'s terrorism succeeded only in the US. It failed to convince most of the Security Council members and their public at home. The Anglo-American allies got only five votes for their resolution sanctioning force against Baghdad. Even Mexico, ruled by a conservative president Vincent Fox refused to back Bush. Secondly, in their impatience to overthrow Saddam Hussein, Bush and his team never paid much attention to the history, culture and ethnic and sectarian composition of Iraq. Take the case of North Korea, Mr. Hiro points out: "After the US and Russia, it has the best missiles in its arsenal. It is on the US State Department's list of countries that support international terrorism. It has an appalling human rights record. Yet Bush has not attacked North Korea. Why?"

Do the London bombings complete a cycle of terrorist attacks on all the nations and people supporting the invasion of Afghanistan and Iraq – Bali, Madrid and London? Responding to this issue Mr. Hiro needs to make a distinction between pre-9/11 and post-9/11. Also between Iraq and Afghanistan, where the US had unanimous support at the UN Security Council. He further discussed that senior British police officers often warned that an attack in Britain was inevitable. Britain contributed proportionately more to the invasion of Iraq than did the US (a third of the total military force compared to one-tenth of the Pentagon's). In post-war Iraq, Britain continues to deploy the second-largest force there after the US, with whom it shares the status of being an occupying power. Equally vital was Britain's contribution in the diplomatic arena. When it came to convincing the world of Saddam Hussein's allegedly malevolent plans, Blair produced a dossier in September 2002 to establish that Iraq was producing weapons of mass destruction.

The interviewer asked: how appropriate is it to call the retaliatory action by *Al-Qaeda* as terrorist attack when the Iraq invasion is regarded as just a pre-emptive exercise? Particularly when no WMDs were recovered from Iraq? Mr. Dilip Hiro to this explicitly declared: "According to UN Security General, Kofi Annan, the Anglo-American war on Iraq was illegal. He said so in his interview with the BBC World Service Radio on September 15, 2004. It is worth noting that while Bush refers to "thugs and assassins" in Iraq, his military commanders and even Rumsfeld invariably refer to "insurgents and insurgency". In a recent interview Rumsfeld said that insurgencies tend to go on for "five, six, 10 or even 12 years". So the scene in Iraq has escalated from "retaliatory attacks" to a sustained insurgency against the occupying powers. By now the failure of the Anglo-American occupiers to find WMDs in Iraq, or find a link between Saddam Hussein and *Al-Qaeda* has been well dissmented by official bodies in the US, Mr. Dilip Hiro clearly commented.[10]

Imaginary Homelands

Why are Muslims in Europe angrier than those in Malaysia, Indonesia and India? India has been mentioned repeatedly as a country with the world's second largest Muslim population but not one national or the international list of the suspects. The Indian Muslims do face disadvantages as a minority and the country has a history of terrible riots. But even the angriest have not turned to Osama for solace. Why? That was well answered by Ranjon Roy saying: "Perhaps one of the reasons is that independent India and especially Jawaharlal Nehru, despite the trauma of Partition, ensured that Muslims had cultural, political and social space. Also there is not an identity crisis among most Muslims that would force them into violent radicalism, which we see happening to sections of Muslim youth in Europe." It perhaps is not a necessary and sufficient condition to prevent radicalisation, but it does help when besides being Muslims in India, they are also men and women from U.P., or Biharis, Gujaratis, Tamils and Bengalis, sharing a language and culture with their neighbours from other religions. Advocating the democratizing process more in order to combat terrorism, Ranjan Roy argues, where there is a degree of alienation, it is nothing compared to being flung into a white neighbourhood of Flemish Belgians or locked into a Turkish ghetto in Germany. Muslims have lived in India for centuries and the subcontinent has been ruled by Muslim rulers who embraced this land as theirs. The writer quotes Robert S. Leiken who argues in one of the issues of *The Foreign Affairs* that Muslims in Europe are most likely to get radicalised because of a range of factors stretching form alienation to dissidence. And many among this group could become the new agents of terror. Post-Westphalia Europe, according to this analysis, split up into tiny nation states with homogeneous communities and one or two languages. Yet, the hunger for workers forced them to open borders and thousands of Muslims migrated to Europe in the post-war years. Algerians and Moroccans headed for France to seek jobs, Turks walked into Germany and Pakistani into Britain. But few fond a warm welcome. While that generation, Leiken argues, "accepted its fate, the newer generation, although more Western, is aggressive". It is actually aware of being brought up in racially-defined ghettos and barbs from right-wing supremacists.

Other scholars to Ranjan Roy have discerned a trend in many of the terrorists or their ideologues having Western exposure. If the Egyptian radical Sayyid Qutb went to the United States as far back as 1948, Ramzi Yusuf, the allegedly mastermind of the first World Trade Centre bombing, was an electronics engineer with a degree from Britain. Others are known to have spent time in France or studied in Germany before turning to radical ways.

Olivier Roy, a French scholar of Islam, says that traditional Islamic societies rarely advocate a move towards militancy and terrorism and are far more tolerant of the status quo. This project for what he calls "Imaginary Islam" is a modern one, discussed, calibrated and implemented against Western imperialism by people who themselves are products of modern ideas and a modern education system. Whether in Iran or Afghanistan, the radicals are usually the ones exposed to modern thinking, Ranjan Roy concludes.[11]

It is unfortunate that Muslims are under the scanner, from Leads to Amsterdam, in the tiny bylanes around Ramblas in Barcelona and around the Algerian Quarter near *Gare du Nord* in Paris. They are being scrutinised to border crossings and airports by officers. But what many will be looking for is not the stereotype. The terrorist is less likely to be a national of a country with a large Muslim population. Ranjan Roy refers a report to explain the case. Recently, the Nixon Centre in Washington DC came up with figures that made US homeland security experts sit up. A study of 373 *mujahideen* in Western Europe and North America between 1993 and 2004 showed there were "twice as many Frenchmen as Saudis and more Britons than Sudanese, Yemenis, Emirates, Lebanese or Libyans". What frightened the Americans was that there were many more of these people who could fly in and out of any Western country without visa checks. But that is just one part of the story. Buried in these numbers is the fact that perhaps Muslims who have migrated to a new homeland are more prone to fall victim to radical brainwashing. It is a scary scenario for Europe at least. The migrants were not welcomed by the European citizens. They were rather treated as strangers mentally and psychologically at least. This created an intolerant reaction against the imperialist Europe.

Continental Drift

Rajesh Sharma speaks on the issue in term of continental drift and is of the view that integration of Muslims in the Western World leaves a lot to the desired. He narrates few specific examples in this context. The case of Rachid Ramda has strained judicial relations between France and Britain for the last decade. On July 25, 1995 a bomb blast in the Paris metro at Saint Michel Station killed eight people and injured over 150. This signalled the beginning of a wave of bomb attacks by the Algerian Islamic Armed Group, the GIA. But despite four international arrest warrants and never-ending court cases, Rachid Ramda, who allegedly financed this wave of terror, has astutely managed to evade extradition to France, much to the frustration of the French authorities. In 2002 a British court cancelled the extradition order, ruling that as Ramda was suspected of terrorist attacks, he could be subjected to degrading and inhuman treatment in France. Now with London itself being targeted by suicide bombers, the French authorities feel that their request for extradition is finally likely to go through.

Again only a few weeks back, the federal constitution court in Germany refused to extradite Mamoun Darkazanli, suspected *Al-Qaeda* financier, to Spain, saying that a European arrest warrant would violate the German Constitution. Norway, on its part, has been struggling for two years to expel Mullah Krekar, the Iraqi Kurd leader suspected of having links with *Al-Qaeda.* Norway granted his family political asylum over ten years ago, but the refugee status did not stop him from returning regularly to Iraq to wage *Jehad.*

Despite terror having invaded virtually every continent and country after country, such disputes are difficult to understand or accept. The legislative frame work needs to be reworked and it is up to the European Union to ensure that all member-states work in harmony as far as anti-terrorism measures are concerned. If every country waits for terrorism to strike its soil before taking harsh measures as Britain is taking today, Europe will be incapable of effectively countering this menace. Europe suddenly seems vulnerable to serious threats, though terrorism is not unknown here. Basque terrorism in Spain, Corsican in France, Irish in Britain or the November 17 movement in Greece are instances of domestic terrorism that have carried on for years. But this time, Sharma argues, the nature of the 'game' has changed.

The London bombings, the writer continues, have sent shockwaves through West European nations. London was considered one of the most tolerant, cosmopolitan and well integrated cities and the British multicultural model superior and most successful than the French republican model that calls for assimilation of all nationalities and communities. But that apparently did not shelter the country from extreme forms of religious fanaticism. Soon after the terror attacks in Britain, France and Italy heightened security measures, reinforced information gathering procedures and cracked down on militants. But what has been immediate and hard-hitting is the action taken against *imams* who were found to be preaching hatred and violence as reported by the media.

Sharma found the European nations that were proud of their policy of freedom of expression and defence of human rights and were always open to receiving dissent amongst their midst, now realizing the consequences and checking and revising their policies. France was now first to embark on an aggressive policy of expelling any religious teacher whose teachings were not in conformity with the "values" of the French Republic. "Zero Tolerance", as the Minister of Interior, Nicolas Sarkozy, terms it. Three *imams* have been expelled and ten more have been identified from a total of 1100 *imams* – the vast majority being a Moroccan, Algerian, Turkish and a small minority of French nationality. Of the over 1500 mosques or the shrines, only about 40 are under the influence of a fundamentalist strain, at times violent. For its part, Austria, with a 5 per cent Muslim population, has decided to expel, starting January, all imams whose teachings are a 'danger' to national security. Denmark, too, intends to strengthen immigration laws, curbing the activities of 'radical religious leaders', obliging them to be financially self-sufficient, speak Danish and respect 'Western values'. However Italy directly threatened for its presence in Iraq, has no specific legislation against radical Islamic teaching and Spain, despite the terrorist attacks of March 2004, has no serious inventory of mosques or *imams*, Sharma goes into the details.

It is actually quite complicated to make an accurate estimate of the number of Muslims who call Europe home. The census of most West European nations has no question on the religion of citizens. But depending on the countries one includes, a figure of well over 12 million is often suggested. France has the largest proportion of Muslims, closely followed by Germany, Denmark, Holland, Sweden, Britain and Italy. But in this battle against terror, the immigrant who concerns this topic most today is the second generation young Muslim: normal youngsters born and brought up in their country of adoption, leading regular family lives who can hardly be suspected of any wrong-doing. But it is in their country of adoption that they discover or rediscover Islam, rather a simplified, radicalised version of Islam and become 'good Muslims'. This new generation of disaffected, alienated and marginalised young Muslims, Sharma evaluates, has fallen prey to radical teachings and taken the *Jehadi* path. He takes the example of France: of the two million second generation immigrants who were either born in France or who arrived in France fairly young, barely 4 per cent reach the university compared to 25 per cent of their classmates who come from similar social and economic backgrounds. Though these immigrant children go to the same schools and receive the same education, they rarely succeed the same way. Whether it is their family background where the parents are unable to provide adequate academic support or other factors, the boys soon sink into despair and delinquency, while the girls, often more mature and committed, seek jobs and rapidly become self-sufficient.

At no stage have we found mention of young girls or women participating directly or indirectly in the recent and not so recent terrorist activities across Europe, whether it is Britain, Spain, Italy, Holland or France, Sharma discusses further. And this has nothing to do with the position of women in Islamic societies. For Muslims who migrated to Europe from Africa, Asia or even West Asia, Islam is much more than a religion; it has become an identity and a cultural refuge. The much discussed story of Islamic head scarf in France is a testimony to that. But irrespective of the Europe they live in, girls from immigrant Muslim households are determined to succeed and seize the chance their adopted countries offer them, an opportunity they are not likely to get in the land of their forefathers. And they have shown little sign of being swayed, as Sharma puts the case.

Reading about this new generation of Muslims, concludes Sharma, "it must be admitted that whatever be their approach, integration of Muslim communities in the Western world leaves a lot to be desired. Europe cannot seal itself off from immigrants. With its ageing population and falling birth rates, immigration is no inevitable but also desirable. As Tahar Ben Jelloun, one of the North Africa's most successful post-colonial writers of Moroccan parentage, now settled in France, once said, "Integration is not necessarily love, it is sharing, a commitment on both sides, it is respect and mutual consideration; putting into practice the principle of rights as well as duties."[12]

No Double Standards

The Hindu's editor "responding to the barbaric attacks" on the London transport network has reminded the 9/11 attack in America and also the March 2004 Madrid bombings. He has analysed these incidents as the sharp reaction against the participation of these countries in the war on Iraq. "All this is more tragic evidence – as if more were needed that the world has become a much less safe place than it was before".

Most in India, long a target of terrorists of all hues – even as recently as two days before the London attacks – would share this sentiment, and appreciate the importance of a united response by the international community to a global scourage. But to continue with the type of response the US and Britain have imposed on the world over the last four years would be monumental folly." The editorial further suggests: if the world is to prevail over terrorism, it is first vital that Prime Minister Blair and President Bush acknowledge the truth that their military project to "make the world a safer place" has only increased the numbers of those in Muslim-majority countries who feel marginalised and threatened by the West, provided more recruits to the cause of "Islamist terrorism", and contributed to its growth as a hydra-headed force that knows no borders and that will stop at nothing to vent its rage. Recognising this and making a course correction now may be the only way to bring in peace, this writing concludes.[13]

The editor was anxious about growing a racial relationship in the future because the three of the terrorists, though all British citizens, were alleged of being Pakistani origin and the fourth was of Jamaican descent, even though all the major political parties have reacted in responsible fashion. However, the political leadership and intelligence services have to perform another task just as expeditiously. The editor emphasizes upon them to find out how propagators of the "ideology of terrorism" and the handlers were able to influence youth from an Asian Muslim community that has been granted a decent measure of political and economic opportunity. Little has been identified in the personal histories of three young men that suggests they were capable of killing their compatriots by exploding the high-yield bombs. Their ordinariness and familiarity with Western mores might have made them the "perfect sleepers" who could be activated at short notice. More insights are likely to emerge if the British police capture a fifth man who alleged gave last minute instructions to the suicide bombers, the editor argues.

The facts available suggest that shadowy operatives who incite terrorist acts in different parts of the world have developed their capabilities sophisticated, almost-impossible-to-guard-against levels. They have the capability to recruit, train, equip and motivate potential suicide bombers within a short period. These operatives can now form autonomous "cells" that can function without overt assistance from networks like *Al-Qaeda* since the Internet provides them easy access to what it takes – from inspirational tracts to bomb-making manuals. The editor further asserts that the Musharraf Government must exert itself further in the campaign against terror since the London bombers apparently had links with *madrasas* in Pakistan – an off-quoted phrase initiated through American foreign policy. In another area, the editor finally concludes, the Western powers, above all the United States, promoted *Jehadism* and un-adulterated terrorism in the name of the liberation from the Soviet troops in Afghanistan. "Today, as has been pointed out by many Western voices of sobriety, reason and justice, the Bush and Blair administrations bear of heavy responsibility for terrorist incidents – through their invasion of, and war crimes committed in, Iraq, compounded by their strategic support for Israel's atrocities against the Palestinians".[14]

The editor severely criticizes the double standards on terrorism being demonstrated by the United States and the U.K. especially in the cases of non-Western countries. It is common that when governments promise "strong" action against terrorism, they come up with "Knee-jerk responses" that inevitably undermine civil liberties. The British Government is not an exception, despite the plausible assurances by Prime Minister Tony Blair that this new anti-terrorism measures are directed at "extremism and extremism only". If anything, the Blair Government has shown a readiness to compromise on human rights and the much cherished British tradition of freedom of expression and liberal values for the very first of the measures that will be implemented – deportation of foreigners for "unacceptable behaviour" that includes "fomenting, justifying or glorifying terrorist violence (and) other serious criminal activity". A signatory to the European Convention on Human Rights, Britain can not return people to countries where they might face death penalty, torture or other mistreatment. The British Government's assurances that the safety of those it sends back will be guaranteed by "memoranda of understanding" with the countries concerned have not satisfied many. In the age of advanced communication, does it help that hate-mongers will not be able to preach in Britain? They could easily propagate their message of violence from anywhere else in the world, the editor argues.

The editor is very much worried about the American and British double standards when the terrorism is defined. The United Kingdom Terrorism Act 2000, describes terrorism as acts that involve "serious violence" against a person or "serious damage" to property, endanger a person's life, create a "serious risk" to public safety or health, or interfere with or disrupt an electronic system and are used to influence the government or intimidate the public and to advance a political, religious or ideological cause. The legislation covers terrorism within and outside the U.K. It makes an offence of inviting financial and other support for a proscribed organization and of addressing a meeting in support of such an organization. Under this act, the British Government should have long ago acted against Anton Balasingham, political adviser to the Liberation Tigers of Tamil Eelam and a British citizen normally resident in Britain, the editor criticises. The LTTE is banned in the U.K., but Mr. Balasingham routinely addresses meetings in its support. The British Government, the critic continues, did not invoke this law even when the LTTE carried out the outrageous July 2001 attack on Sri Lanka's international airport; instead it advocated that Sri Lanka should begin peace talks with the Tigers. Now that the Blair Government has proposed fresh measures that will make an offence of condoning or glorifying terrorism in Britain and abroad, by foreigners as well as British citizens, it is time for an honest debate on a more focussed but also universal definition of terrorism and the types of related conduct that would be unacceptable. This alone, the editor finally concludes, will safeguard human rights, and ensure that the real terrorists do not slip through the cracks anywhere in the world.[15]

The editor simultaneously criticises the state terrorism committed by another name. London or Kashmir, there is something uncivilised about a policing system that, in the name of nation, queen, democracy or whatever, permits its personnel to kill suspects – a system that shoots first, checks later, and gets away with it basically. The plain clothes policemen who shot dead Jean Charles de Menezes, an innocent and upstanding Brazilian workingman, in a London tube station on suspicion that was connected with the London bomb attacks went by nothing more than that he lived in a neighbourhood under surveillance, was dressed unusually for summer, and did not stop when challenged. Thousands of kilometres away, soldiers in the vicinity of a Kashmir village shot dead three children suspecting they were militants – on the basis of nothing more than that they did not respond soon enough to a call for identification at a checkpoint. Motive apart, the substance of both acts, the editor analyses, was indistinguishable from cold-blooded murder, especially as there was no question of pleading any right to self-defence in the circumstances.

Both security forces – London's Metropolitan police and the Indian Army – as the editorial points out, have expressed the minimum quantities of 'regret' judged to be necessary to assuage outraged public opinion. And both seem determined not to be held accountable for the 'tragedy'. In both cases, authorities has sought to rationalise the horrifyingly irreversible actions of their men by calling attention to the prevailing situation in which they were taking 'fast time' decisions, and therefore, could not be expected to follow normal procedure. The London police commissioner has gone so far as to say that such is the contingency after the string of bombings in the city that the 'shoot to kill' policy currently in force will continue, and more innocent lives could be at risk.

If things go badly for the security forces in the official enquiries, admissions may follow that, in a pressure cooker situation created by terrorist acts, their personnel may have 'over-reacted', the editorial continues. It is more than likely that a case will be made out for providing a substantial measure of protection to these privileged, patriotic killers. A system that rationalises horrible human rights offences by claiming that the only way to protect citizens' lives from terrorism is to take out suspects can be characterised as not worth having. Much like the scourage it seeks to fight, no one known who, or where, it will strike next. There is even a name for it – state terrorism, the editorial defines. "It is shocking that Ken Livingstone, Mayor of London and champion of human rights the world over, has jumped to the defence of his city's police force by declaiming that the tube killing really has to be blamed on the London bombers. In India, the gunning down of three children near the village of Bangargud in deeply alienated Kashmir calls attention to the urgent need to strengthen the law, including the Human Rights Act 1993, to make security forces accountable for offences against common humanity."[16]

It is appreciable the editor's criticism is not limited to the terrorism committed by US and UK; he rather pays full attention to the atrocities of police administration in the most sensitive area like Kashmir. He targeted both the security forces – London's Metropolitan Police and the Indian Army – as irresponsible and unaccountable specially when they left no chance of pleading any right to self-defence. He declared both the authorities rationalising their horrifying irreversible actions. In that case the editorial may be thought an honest treatment with the issue.

Coinciding with G-8 Summit

Shelley Walia talks and comments on the G-8 summit at Gleneagles when the July 6, 2005 was the day of marches and protests in the city. Hundreds of scholars walked out of their class rooms; an estimated 2 lakh people converged on the hotel for a rally organized by "Make Poverty History", a coalition of about 450 non-governmental organizations. This is understandable says the writer. Considering that on the top of the agenda is the worldwide concern with death and hunger in sub-Saharan Africa, the mammoth rallies were intended to draw attention to. As pointed out by Jeffrey Sachs, adviser to Secretary General Kofi Annan on the U.N. Millennium development goals, "Africa's investment priorities lie in four main areas: health, education, agriculture and infrastructure." If no concrete steps are taken, the countries of Africa will miss the deadline of 2015, which is the year fixed by the UN to halve the poverty in the world, in these areas by a wide margin.

Noticeably, aid alone, the writer argues, will be of no use if the G-8 do not realise that lifting trade barriers and allowing free flow of needy migrants across borders are of crucial importance in making poverty history. Indeed "the people have roared, but the G-8 has whispered" as Kumi Naidoo, Chair of the "Global Call to Action against Poverty" so tersely put it.

To the writer, no war and no bloodshed can ever be justified. The terrorist attacks on New York, on Madrid, on London, on Ayodhya or the bomb blasts in Mumbai are as unpardonable as the war on Afghanistan or Iraq. It is clear that there is no way that a highly sophisticated weaponry can successfully wage a war against the guerrilla tactics of a terrorist onslaught. And there are no national borders for the operation of terrorism and no set time, though the attack on London is certainly intended to coincide with the G-8 summit. This is what the leaders who had assembled at Gleneagles must strive to realize.

In the backdrop of the terrible tragedy in London, the leaders deliberated over the pressing issues that pre-occupied the world community in the recently years. Terrorism, which was not on the agenda, can now in the wake of 7/7, be put on the top demanding a new alertness from the leaders, Shelley Walia argues. "But I wonder", the writer concludes, "if the solidarity expressed in Gleneagles is a way out or one more step towards the further intensification of the conflict between the "civilized" forces and the *Jehadi* ideology".[17]

Sweeping Judgements about Islam

Vidya Ram talks in detail about the Londoners whose mood dramatically changed in the first week of July 2005. Less than 24 hours after thousands of elated Londoners poured into Trafalgar Square to celebrate the Olympic coup, four suicide bombers blew themselves on three busy underground trains and a bus, killing 55 commuters and injuring hundreds more on their way to work. More unfortunate were the sweeping judgements about Islam and Muslim community made in the wider society, a situation not helped by a statement by a former police commissioner warning that between 2000 and 3000 British citizens have been to *Al-Qaeda* training camps. There have been calls, the analyst is surprised, from some politicians and political commentators, for Muslims to "root out" the terrorists among them, as though the terrorists' actions could somehow be blamed on a failure by the Muslim community. British Muslims rightly argue, the writer further says, that there should be no "collective guilt" – not for an attack whose victims included several Muslims – and leaders of the community have been swift and vocal in their condemnation of the bombings. Nevertheless, suspicion and blame, as the article analyses, will continue to be placed on their shoulders by sections of society unless an effort is made to consider the political and international dimensions of the problem.

The backlash from Right wing extremists is expected and understandable. The citizens of "Asian" appearance were subjected to racial attacks, mosques in northern England were targeted and others had received bomb threats. The far-Right, anti-immigration, British National Party (BNP), whose leader was arrested in the past for inciting racial hatred, used pictures of the bus bomb in a local election campaign with the slogan: "Maybe now it's time to start listening to the BNP". But the reactions of the multicultural Londoners are very amazing to the writer.

Prime Minister Blair, Vidya Ram criticizes, has observed that the "shoddy perversion" of Islam, caused by hatred of the Western way of life and freedom, had driven a small minority of Muslims to turn to terrorism. There was absolutely no reference to Britain's foreign policy, particularly in West Asia, and therefore more susceptible to those eager to exploit their sense of alienation and injustice. Nor was there reference, the criticism goes on, to the fact that it is countries with troops in Iraq, like Spain, the United States and Italy, and not other democratic Western countries such as Sweden or Norway, which face the terrorist threat.

Responsibility for the dreadful events on 7/7, the writer further comments, lies squarely and solely on the shoulders of the bombers, and those who masterminded the attacks. However, these attacks will continue unless urgent steps are taken to combat some of the underlying political context. While the Blair Government's response has, in many ways, been "milder and more reasoned" than that of Bush administration following 9/11 if it continues to ignore international factors, it will fail to prevent future attacks, the author views. ID cards, which the government is eager to introduce and civil liberties groups strongly oppose, did not prevent the Madrid bombings, he quickly offers the case.

A clamp down on immigration and a raft of stringent anti-terrorism and intelligence measures, which are now unlikely to face much scrutiny or opposition from other political parties, the writer suggests, will only serve to alienate minority groups even further. He quotes Robin Cook M.P., the former Foreign Secretary who said explicitly, the single most effective action to reduce the threat of terrorism would be to withdraw British troops from Iraq. The Italian government has already begun the process of withdrawal. The people in London and other cities will go to work knowing there is a strong possibility of the attacks continuing. It is the lives of ordinary working people, the majority of whom value Britain's multicultural society and oppose the government's war in Iraq, that are under threat, the analysis concludes.[18]

Lexicon of Terror

In the few years that have following 9/11, the litany of tragedy has lengthened around the world. What can one do to respond meaningfully to such meaningless violence? Shashi Tharoor in his write up argues. The tragedies like those of Bali and Beslan, Madrid and Moscow, Baghdad and Bombay, London and Delhi, to name just a few, have added their stories to the global narrative of terror. "9/11" entered our lexicon; "13/12" in Delhi, and "7/7" in London have threatened to follow suit, Tharoor argues. "But we might as well find ourselves using up all the dates in the calendar. Terrorism is a threat to all of us, all the time; its particular horror lies in its randomness, in the knowledge that it can strike anything, anywhere. When terror strikes, it leaves survivors with unanswerable questions".

Tharoor further says that as one who has spent his entire working life at the United Nations, he has to say that terrorism denies everything the U.N. stands for: the rule of law; the protection of civilians; mutual respect between people of different faiths and cultures; the peaceful resolution of conflict. And the response to it also places in jeopardy all the hard fought civil liberties and protection that have come to distinguish contemporary civilization. As understandable fear and suspicion dominate the law-enforcement response, human rights, the presumption of innocence, the rejection of stereotyping, all risk going by the board, as the writer elaborates.

Earlier this year U.N. Secretary-General Kofi Annan, the writer further says, set out the main elements of a global counter-terror strategy, in terms of five goals: to dissuade disaffected groups from choosing terrorism as a tactic to achieve their goals; to deny terrorists the means to carry out their attacks; to deter states from supporting terrorists; to develop state capacity to prevent terrorism; and to defend human rights in the struggle against terrorism. Of course all this is much easier said than done, Tharoor goes on. Terrorists kill because they think that terrorism is effective, and that it advances their objective of sowing fear in the targeted populations, and including the affected societies and governments to change a policy or reverse a course of action. "The world has to prove to them", the author says, "that they are wrong: but until the terrorists are convinced that terrorism is futile, it will continue. So we have to show any future terrorist that terrorism never gets what it wants because terror only hardens the resolve of the targeted society. We have to demonstrate in word and deed that terrorism is so unacceptable that to resort to it undermines our sympathy for the cause on whose name it is undertaken. No rightful cause, no flagrant wrong, justifies the deliberate killing or maiming of non-combatants."

Tharoor then concludes: for years India has advocated the adoption of a comprehensive international convention on terrorism that makes this clear. Governments have yet to agree on one, though the impetus in now showing. Ordinary citizens, civil society and religious leaders should also join the cause: the time is ripe for a truly global "people's campaign" against terrorism. Let us all be resolute. But at the same time, the author cautions, let us promote and defend human rights – the best bulwark against the very injustice that is sometimes cited by the terrorists to defend their actions.[19]

Pakistan: A Repeat of the post-9/11

B. Muralidharan Reddy talks in term of Pakistan's behaviour which is repeating the post-9/11 rhetoric. To the writer, the Pakistani establishment's response post 7/7 is similar to what it did after 9/11: all the right noises but little else. The same fiery statements on the global threat posed by terrorism and the same talk of brand new action plans to uproot it from Pakistani soil. More so in the past few days after it became known that three of the four suspected bombers visited the country in recent months. Eight day after the London carnage, President Pervez Musharraf presided over a meeting of the country's top police officers to decide what needed to be done to contain the extremist menace. Declaring a firm commitment to combat extremism and terrorism, Gen. Musharraf directed law enforcement agencies to launch a "countrywide" campaign against the collection of donations, display of arms, holding of gathering by banned outfits, and to remove all hate material from the markets by December 2005 at the latest. These were precisely the tasks he assigned the law-enforcing agencies post 9/11.

Obviously there is a huge gap between promise and practice, Reddy says. During last Friday's meeting with police officers, Gen. Musharraf reiterated the Government's resolve not to allow banned militant organizations to resurface using any other name. The reference was clearly to the outfits banned in early 2002. Some had to be banned a second time after they re-surfaced under different names. The government machinery, the writers criticizes has been half-hearted in dealing with the problems of fundamentalism. The proposed reform of *madrasa* education system best illustrates the point. In his path-breaking speech in 2002, Gen. Musharraf had identified *madrasa* reforms as the key to tackling extremism. Yet except for a few showcase "reformed" *madrasas* no sign of change is visible. The military-led government's proposal measures, from curriculum changes to a few registration law, have been dropped in the face of opposition from the MMA (*Muttahidah Majlis e Amal*) and its *madrasa* subsidiaries. "You must enforce an end to publication and distribution of hate material including pamphlets, booklets,

CDs, etc., writers, publishers and distributors of all such literature must be held accountable in accordance with the law. You must ensure that such material is not available in markets latest by December, this year." Gen. Musharraf told the top police officers on Friday. Why did the Government not demonstrate this urgency immediately after 9/11? Why should it require a wake-up call in the form of 7/7, Reddy asks.

Can the Government hope to succeed in its ambitious agenda without enlisting the cooperation of the country's mainstream political forces? Given the state of Gen. Musharraf's relations with former Prime Ministers Benazir Bhutto and Nawaz Sharif, their parties are out of the loop in the so called fight against fundamentalism. In a bid to keep mainstream parties and their leaders at bay, Gen. Musharraf and his managers have been forced to embrace parties that preach and practice a division agenda. As a result, there is an impression, argues Muralidharan Reddy, the President is more comfortable with the MMA than the mainstream parties. However, the MMA's policies could come in conflict with the concept of 'enlightened moderation' the General is trying to promote. Restoration of the religion column in passports after religious parties threatened an agitation best illustrates the point.

In its recent report on sectarianism in Pakistan the International Crisis Group, (ICG) a cross country NGO reporting from conflicting zones, said the political use of Islam by the state promoted an aggressive competition for official patronage between and within the many variations of *Sunni* and *Shia* Islam, with the clerical elite of major sects and sub-sects striving to build up their political parties, raise *Jihadi* militants, expand *madrasa* networks and, as has happened on Gen. Musharraf's watch, become part of the Government. The report said administrative and legal action against militant organizations has failed to dismantle a well-entrenched terror infrastructure. "All banned extremist groups persist with new labels, although old names are still in use. The *Jihadi* media is flourishing, and the leading figures of extremist *Sunni* organizations are free to preach their *Jihadi* ideologies. Leaders of banned groups such as the *Lashkar-e-Taibah, Sipah-e-Sahabah* and *Jaish-e-Mohammad* appear to enjoy virtual immunity from the law. They have gained new avenues to propagate their militant ideas since the chief patrons of *Jihad*, the *Jamiat Ulama-e-Islam* (JUI) and the *Jamaat Islami* (JI), have a acquired prominent and powerful roles in Musharraf's political structure", the ICG said. Would Team of Musharraf act differently post 7/7 given the experience of taking on fundamentalists in the last three years, Muralidharan Reddy concludes in an interrogative style.[20]

Al-Qāeda or Al-Fāyda?

"These gentlemen are the moral equivalents of America's founding fathers". (Ronald Regan while introducing the *Mujahidin* leaders to media on the White House Lawns in 1985). "Americans are asking: why do they hate us? They hate our freedoms – our freedom of religion, our freedom of speech, our freedom to vote and assemble and disagree with each other." (George W. Bush, in his speech in U.S. Congress in the aftermath of 9/11, 2001).

These two statements, Ram Puniyani comments, reflect the so-called transition of freedom fighters of which U.S. administration was proud to the same one's being called enemies of U.S. when Tony Blair in the aftermath of 7/7 uttered his feelings that our resolve to uphold our values is stronger than their resolve to break it, he was referring to the people with same ideology and politics whom Regan praised to the sky and about whom G.W. Bush had the totally contrary view.

What has changed during last one and a half decade, have 'they' changed? Or is it that U.S. needs have undergone a rapid transition during this decade? Mr. Puniyani surprisingly asks the question and then goes ahead discussing: the reference to the ghastly acts of terrorism of 9/11 and 7/7 does send the shivers down one's spine. Not only the killings of innocents, non combatants in 9/11 and 7/7 is extremely heinous and cowardly, but also the aftermath of such actions is something one needs to mull over. The ongoing extremism and 'war on terror' both are affecting the societies in a painful manner. While on one hand killing of innocent is a matter of deep anguish the post terror polarization of communities on religious ground and the demonization of Islam are the consequences, which have deeper impact on the lives of people world over.

The begin with, the question is, who did it? The author puts the basic question. Surprisingly after 9/11 the investigation has not been very definitive. It was presumed, Osama bin Laden, *Al-Qaeda* are the one's behind the tragic event. Afghanistan was invaded on the pretext of catching hold of Osama, nearly sixty thousand people were killed by the U.S. attack, but could not be caught hold of. Incidentally it was Bin Laden who was projected to be the primary culprit against whom the war is being waged. U.S. did succeed in installing its puppet government in Afghanistan and also in taking control of the huge oil reserves around Afghanistan.

On the ground that Iraq is a threat to U.S. security, and also that it is harbouring *Al-Qaeda*, it was invaded, thousands of Iraqis have since then perished and hundreds of U.S. armed personnel have been killed, the writeup continues. The sexual torture of Abu Gharib prison might have been just a tip of the iceberg hiding more, which we will never come to know. There are also doubts about the real culprit of 9/11 so to stay, as conclusive evidence has not been produced by the U.S. Tony Blair did not loose even minutes to hint that 'same' culprits are involved. Some reports pointed out that it is the act of Secret Organization Group of *Al-Qaeda*, which in its temporarily put up website, claimed, "We continue to warn the Governments of Denmark and Italy and all crusader governments that they will be punished in the same way if they do not withdraw their troops from Iraq and Afghanistan.

Even in the aftermath of 9/11, the analysis goes on, there were serious doubts raised about the perpetrators of the event, whether it was *Al-Qaeda* or was it some other agency. Anyway, a pretext to attack Afghanistan could be cooked up with ease. Even now doubts are being raised that since there is a pressure on the U.K. Government to withdraw the troops from Iraq and Afghanistan and this incident will ensure that troops continue to be in Iraq. On one hand we have *Al-Qaeda* and the like, who in the name of *Jihad* are committing havoc. These actions in the name of *Jihad*, are the worst enemies of Muslims as a community. These create hatred against this community and the demonization process against Muslims and Islam gets a boost after every such event. The targeting of average Muslims as terrorists and criminals gets biggest justification from such acts. These actions are the one's which have laid the foundation of the ideology guiding many Western powers and also other countries, Mr. Puniyani explains the Western justification for crusading against Islam.

The other factor is the policy of Western powers, which so far has been steadfastly supporting Israel's violation of the rights of Palestinian people and its blatant vandalism in the neighbouring region, Mr. Puniyani further argues. The *Jihadi* terrorism as such was consciously brought up and promoted not by any Muslim country. It was the handiwork of U.S., C.I.A. in its goal to contain the influence of communism during the era of cold war. During that period many a countries strived for nationalism to get rid of the clutches of colonial powers. Most such endeavours were opposed by Western powers with U.S. in the lead. With the success of communists, says the writer, coming to power in Afghanistan, U.S. administration started promoting the opponents of communist regime. Communists tried to bring in land reforms, curtail opium cultivation, and this hurt the interests of the feudal and orthodox elements, the author goes into the details of the history.

These opponents to communist regime the elite, according to this study, were right wing Islamists. It was from this Muslim right wing that *Al-Qaeda* was formed with the direct patronage of U.S. Billions of dollars of aid and armaments, including stringer missiles were given to *Al-Qaeda* by US. *Al-Qaeda* grouped together with the help of Pakistan and Saudi Arabia. With the defeat of communist forces US became more assertive and started interfering in the region with vehemence, the attack on Iraq in 1993 was the first manifestation of the same. The right wing Islamists felt the threat of US presence and the rest is too fresh in our memories to be recounted. "Anti-Islamism now came to substitute Anti-Communism as the 'other' of imperialist powers. Lured by the oil wealth of the region US-UK axis has violated every possible international law and has removed all roadblocks to its pursuits for profit (*Fāyda*). This axis also attacked Afghanistan and Iraq telling the world that this is the only way to make their countries safer for themselves. Can such blatant violation of human and international norms make the world safer? And pray tell me, which is the bigger curse of the world today: *Al-Qaeda* or Al-Fayda?"[21] The analysis thus concludes.

Justice not more Terror

Milon Rai, the famous journalist and writer is determined that in order to stop Bin Laden and the like it is essential to do justice. The world needs justice, not more terror. Explaining *Al-Qaeda* is the wrong answer to terrorism the US Government's official '9/11 Commission' reported that Bin Laden's grievance with the United States 'started in reaction to specific US policies'. Bin Laden and his group 'say that America had attacked Islam... Americans are blamed when Israelis fight with Palestinians, when Russians fight with Chechens, when Indians fight with Kashmiri Muslims, and when the Philippine government fight ethnic Muslims in its southern islands'. The US is also 'held responsible for the governments of Muslim countries, derided by *Al-Qaeda* as 'your agents'. Such charges, says the Commission, 'found a ready audience among millions of Arabs and Muslims angry at the United States because of issues ranging from Iraq to Palestine to America's support for their countries' repressive rulers'.[22]

The Commission's analysis may have drawn on the writings of Michael Scheuer, who served in the C.I.A. for 22 years, and who headed the CIA Counter-Terrorism Centre's Bin Laden task force (1996-1999). Scheuer, who retired in November 2004, wrote two recent books as *Anonymous: Through Our Enemies' Eyes*, and *Imperial Hubris: Why the West is Losing the War on Terror*. (He was unmasked in the Boston Phoenix).

Scheuer contests the view put forward by George W. Bush and Tony Blair: We in the United States and the West make a mistake when we argue, as has (*New Yoark Times* Columnist) Thomas L. Friedman, that Bin Laden's attacks are "not aimed at reversing any specific U.S. foreign policy," or as Steve Simon and Daniel Benjamin did in *Survival* in early 2002, that Bin Laden has "no discrete set of negotiable political demands."[23]

Scheuer argues that Osama bin Laden has 'clear focused limited and widely popular foreign policy goals' including: 'the end of US aid to Israel and the ultimate elimination of the state; the removal of US and Western troops from Iraq, Afghanistan and other Muslim lands; the end of US support for the oppression of Muslims by Russia, China and India; the end of US protection for repressive, apostate regimes in Saudi Arabia, Kuwait, Egypt, Jordan, etc., and the conservation of the Muslim world's energy resources and their sale at higher prices.'

Scheuer observes that, "Bin Laden is out to drastically alter US and Western policies toward the Islamic world, not necessarily to destroy America, much less its freedoms and liberties. He is a practical warrior, not an apocalyptic terrorist in search of Armageddon".[24] He wrote, while still a serving CIA officer, "Bin Laden has been precise in telling America the reasons he is waging war on us. None of the reasons have anything to do with our freedom, liberty and democracy, but have everything to do with US policies and actions in the Muslim world".[25] Scheuer goes further, arguing that 'the United States and its policies and actions are Bin Laden's only indispensable allies".[26]

The 9/11 Commission also asked the question, 'what can we do to stop these attacks'? It suggested that, while Bin Laden's campaign had begun in reaction to US policies, 'it quickly became far deeper': To the second question of what America could do, *Al-Qaeda*'s answer was America should abandon the Middle East, convert to Islam, and end the immorality and godlessness of its culture... if the United States did not comply, it would be at war with the Islamic nation".[27]

The Commission produced no evidence that *Al-Qaeda* had such a maximalist programme. Michael Scheuer vigorously disputes this view, drawing a distinction between 'the things a Muslim world find offensive' and things which a Muslim might regard as an attack on Islam or on Muslims. 'Part of Bin Laden's genius is that he recognized early on the difference between those issues Muslims find offensive about America and the West, and those they find intolerable and life threatening'.[28]

Jason Bruke, Chief reporter for the *London Observer*, points out in his book *Al-Qaeda*, 'while Bin Laden's discourse may be based on interpretation of Islamic history, his power is derived from playing on the current social, economic and political problems of the Muslim world'.[29] In the case of Soviet invasion of Afghanistan, Bin Laden and other non-Afghan Muslims 'went there to fight the Red Army not because the Soviets were atheists and communists but because of their brutal invasion.[30] After the invasion was reversed the *mujahideen* did not continue armed action against the atheist and anti-Islamic Soviet Union. When the grievance ended, so did the mujahideen war. Scheuer argues that Osama bin Laden has 'clear, focused and limited' foreign policy goals. The goal is not the establishment of an Islamic fundamentalist state in the US, whatever the 9/11 commission asserts, but deep change in US foreign policy.

After 9/11 Bin Laden said, 'Just as they are killing us, we have to kill them so there will be a balance of terror... We will do as they do. If they kill our women and innocent people, until they stop'.[31] Intervening in the closing days of the 2004 presidential election, Bin Laden told the American people 'your security does not lie in the hands of Kerry, Bush or *Al-Qaeda*. Your security is in your own hands. Each and every state that does not tamper with our security will have automatically assured its own security (BBC translation). This was translated by CNN as 'Any nation that does not attack us will not be attacked'. 'Us' is meant to refer to the community of Muslim nations and populations, and 'attack' has a broad meaning, as former CIA official Michael Scheuer explains.

Writing before the invasion of Iraq, Scheuer commented: "How will (*Al-Qaeda*) recognise victory? Easy, by forcing drastic changes in US foreign policy... when US and British forces evacuate Saudi Arabia and the rest of the Arabian peninsula; when the United States has terminated all aid to Israel; and when the US and UN embargoes on Iraq are lifted". (These achievements Bin Laden has called the regimes of 'hypocrites' in Saudi Arabia, Egypt, Jordan and elsewhere).[32] To these goals, one might add the ending of the US-UK occupation of Iraq and presence in Afghanistan.

Underlying these demands are legitimate grievances against the West, as Mr. Milan Rai has argued with the authentic sources, Western support for Israeli oppression of the Palestinians; the invasion of Iraq and Afghanistan; the brutal sanctions imposed on Iraq (now lifted); and US-UK support for dictatorial regimes in the Middle East are quite genuine demands. These are immoral policies which should be reversed because they are wrong. So is the policy of ignoring or supporting – oppression in Chechnya and elsewhere. It also happens that reversing these immoral policies would drain most if not all of the hatred which fuels *Al-Qaeda*. This is how we can stop Bin Laden. War, retaliation and violence simply adds to his appeal, Mr. Milan Rai honestly and unhesitatingly suggests.

The governments of Britain and the United States can pursue the path of punishment and preventive violence, or they can seek to bring this wave to terrorism to an end, Mr. Rai discusses both the options. Bringing *Al-Qaeda* style terrorism to an end means, above all, reducing the motivation that exists to carry out terrorism. This does not mean 'negotiating with terrorists' or capitulating to their demands', but seeking justice and human rights for all, including the peoples of Palestine and Iraq, Mr. Rai further explains.

"The answer to terrorism is justice, not more terrorism", the author concludes his remarks. "London and Washington must also stop practising the terrorism of the powerful invasion, occupation, and indirect terrorism via oppressive states. "We should recognise that in much of the world the US is regarded as leading terrorist state, and with good reason."[33]

Notes and References

1. Jawaharlal Nehru, *India's Foreign Policy Selected Speeches*; September 1946 – April 1961, New Delhi, 1961, p. 79.

2. *Ibid.*, pp. 79-80.

3. See for a detailed study of the non-aligned policy of India and its involvement in various issues, Dr. H.M. Wajid Ali, *India and the Non-Aligned Movement*, New Delhi, 2004, 273 pp.

4. *The Times of India*, July 26, 2005 p. 14. The Prime Minister Manmohan Singh in a statement on his recent visit to the U.K. said in New Delhi that a collective strategy needs to be evolved to free the world from the scourage of terrorism, now a global phenomenon as demonstrated by the London blasts. "This (the terror attack in the British capital) is a vivid demonstration that terrorism is a global phenomenon. We have suffered from this scourage for nearly 20-25 years. The blast is a demonstration that all of us will have to work together to evolve a collective strategy to free the world from this scourage." Singh said he attended a meeting of group of five countries – India, Brazil, Mexico, South Africa and China – in Scotland where a consensus emerged on working towards performing the international trading system, transfer of resources to developing countries and transfer of technologies from the rich to poor nations. He said that during his meeting with G-8 leaders, he expressed concern about the way the international system was functioning and paying inadequate attention to needs of poor countries. "I laid emphasis on reform of the international system and ensuring that Doha round of trade negotiation becomes generally a development round. The PM said he also laid emphasis on the fact that all countries have an obligation to work together to find credible ways to protect and preserve the environment. "But I also said this must be done mindful of devemental imperatives of poor nations", Singh said. *The Times of India*, July 11, 2005.

5. Anita Sen, *The Times of India*, July 11, 2005, p. 16.

6. *The Times of India*, August 6, 2006, p. 14.

7. Jug Suraiya, The Colour of Terror, *The Times of India*, July 28, 2005, p. 12.

8. Rashmee Roshan Lal, Enemy within UK, *The Times of India*, July 17, 2005, p. 13.
9. Swagato Ganguly, Dangerous Liaisons, *The Times of India*, August 31, 2005, p. 14.
10. Ziya us-Salam, Profound Research, *The Hindu*, September 25, 2005, p. 4.
11. Ranjan Roy, Terror and Imaginary Homelands, *The Times of India*, July 22, 2005, p. 16.
12. Rajesh Sharma, Eyes wide shut, *Hindustan Times*, August 27, 2005, p. 8.
13. Editorial, *The Hindu*, July 9, 2005, p. 10.
14. Editorial, *The Hindu*, July 18, 2005, p. 10.
15. Editorial, *The Hindu*, August 31, 2005, p. 10.
16. Editorial, *The Hindu*, July 26, 2005, p. 10.
17. Shelly Walia, In the Wake of 7/7. *The Hindu*, July 17, 2005.
18. Vidya Ram, British Society grapples with aftermath, *The Hindu*, July 18, 2005, p. 11.
19. Shashi Tharoor, The Lexicon of Terror, *The Hindu Magazine*, September 11, 2005, p. 11. Very interesting case in this regard is the report prepared seriously by Lewis M. Simons, an ex-Marine who covered the Vietnam war for the *Associated Press* and *The Post*. He says that he had an "early reminiscent experience" when he visited Iraq recently to write a piece for *National Geographic*. After a month in Iraq, he returned home and said "certain that this war, like Vietnam, will never be won... Since in my judgement, we were wrong to go in, I am afraid there's no good way to get out". In an attempt to understand the concept of winning the war in Iraq, the writer asks: 'what would 'winning' in Iraq mean, anyway? A democratic society that's free to elect an anti-American, pro-Iranian, fundamentalist Islamic government? A land of gushing oil well feeding international oil company profits at U.S. taxpayers' expense? *Shia*s, Kurds and *Sunni*s joining hands to end terrorism around the world?" Like Vietnam, says Simons, the Americans do not understand Iraq. "The truth – that Iraq

was not a terrorist haven before we invaded, but we're making it into one today – has been thickly painted over with unending coats of misinformation". Comparing the two wars, the author notes that "where 392 Americans were killed in action in Vietnam from 1962 through 1964, the first three years of the war, (and 58000 by the time of the US withdrawal in 1975), after two years in Iraq we have nearly 1900 Americans killed in action. Where two million Vietnamese were killed by the war's end, we have no idea how many Iraqis have died since we unleashed 'shock and awe'. Is it 10,000, 20,000, 30,000? More?" Simons says that this 'blithe American disregard' for their lives infuriates Iraqis. He warns that what Americans failed to understand in Vietnam – 'that people who want foreign occupiers out of their country are willing and prepared to withstand any kind of privation and risk for however long it takes – are failing, once again, to grasp in Iraq". Discussing his experience in Iraq, the author says that in a country where planes have to make emergency landing to avoid being hit by the enemy's rockets and where American soldiers and citizens have to be protected by humvees or helicopters when going out in the streets, 'there can be no military solution". The auther also notes that some American soldiers in Iraq are most bitter about their perception that the Bush administration's effort to wage the war on the cheap applies only to them, while private contractors grow rich. "On the green plastic wall of a portable toilet at Baghdad military airport, I read the following graffiti, scrawled by a civilian contract employee: 'In months, $ 200,000. I am out of here. (expletive) you Iraq". Beneath it was response from the ranks: '12 months. $ 20,000. What the (expletive) is going on here?" Arguing that there's no 'good way' to quit Iraq, the author says that if America stays, the 'insurgency' continues. If it leaves, the insurgency will likely expand into an all-out civil war, the fragmenting of Iraq and the intervention of Iran, Turkey and Syria, followed by the collapse of promised democracy in the Middle East: a kind of reverse domino theory. He says that before the mid-term elections next year President Bush may withdraw several thousand US troops, but the bulk of the US forces will stay, giving the guerrillas an excuse to fight. The author believes that the Bush administration will leave this mess for the next administration, which may find equally difficult to deal with it. This analysis was published in the *Washington Post* on Sunday on August 28, 2005. *See* for its reprint *The Times of India*, August 30, 2005 (Iraq War like Vietnam).

In India over the past 15 years brought them grief in recent years? The Indians genuinely marked a question. It would appear so, they hoped going by the action replay of terrorist acts in India that one is now witnessing in various parts of the world. The serial blasts that shook London on Thursday (7/7) show once again that India has been used as a laboratory by terrorists, writes Chidanand Rajghatta (*Hindustan Times*, July 10, 2005). The Mumbai serial blasts of 1993 and subsequent incidents of bombing commuter transport in the city and in Delhi may well have been a dryrun for attacks in Madrid and London among other places. It does not stop there, Rajghatta further says. The hijacking of an Indian Airlines plane from Kathmandu to Kandhar also seemed a practice run for what happened on 9/11 – five men to a plane armed with nothing more than box-cutters managed to commandeer a flight. The only difference was they did not fly and crash the planes into any buildings. Such acts of terrorism have often been dismissed in the West as "separatist violence", "insurgency attacks" and "militant reprisal". Even to this day, the writer continues, terrorist incidents in India – such as last weeks attack on the Babri Masjid – Ram Janambhoomi complex – barely cause a ripple there. All that may be changing, now that the scourage of terrorism has spread across the world. Last year, one methodology used by CIA's Counter-terrorism Centre to tabulate terrorist incidents showed that India was the worst victim of terrorism in the world. Of the 651 incidents reported during the year, more than 40% (295) took place in India with Iraq coming next at 201. By that measures US and UK were not even on the board.

20. B. Muralidharan Reddy, A Report of the post-9/11 rhetoric. *The Hindu*, July 19, 2005.

21. Ram Puniyani, Roots of Global Terror, *The Milli Gazette*, 1-15 August 2005, p. 22.

22. *The 9/11 Commission Report*, New York, Norton & Co. 2004, p. 51.

23. Michael Scheuer, *Anonymous: Through Our Enemies Eyes*, p. 256.

24. Michael Scheuer, *Imperial Hubris: Why the West is losing the War on Terror?*, p. XVIII.

25. *Ibid.*, p. X

26. *Ibid.*, p. XI

27. *The 9/11 Commission Report*, *op. cit.*, pp. 50-51.

28. *Imperial Hubris*, p. 10.

29. Jason Bruke, *Al-Qaeda*, Penguin, 2004, p. 25.

30. *Imperial Hubris*, p. 10.

31. Cited in Through Our Enemies Eyes, p. 247.

32. *Ibid.*, p. 256.

33. Noam Chomsky, 9/11, Seven Stones, 2001, p. 23. To read full text of the article of Milan Rai visit: http://electroniciraq.net/news/2038.shtml.

*****

4

MUSLIM APOLOGISTS

Join the Mainstream

Mr. Shahid Malik, Member of Parliament in UK for Dewsbury insists on the young men to join the mainstream. His expressions on the issue were reactionary and agitating. The knowledge that there were young men, born and bred in the country of the writer, angry enough and fanatical to blow innocent commuters to pieces had been hard to digest. Since it emerged that one of the suicide bombers of July 7, widely assumed to have been the ringleader, was from Dewsbury in West Yorkshire, many people asked the M.P. from the same constituency, what elements in that area could have spawned such radicalism? What influences could lead a husband and father, a primary school assistant to detonate a bomb, killing seven innocent persons and himself in the process?

"Apart from pointing out the obvious – that Mohammad Siddique Khan was born in Leeds, attended mosques there, and only moved to Dewsbury recently – I have to tell people that none of us in Dewsbury can understand it either. It is true that some young Muslims in my constituency have been angered, and frustrated by what they see as the double standard of the "West" in relation to international Muslim areas of conflict: Palestine, Kashmir, Afghanistan, Iraq or Chechnya" the Member of Parliament admits.

The author further confesses: "There is a feeling of alienation, often alienation; a feeling that some how you do not belong; a feeling made much more acute by the fact that the party that came second in last year's local elections – the British National Party – says it wants an "all-white Britain". No wonder young Muslims who travel to Pakistan come back with a sense of belonging and an inner peace that eludes them in their own country."

But, the author asserts, none of this is meant justify or excuse terrorist actions. "Those of us in leadership roles must make it clear to our young people that in a democracy the way we express such feelings is by debate and through democratic institutions, not through violence. We must drag them into the political mainstream." "The attacks of July 7", he further asserts, "have shown us the danger that words can become deadly deeds. We must confront head-on those few who preach violence and hatred in the name of Islam and, in doing so, poison the minds of vulnerable young men."

"When I, and other British Muslims voiced condemnation of extremists in the past, we feared giving ammunition to far-right extremists. Equally some feared stoking up tensions within the community." Hence, when the speaker challenged the perceived status quo within Britain's 1.8 million – strong Muslim community, he expected to provoke a wave of disapproval. But it seemed he tapped into a nerve. Challenging the community to confront this evil gained widespread approval from everyone except extremists, he narrated.

For British Muslims there was a sense of relief. They were no longer in denial. They would no longer pretend not to see or hear the fanatical view who stood outside their mosques, polluting young minds. The events of July 7 had changed that "The choices are stark yet clear – we neither confront the enemy within, or are seen to condone", he says. "On July 14," the author narrated his experience," I stood with some of my constituents outside Mohammad Siddique Khan's home in Dewsbury to observe a two-minute silence in memory of his victims. In doing so we sent a powerful message: the battle for the hearts and souls of British Muslims, here in Dewsbury and across the country has truly begun", he concludes.[1]

The Price of Occupation

The British activist and writer of *Speaking of Empire and Resistance* Mr. Tariq Ali does not consider the anti-terror laws made by troubles in Northern Iceland, the Irish Republic Army targeted mainland Britain, it came close to blowing up Margaret Thatcher and her Cabinet in Brighton. Some years later a missile was fired at No. 10. London's financial quarter was also targeted. There was no secret as to the identity of the organization that carried out the hits or its demands. And all this happened despite the various Prevention of Terrorism Acts passed by the House of Commons. The same situation may be repeated in the cast of 7/7, Mr. Ali evaluates.

It may be safely assumed, Mr. Tariq Ali goes on, the cause of these bombs is the unstinting support given by New Labour and its Prime Minister to the United States' wars in Afghanistan and Iraq. Most Londoners (as the rest of the country) were opposed to the Iraq war. Tragically, they have suffered the blow and paid the price for the re-election of Mr. Blair and a continuation of the war.

Ever since 9/11, Tariq Ali has been arguing that the "war against terror" is immoral and counter productive. It sanctions the use of state terror – bombing raids, torture, countless civilian deaths in Afghanistan and Iraq – against "Islamo-anarchists" whose numbers are small, but whose reach is deadly. The solution then, as now, is political, not military, he suggests. The British ruling elite understood this perfectly well in the case of Ireland-curtailment of civil liberties, that did not solve the problem.

The real solution lies, Mr. Tariq Ali advises, in immediately ending the occupation of Iraq, Afghanistan and Palestine. Just because these three wars are reported sporadically and mean little to the everyday lives of most Europeans does not mean the anger and bitterness they arouse in the Muslim world and its diaspora is insignificant. At the beginning of the G-8 summit,

Mr. Blair suggested that "poverty was the cause of terrorism". It is not so. The principal cause of this violence is the violence being inflicted on the people of the Muslim world. And unless this is recognised, the horrors will continue, Mr. Ali fears.[2]

Terror Links

Mr. Salim Lone, the former spokesman for the United Nation's mission in Iraq, clearly declared that the Gleneagles summit's grand stage might well have shown up George W. Bush's hypocrisy in proclaiming an "ideology of compassion" over African poverty and global warming. Instead, the London bombings allowed the U.S. President and Tony Blair to strut as anti-terror champions again, when infact their policies continue to produce thousands of new terrorists, as he criticized.

One hardly expected British and U.S. officials to admit the Iraq-terror link. Mr. Blair and U.S. Secretary of State Condoleezza Rice denied this linkage by recalling that the 1998 U.S. embassy bombings in east Africa and the 9/11 attacks took place before the 2003 Iraq war. But not one interviewer or reporter pointed out that both these attacks were preceded by another war against Iraq, following its 1990 invasion of Kuwait. Indeed it was that that war and the accompanying United Nations sanctions, plus the sanctioning of U.S. troops in Saudi Arabia, that ushered in our age of global terror with the attempt to blow up the World Trade Centre in 1993, the writer added.

Mr. Bush and Mr. Blair were also back in full throttle over the terrorists' barbarity in contrast to the West's superiority of culture and values. Terrorists were motivated by hatred for the Western way of life, they insisted. There appeared to be no memory of the half a million Iraqi children killed by sanctions ruthlessly maintained by the U.S. and U.K. Indeed this slaughter was defended as necessary fo advance U.S. interests by the former U.S. Secretary of State, Madeleine Albright. It was "worth it", she told CBS in 1996. While repeatedly reporting comments asserting the other side's inhumanity in recent days, Western TV networks have not even hinted at the images they possess of more recent of crimes against humanity committed in

Fallujah, Najaf, Qaim, the mountain villages of Afghanistan, Jenin. Yes, the terrorists are barbaric – but who is more so?

Mr. Lone further says that Muslims in particular want to see an end to terrorist carnage: after all, the principal victims of terror and the U.S. – British aggressions disguised as a response to it are Muslim countries. Forever Westerner killed by Muslim terrorists since the end of the cold war, at least a hundred Muslims have died in wars and occupations perpetrated by the West. Action against terrorism is imperative, but will only succeed if accompanied by steps to address intense Muslim grievances, including curbing wars of aggression and occupation, which are among the central causes of the exponential growth in terror. But no one dares to put these items on the international agenda because of U.S. Power – and the support given to the U.S. by Britain. Without that British support, the U.S. would be comprehensively isolated and forced to reconsider its policies, Mr. Lone concluded.[3]

Bombs with Lessons

Throughout the 1980s and 1990s, foreign intelligence services were complaining about the U.K. The editorial staff of *Leader* syas that we had allowed our capital city to become a heaven for resistance fighters and/or terrorists. The French were particularly incensed, tracing the origin of the bombings of the Paris Metro to cells operating, with apparent impurity, from London.

The *New Statesman* revealed in December 2002 that, even a year after the attack on the World Trade Center in New York, Britain was still seen as excessively tolerant. In a cover piece entitled "Londonistan", we quoted European and American officials as suggesting that the UK had come to a non-aggression pact with Islamist oppositionists dating back to the *mujahedin* rebellion against the Soviet-backed regime in Afghanistan – let them act with impunity as long as they did not launch any attacks on our soil.

As we ponder the horror of the events of 7 July, the callousness and the arbitrariness of the violence visited on our vibrant and cosmopolitan capital city, it is worth reminding ourselves of the inconsistencies of our policies, not least policies to protect the security of our citizens. This is not a time for point-scoring – the roots of many of the problems reach back years. This is a time for pulling together, as Tony Blair and Ken Livingstone in their different ways have declared. But it is also a time to air some hard and unpalatable truths. This week the writer Ziauddin Sardar warns his fellow Muslims that they can no longer hide behind hollow declarations that the suicide bombers, and those who masterminded and supported them, are deviants within Islam. Incitement to jihad, to exact revenge for injustices, real or perceived, in the Middle East, must no longer be tolerated within the Muslim community or outside it as part of freedom of speech. At the same time, far greater efforts should be made towards cohesion. We cannot wish away problems of alienation and anger. We now know that we cannot pass by on the other side. Hard truths apply to all. Inevitably, that brings us back to Iraq. The spin of the past few days – that the invasion of Iraq had no galvanising effect on Islamist radicals – is as fatuous as were the promises before the war of a mission to "democratise" countries at the barrel of a gun. The consistent opposition of the *New Statesman* to the war was, and is, based not on anti-Americanism but on a thorough understanding of international security. By far the most convincing argument against the war (and there were so many) was that it would make the world far less safe. Almost everything that has happened in the past three years has vindicated this view. Here are just a few reasons: the deceptions and hubris that surrounded the warnings of weapons of mass destruction made it all the more difficult for the public to believe ministers and security chiefs when they warned that a terrorist attack on British soil was inevitable; the lack of international support for the invasion made it all the more difficult for democratic countries to unite behind a common approach that included counter-terrorism; the asymmetric nature of the original warfare, plus the abuses at Abu Gharib and Guantanamo Bay and the assault on Fallujah last November, at a cost of more than

700 lives, reinforced the resolve of those who sought a perverted form of retaliation.

Most important of all, a link between terrorism and failing state' that did not exist before the war now does exist in abundance. Our deliberate encouragement of Islamists in Afghanistan helped foster much of the terrorism of recent years. Iraq has provided it with a new lease of life spanning, who knows, perhaps a couple of decades. That the consequence was unintended does not make it any less forgivable.

These policy calamities were predicted not just by many on the left. British ambassadors, parliamentary committees, intelligence officials and police chiefs expressed their fears and frustrations at the simplicity of the Bush-Blair world-view, sometimes publicly, usually discreetly. They should have been more candid. So should members of cabinet and parliament. So, also, should a media that has replaced bellicosity in the run-up to war with a reluctance to engage in debate since the London bombings.

The Prime Minister has responded to the atrocities with admirable calm and sure-footedness. That is not an optional extra. That is a prerequisite for leadership for which the nation should be grateful. But there is another important manifestation of leadership as well – to think strategically, to pursue policies that are predicated on more than a hunch that "good will prevail". Out of this horror we cannot find solace in certainty, either for our future security or an analysis of the past. We can learn lessons, however, both from an excess of complacency at home and an excess of zeal abroad. No politician can guarantee our safety in any of the world's great cities at a time when anyone can download bomb-making instructions from the internet. No politician can remove an individual's sense of grievance, however warped. No state can prevent wanton acts of murder, terrorist or otherwise.

The events of 7 July have led to further calls for "clampdowns". The ease with which the four bombers planned and executed their attacks reinforces the need for better intelligence. If specific new laws are required, they should be scrutinised speedily and dispassionately, and not be dismissed out of hand. The immediate focus is naturally on security at home. In the longer term, we must reassess our actions abroad. What we can demand of our politicians than they have displayed internationally to date.[4]

Earlier after 9/11 attacks Ziauddin Sardar could not recognize his religion in either the fanatics' deeds or in the media descriptions of "these people". He quickly responded in the *New Statesman*:

The fallout has already begun. American Muslims have started to receive threatening phone calls. Muslim websites have been brought down with hate mail. Muslim areas in New York have asked for extra police protection. My own relatives in various American cities are afraid to go out for fear of being beaten. In the UK, the Muslim council of Britain has also been inundated by hate mail. Headlines proclaim "declaration of war" and lead inevitably to innumerable invocations of the "clash of civilisations", the assumption that all Muslims somehow hate the West and are inimical to the values of western civilisation. "These people", the recurrent phrase that punctuates all references to the perpetrators, is not a specific accusation; it is a general charge. Not surprisingly, fear has spread among all Muslims who, for no fault of their own, will be classed among the perpetrators.

Muslims fear that the scale of the outrage will dictate the logic of the countermeasures. In its determination to punish the terrorists and those who harbour terrorists, the US will lose the distinction between the innocent and the guilty. Its anger is such that it will blanket everyone; it already allowed Lawrence Eagleburger, a former secretary of state to the first President George Bush, to declare: "You have to kill some of these people; even if they were not directly involved, they need to be hit." Yet Muslim organisations in Europe and America were among the first to declare their outrage. The Muslim Council of Britain described the attacks as "senseless and evil acts that appal all people of conscience." "Unbelievable" was the common sentiment expressed by leaders throughout the Muslim world, from Palestine's Yasser Arafat to Pakistan's General Musharraf.

As a Muslim, I wince at the prejudice that the media are peddling, seemingly everywhere. And yet, senseless suicide and slaughter by fanatics are no part of my faith. Justice is the supreme value of Islam, but seeking justice demands, requires and bears the duty of just means. The matching of ends to means in one inseparable body of values and ethical restraints is the essence of Islamic teaching.

How am I to comprehend, I ask myself, this colossal act of terrorism if the perpetrators turn out to be Muslims? How am I to cope with the presumption that, at some level, all Muslims must be able to understand the minds of terrorists and suicide bombers, because in some dark corner of their psyche they share a common core of ideals?

Clearly, the terrorists do not follow the same Prophet Mohammed (SAW), who as unequivocally forbade the killing of civilians, women and children, the old and the infirm, the destruction of property, burning of crops, and slaughter of animals in any act of war. And I do not for a moment believe they undertake these acts for the services of 72 virgins, permission to see the face of Allah (SWT) and other nonsense that I keep reading in the press.

As the novelist Tom Clancy said on CNN, it is simply ridiculous to talk of "Islamic" terrorists, the media's favourite epithet. "These people don't act because of their religion; it's because they are fools" Clancy noted. It is quite futile to seek some explanation of terrorist acts in the world-view of Islam.

What we need to understand is that terror is an aberration, that it isolates those capable of such horrendous inhumanity from the rest of the community, that it makes them different from everyone else. The terrorists harm those they perversely claim to defend, whose causes they allege they seek to further.

So, how are we to cope with terrorism, including Muslim terrorism? To leave no hiding place for the guilty, we have to address the injustices that provide the noxious fumes in which terror is conceived. We have to face the awful disparity of compassion that is so commonplace among those who could never conceive of themselves becoming terrorists. In so many parts of the world, we neglect the legitimate needs, basic rights and awful circumstances of people without hope, without justice, jobs or any proper provision. It is not terrorists who spread the seeds of such appalling human waste, oppression and tyranny. Good people who walk by on the other side, who fail to engage and care for just resolution, who tolerate the intolerable, bear responsibility for the ongoing evil of injustice. The inaction of these good people creates the void in which the aberrant, the abnormal, the terrorists seek to assert their monopoly of compassion through evil deeds.

How do we counter the threat of terror? Already we are being told that the implosion of intelligence gathering on the ground is a casualty of peace which, far from bringing any dividends, has led to the devastation at the World Trade Center and the Pentagon. America has put its faith in technology, in remote sensing, in isolation, in dreams of a shield that will keep it safe from "rogue states" and whatever else stalks the globe seeking its downfall.

The truth is, better intelligence cannot fight terrorism. The best weapons are compassion for the neediest and a willingness to form a partnership with the oppressed and tyrannised, so that they can seek a better existence.

Unless we have a different kind of intelligence – to make common cause, through our differences, across communities – we shall all be victims of terror.[5] Sardar had concluded.

Can Islam Change?

Beslan and 9/11 are leading millions of Muslims to search their souls. Even clerics now question the harshest traditional laws and look for a more humane interpretation of their faith. It is claimed by Ziauddin Sardar.

The Muslim world is changing. Three years after the atrocity of 9/11, it may be in the early stages of a reformation, albeit with a small "r". From Morocco to Indonesia, people are trying to develop a more contemporary and humane interpretation of Islam, and some countries are undergoing major transformations.

Much of the attention is focused on reformulating the *Shariah*, the centuries-old body of Islamic law deeply embedded in a medieval psychology. The *Shariah* is state law in many Muslim countries such as Saudi Arabia, Iran, Pakistan and Sudan. For many conservative and radical Muslims, the *Shariah* is Islam: it cannot be changed and must be imposed in exactly the shape it was first formulated in the ninth century. Since 9/11, there has been a seismic shift in this perception. More and more Muslims now perceive Islamic law to be dangerously obsolete. And these include the *ulama*, the religious scholars ands clerics, who have a tremendous hold on the minds of the Muslim masses.

In India, for example, where the secular state allows Muslims to regulate their communal affairs according to their own law, the "triple *talaq*" is being changed. Triple *talaq* gives a man the absolute right to divorce his wife by uttering "I divorce thee" three times. He can do it by letter, telegram, telephone, fax, even by text message. Quite apart from denying women's rights, the law has inherent absurdities. For example, as one critic has explained, "The moment a Muslim male utters '*talaq*, *talaq*, *talaq*', his wife becomes unlawful to him, even if he has uttered those words under coercion, in a fit or rage or a drunken state, and regrets his utterance the very next moment." The only way out is for the woman to marry someone else, consummate the marriage, get the second husband to divorce her and then remarry the first husband.

But in July, the All India Muslim Personal Law Board declared that triple *talaq* was wrong, promised to prepare a model marriage contract (which would require both husband and wife not to seek divorce without due legal process) and asked Muslim men to ensure that women get a share in agricultural property.

These may look like minor changes, but there are enormous implications to the board's implicit admission that Islamic law is not immutable. Certainly, it has set defenders of the pure faith at the throats of members of Muslims for Secular Democracy (MSD), who are campaigning for root-and-branch reform. "Remain in your senses," the conservative *Urdu Times* warned Javed Akhtar, the poet and Bollywood screenwriter who is MSD president. "The day is not far when you too will be counted among the infamous blasphemers such as Salman Rushdie."

Yet in India, at least, the purists – both the conservatives and the more aggressive radicals – are on the retreat. Uzma Naheed, an activist for women's right and Personal Law Board member, says that even the religious scholars are changing. "It is not just that a person like me is invited to address large gatherings of the *ulama* in different parts of the country, where I am given a very patient and sincere hearing. It is what the *ulama* themselves have started saying in public meetings that is more significant."

In Pakistan, however, the *ulema* are still predominantly hardline and are locked in a virtual civil war with reformers. The contentious issue here is the Hudood Ordinance, which states the maximum punishments for adultery (stoning), false accusation of adultery (80 lashes of the whip), theft (cutting off the right hand), drinking alcohol (80 lashes) and apostasy (death). The ordinance was imposed on Pakistan in 1979 by the military ruler Muhammad Zia ul-Haq, under pressure from Islamic parties. It makes no distinction between rape and adultery; thus women who are raped often end up being shipped while the rapists are exonerated. Girls who have reached the age of puberty are treated as adults. Worse, women are not allowed to give evidence on their own behalf. Among the high-profile injustices was the case in 1983 of 15-year-old Jehan Mina, raped by an uncle and his son. She was sentenced to ten years in prison and 100 lashes, reduced to three years and 15 lashes in view of her age. In 1985, a blind maidservant, Safia Bibi, was sentenced to a similar punishment. In both cases, the girl's pregnancy was used as proof that the sex act had been committed but the men were acquitted on the benefit of the doubt. Several women have been sentenced to death by stoning, the most recent being Zafran Bibi in Kohat in 2002, although that sentence was quickly overturned on appeal.

In the past three years, protest against the Hudood Ordinance, which was never popular, have reached a crescendo. The Joint Action Committee, a network of NGOs which has held a string of demonstrations across Pakistan in the world". Though he has often promised to repeal the laws, the country's military ruler, General Pervez Musharraf, always caves in under pressure from puritan Islamist parties. "No one can deny," he told a recent meeting in Karachi, "that we have to adhere to the *Qur'ān* and the example of the Prophet Muhammad (SAW). The question is of correct *ulama* who dominate it have never previously voted for justice and women's rights. However, they cannot be left out of the equation. For the vast majority of Muslims, changes to Islamic law have to be made within the boundaries of the *Qur'ān*'s teachings if they are to be legitimate. Without the co-operation of the religious scholars, who bestow this legitimacy, the masses will not embrace change.

This is where Morocco has provided an essential lead. Its new Islamic family law, introduced in February, sweeps away centuries of bigotry and bias against women. It was produced with the full co-operation of religious scholars as well as the active participation of women. Morocco retained much of the colonial legal system that France left behind but, in family law, followed what is known locally as the Moudawana – the traditional Islamic rules on marriage, divorce, inheritance, polygamy and child custody. At first, King Mohammed VI had to abandon plans for change because, protesters claimed, he was trying to impose secular law and Western culture on Morocco. In spring 2001, however, he set up a commission, which included women and was given the specific task of coming up with fresh legislation based on the principles of Islam. Given enormous impetus by 9/11 and its aftermath, it produced a report that many see as a revolutionary document. The resulting family code establishes that women are equal partners in marriage and family life. It throws out the notion that the husband is head of the family and that women are mere underlings in need of guidance and protection. It raises the minimum age for women's marriage from 15 to 18, the same as for men.

The new Moudawana allows a woman to contract a marriage without the legal approval of a guardian. Verbal divorce has been outlawed: men now require prior authorisation from a court, and women have exactly the same rights. Women can claim alimony and can be granted custody of their children even if they remarry. Husbands and wives must share property acquired during the marriage. The old custom of favouring male heirs in he sharing of inherited land has also been dropped, making it possible for grandchildren on the daughter's side to inherit from their grandfather, just like grandchildren on the son's side. As for polygamy, it has been all but abolished. Men can take second wives only with the full consent of the first wife and only if they can prove, in a court of law, that they can treat them both with absolute justice – an impossible condition.

Elsewhere, the focus is not so much on Islamic law as on Islam as a whole. In a general election last March, the Malaysian Prime Minister, Abdullah Ahmad Badawi, argued that Islam was almost totally associated with violence and extremism and needed to be formulated anew. He called his new concept "*Islam Hadhari*", or progressive Islam. It was pitted against the "conservative Islam" of the main opposition party, the Islamic PAS. For the first time, the governing coalition won more than 90 per cent of federal parliamentary seats. PAS, and its version of Islam (full implementation of the *Shariah*, without modification; a leading role in the state for religious scholars; and so on), were routed.

Badawi, who is a trained religious scholar, took the term "*hadhari*" from Ibn Khaldun, the 14th Century Muslim historian and founder of sociology. The term signifies urban civilisation; and *Islam Hadhari* emphasises economic development, civic life and cultural progress. When Muslims talk about Islam, says Abdullah Mohd. Zain, a minister in the prime minister's department, "there is always the tendency to link it to the past, to the Prophet's time". Islam Hadhari gives equal emphasis to the present and future. "it emphasises wisdom, practicality and harmony," says Zain. "It encourages moderation or a balanced approach to life. Yet it does not stray from the fundamentals of the *Qur'ān* and the example and sayings of the Prophet (SAW).

Both Malaysia's *Islam Hadhari* and Indonesia's deformation emphasise tolerance and pluralism, civic society and open democracy. Both are likely to spread. Malaysia is trying to export *Islam Hadhari* to Muslim communities in Thailand and the Philippines. Meanwhile Morocco is trying to persuade Egypt, Jordan and the United Arab Emirates to adopt its model of family law.

Muslims worldwide are acknowledging the need for fundamental change in their perception of Islam. They are making conscious efforts to move away from medieval notions of Islamic law and to implement the vision of justice, equality and beauty that is rooted in the *Qur'ān.* If such changes continue, the future will not repeat the recent past.[6]

Fatwa on Fanatics

Ziauddin Sardar himself issued a *fatwa* against 'fanatics' and those who involved in terror. He was of the view that *fatwas* were always misused to damage the real image of Islam. So the moderate Muslims should come forward and fight against these elements. His full text is as follows:

"The magnitude of the terrorist attack on America has forced Muslims to take a critical look at themselves. Why have we repeatedly turned a blind eye to the evil within our societies? Why have we allowed the sacred terms of Islam, such as *fatwa* and *jihad*, to be hijacked by obscurantist, fanatic extremists?

Muslims are quick to note the double standards of America-its support for despotic regimes, its partiality towards Israel, and the covert operations that have undermined democratic movements in the Muslim world. But we seldom question our own double standards. For example, Muslims are proud that Islam is the fastest growing religion in the West. Evangelical Muslims, from Saudi Arabia to Pakistan, happily spread their constricted interpretations of Islam. But Christian missionaries in Muslim countries are another matter. They have to be banned or imprisoned. Those who burn effigies of President Bush will be first in the queue for an American visa. The psychotic young men, members of such extremist organisations as Al-Muhajiroun and 'Supporters of Sharia', shouting fascist obscenities outside the Pakistan Embassy, are enjoying the fruits of Western freedom of expression. Their declared aim is to establish 'Islamic states'. But in any self-proclaimed Islamic state, they would be ruthlessly silenced.

This is not the first time concerned Muslims have raised such questions. But we have been forced to ignore them for two main reasons. In a world where it is always open season for prejudice and discrimination on Muslims and Islam, our main task has seemed to be to defend Islam.

The other reason concerns Ummah, the global Muslim community. We have to highlight, the argument goes, the despair and suffering of the Muslim people-their poverty and plight as refugees and the horror of war-torn societies.

So, all good and concerned Muslims are implicated in the unchecked rise of fanaticism in Muslim societies. We have given free reign to fascism within our midst, and failed to denounce fanatics who distort the most sacred concepts of our faith. 'We have been silent as they proclaim themselves martyrs, mangling beyond recognition the most sacred meaning of what it is to be a Muslim.

But the events of 11 September have freed to us from any further obligation to this misapplied conscience. The insistence by the Muslim Council of Britain that the Islamic cause is best served by the Taliban handing over Osama bin Laden, is indicative of this shift.

The devotion with which so many Muslims, young and old, in Europe and America, are organising meetings and conferences to discuss how to unleash the best intentions, the essential values of Islam, from the rhetoric of *jihad*, hatred and insularity, is another.

But we have to go further. Muslims are in the best position to take the lead in the common cause against terrorism. The terrorists are among us, the Muslim communities of the world. They are part of our body politic. And it is our duty to stand up against them.

We must also reclaim a more balanced view of Islamic terms like *fatwa*. A *fatwa* is simply a legal opinion based on religious reasoning. It is the opinion of one individual and is binding on only the person who gives it. But, since the Rushdie affair, it has come to be associated in the West solely with a death sentence. Now that Islam has become beset with the *fatwa* culture, it becomes necessary for moderate voices to issue their own *fatwas*. So, let me take the first step. To Muslims everywhere I issue this *fatwa*: any Muslim involved in the planning, financing, training, recruiting, support or harbouring of those who commit acts of indiscriminate violence against persons or the apparatus or infrastructure of states is guilty of terror and no part of the *Ummah*. It is the duty of every Muslim to spare no effort in hunting down, apprehending and bringing such criminals to justice. If you see something reprehensible, said the Prophet Muhammad (SAW) then change it with your hand; if you are not capable of that then use your tongue (speak out against it); and if you are not capable of that then detest it in your heart.

The silent Muslim majority must now become vocal. The rest of the world could help by adopting a more balanced tone. The rhetoric that paints America as a personification of innocence and goodness, a god-like power that can do no wrong, not only undermines the new shift but threatens to foreclose all our future."[7]

Terror roots in Islam

Hasan Surror, the famous Indian journalist and writer analyses the level of Islamophobia in Britain and finds it a minor stuff isolated acts of individual fanatics. To him, barring a few stray incidents there was "no anti-Muslim backlash" post-7/7. The fact that a number of Muslims had also been killed or injured in the attacks had created an overwhelming sense of unity with victims of other faiths. Indeed, a young British Asian Muslim girl had become the public face of the July of tragedy – a symbol of row it had affected every community.

The family of 20-year-old Shahara Akhtar Islam, who was feared dead was quoted as saying that she had been killed "in the name of the religion that she loved". This was how *The Independent* profiled her in a front-page splash: "Shahara Akhtar Islam was a devout Muslim with all her life before her... And now this young woman, who so confidently straddled the twin cultures of her mosque and her city is... feared dead, a victim of the horrific violence wreaked on London this week, almost certainly by terrorists of Al-Qaeda, murdering and maiming in the name of her faith."

Barring the usual suspects on the Right, Mr. Hasan Suroor says, the British media has acted with great restraint this time and, more importantly, highlighted the apparent change in the Muslim attitude community's willingness to stand up and be counted against fellow Muslims abusing Islam. This makes some of the breathless reporting in the foreign media even more jarring,[8] the writer analyses.

The author realizes that Muslims instead of continuing to play the Ostrich, clearly and explicitly condemned strongly the terrorist attacks without using any 'if' and 'but' and without hiding behind "grievances" and without rationalizing the "anger" of those behind 7/7. What happened that day was seen by Muslims as a "collective shame" and they were willing to go the extra mile to take on suspected extremists within their ranks.

Mr. Hasan Suroor thought it unrealist to expect parents to squeal on their children on suspicion that they are becoming too devout or spending too much time in the mosque and those who are blaming the families in this regard are simply playing to the gallery. But what parents can do, the author suggests, is "to create a climate at home that does not fuel religious passions or deepen the confusion of identity among the young".

In the end, of course, children grow up and go their own ways and even the best – or most authoritarian – of parents lose control. But while they are still learning, there is a lot parents can do to minimise the possibility of their being brainwashed by outside influences. Mr. Suroor further explains this saying: "If the talk in the family – as is generally the case in Muslim families – is constantly about Muslim grievances portraying the community always as a victim of anti-Islamic conspiracy then some of it is bound to rub off on the young who, then, start seeing demons all around them." They begin to attribute their own personal failures to what they have picked up at home; and their sense of injustice and unfairness is compounded when they experience racism in the playground and at work. Along comes a "mad" mullah and tells them that their salvation lies in jihad and, then, through a selective and perverted reading of the Qur'ān he brainwashes them into believing that it is their religious duty to kill *Kāfirs* especially those who may be waging a "war" against Muslims – a reference to the West's "war against terror". And thus another *jihadi* is born – another "nice lad" lost to extremists, Mr. Surror concludes his analysis.

According to the author, the British Muslim perception of terrorism is certainly changed now. So as other people's sons were killing and being killed in Kashmir, Chechnya, Afghanistan, Iraq and Palestine there seemed little wrong with it; if anything there were people who hailed them as martyrs. What 7/7 has done is to bring British Muslims face to face with the horrors of terrorism because, for the first time, their own sons have killed and been killed – literally at their own doorsteps.

The death of a number of innocent and devout Muslims in the explosions, Mr. Surror argues, has generated its own pressures on the community to "do some thing" to prevent such outrages. Muslims have died in terrorist attacks before but this time the victims were people you and me knew. The community can put a face on them and it is shocked. The question people were asking all of last week as they buried their dead was: where, in Islam, is it permitted to wreak mindless violence against innocent people, among them devout Muslims?

And that brings the readers to the crux: the nature of Islam. Muslims routinely claim that the Islamic precepts can not be used to justify violence and that Islam has nothing to do with what is being done in its name. Is this true? To respond this question Mr. Suroor quotes Ziauddin Sardar, "the internationally acknowledged Muslim scholar" who has a "deep knowledge of Islamic theology" and argues in the way that suits perhaps the author that is "Islam has everything to do with it."

Sardar acknowledges that vast majority of Muslims "abhor violence" and believe that "the main message of Islam is peace", but says: "Nevertheless it is false to assume that the *Qur'ān* or Islamic law can not be used to justify barbaric acts. The terrorists are a product of a specific mindset that has deep roots in Islamic history. They are nourished by an Islamic tradition that is intrinsically inhuman and violent in its rhetoric, thought and practice... Only by recognising this brutal fact would we realise that the fight against terrorism is also an internal Muslim struggle within Islam. Indeed it is a very struggle for the soul of Islam."

Mr. Surror further argues that the *Qur'ānic* verses lend themselves to different – and of ten conflicting – interpretations because they were composed in different times and in different contexts; and therefore two different verses on the same subject (for example the status of women) can be interpreted differently. The author, therefore, suggests the *Qur'ān* should be "read in its totality in order to get a true sense of Islamic teachings whereas conservative *ulama* and extremists seize on the passages that suit their agenda". Why the extremists get away with the *Qur'ān*, the author locates the reason and provides its solution also, is because an overwhelming majority of Muslims, even though they have read the *Qur'ān*, do not really know what is in it. The reason is simple: the book is in Arabic, a language ordinary Muslim outside the Arab world do not know and yet, traditionally, the *Qur'ān* is taught in Arabic. The result is that they learnt it by rote without understanding the meaning. Ask an average Muslim and he would recite verse after verse from the *Qur'ān* but ask him what they mean and he is more likely to give you a blank stare.

Mr. Surror therefore concludes that "Muslims, who do not know Arabic, must be encouraged to read the Qur'ān in their own language so that they understand it and are able to challenge when confronted with a selective and self-serving reading. For starters, nothing like a good argument to clear the head."[9]

Defining a Moderate Muslim

The "moderate" Muslim who is routinely urged to stand up and take on the radicals, has become a bit of a cliché in the current debate on Islamist extremism. For few have a clear idea who exactly they mean when they talk about moderate Muslims. Moderate in relation to what and whom? The issue is seriously debated by the scholars and journalists. Mr. Hasan Surror talks on the topic in his own terms.

Admittedly, moderation is a relative term but it has become even more relative in the so-called war on terrorism with its limited aim of putting an end to violence rather than engaging in the more complex task of tackling ideas and issues that breed it. So, any one who does not advocate violence, *ipso facto*, becomes a moderate and an ally even if he or she holds potentially obscurantist views on important issues such as individual freedom, women's rights, and freedom of speech, among others. "Moderation" Mr. Surror observes, "has come to be defined in such narrow terms in the post-9/11 climate that many of those who are now hailed as moderates by Western governments, desperately seeking Muslim allies in their campaign against terrorism, would have been judged rather differently in more normal circumstances."

Mr. Surror quotes the case of Muslim Council of Britain (MCB) the largest Muslim organization in the country which is officially recognised as the most moderate face of Islam in Britain. Its general secretary Iqbal Sacraine has been Knighted in recognition of his contribution to interfaith dialogue, though his critics say that he has been rather more useful in delivering Muslim votes to the Labour Party. But how "moderate" is he, the author explains.

Mr. Surror refers to Salman Rushdie in this regard. As Rushdie has recalled, "this is the same Sacraine" who in 1989, led the book burning campaign over *Satanic Verses*. He endorsed the *fatwa* against Mr. Rushdie saying that given the supposed enormity of his offence, "death is perhaps too easy" for the author. Footage of his inflammatory speeches against the book and Mr. Rushdie was replayed by the BBC recently in a controversial programme that challenged his and the BBC's moderate credentials. Asked whether he would still respond the same way if the Rushdie affair were to be replayed his answer was eloquently vague. But shorn of the many "ifs" and "buts", it amounted to a mumbled yes.

"If Sir Iqbal Sacraine is the best Mr. Blair can offer in the way of a good Muslim, we have a problem", Mr. Rushdie wrote in *The Times* arguing that the choice of Mr. Sacraine illustrated the "weakness of the Government's strategy for relying on traditional, but essentially orthodox Muslims to help eradicate Islamist radicalism"

"True" says Mr. Surror, "but it also highlights a sad truth: the lack of choice when it comes to finding moderate Muslims who also have sufficient influence in the community. There are not too many who fit the bill. Not that the community does not have moderate figures but, from a government's point of view, it is no good promoting leaders who may be epitomes of moderation but are not taken seriously by fellow Muslims whose views it wants to change"

"It is that old leadership crisis" Mr. Surror continues, "and the liberal Muslim intelligentsia has contributed to it by behaving as a "secular" elite afraid of soiling its hands with "sectional" issues – thus handling over the space to opportunistic elements. Essentially, Mr. Sacraine and other mainstream leaders like him are products of a leadership vacuum and they benefit from the crisis situations, which suddenly make them an important link with the community" the author evaluates in his own perspective.

Prime Minister Tony Blair may talk passionately about combating ideas than produce terrorists but his Government's instinctive reaction when bombs are flying around is to get hold of some one who can help put out the fire. The logic is that if someone like Mr. Sacraine and his friends can be of use what is wrong in wooing them? And if a Knighthood here, a peerage there, and invitations to Down Street can help raise their profile and make them more respectable in the community, well, why not?

What Western governments are looking for are orthodox but non-fanatical "insiders" (as against secular "outsiders") – people who have enough acceptability within the community and can invoke the authority of Islam to denounce terrorism, analyses Mr. Suroor. It is argued that a massage couched in an appropriately religious tone and delivered by seemingly "devout" Muslims who are in "communion" with the community has a greater chance of being given a hearing than lecture on reforms by secularists whom the community regards as too elitist and detached.

This approach adopted by the Western governments does not serve the interests and planning of the secularists and goes against their logic and argumentation. Mr. Suroor, therefore, criticises it as "short-termism" that suggests that "there is neither a strategy in place, nor a political will to help Muslims find a more dynamic leadership". But then governments every where tend to prefer to do business with the devil they knew, especially when the choice is limited and it may take years and a lot of hard work to find an alternative, which may or may not live up to the expectations. At least, the frontline leadership of the Muslim Council of Britain can talk the talk and, when under pressure, is good at making appropriate noises. Indeed, it has been doing that rather well since 9/11, sometimes even in the face of opposition from the more hardline groups. The government fears that the alternative to the MCB could be even worse. So in the present climate the choice, really, is not so much between moderates as between whoever is less of a hardliner.

Having said that, he further elaborates, leaders from a traditional mould can – if they wish – play a positive role for the simple reason hat conservative Hindu and Muslim faith group feel more comfortable with them than with secularists who remain on the fringes of community life. It is a mistake to dismiss all traditional leaders as necessarily obscurantist, communal and backward-looking. No doubt, most happen to be *status quoists* and have a vested interest in keeping the community backward in order to maintain their hold on them, but there have been many exceptions both among Hindus and Muslims. Many of the reformers in the Hindu community were spearheaded by traditional and deeply religious figures, and one of the most prominent Indian Muslim reformers, Syed Ahmad Khan, the founder of Aligarh Muslim University, also came from a "traditional" background, Mr. Suroor strongly argued in favour of traditional modern Muslim leader.[10]

Muslims need a Gandhi

Asghar Ali Engineer, the Mumbai - based writer and activist speaks of the terrorist activities spread all over the world – London, Madrid, Delhi and so on. He raises the question why do the terrorists resort to such operations in which, more often than not, they lose their lives in the prime of their youth? The author responds that it is not because of the religious fanaticism. These actions cannot be explained as mere acts of religious fanaticism. No psychologist will agree with the involvement of religion in such phenomenon.

To Mr. Engineer, the US and UK forces are too mighty for these youth belonging to organizations like al-Qaeda or Lashkar-e-Taybah or similar other organizations to take on frontally. The terrorists also use highly destructive weapons manufactured by the West and smuggled or stealthily sold by the manufacturers. These terrorists use same weapons as the forces of US and UK though they certainly do not have access to re-destructive weapons like clear missiles or much more destructive bombs causing death and destruction on much wider scale.

These youths acting as suicide bombers or planting car bombs are not so much fanatics as angry young men boiling with anger at these Western countries destroying their countries and killing and raining death and destruction. In UK we see today that how British people are expressing their anger at Muslims of

UK by attacking their mosques and Gurduwaras (through mistaken identity) because some suspected Muslims planted bombs in Central London which resulted in loss of more than 53 lives and many other injured. Do we call them fanatics? No. They are simply expressing their anger at loss of innocent lives. Just imagine how angry would they have been if UK had been attacked by Iraq or any other Muslim country and it had rained death and destruction on innocent civilians in addition to military targets, the author argues.

This is not to justify the bombing in London or anywhere by terrorists, the writer explains his position. It is only to show that it is not mere religious fanaticism as often described in Western media but only anger at invasion of their countries by US and UK and stationing their forces there. It is in other words more political than religious. Anywhere it is not for spreading Islam that these young men are laying down their lives but to ensure independence of their countries.

I think, the author offers his reflection with determination, the West particularly Bush and Blair better refrain from invading these countries if they really care for their democratic values to prevail as they so often declare from every platform. When London was bombed on 7th July Blair and Bush both again declared, 'our values shall prevail and as we will fight terrorism'. These values must of course prevail but these will not prevail if they destroy others' freedom. The author continues saying: Everyone knows that hatred begets hatred and violence begets violence. In modern world violence should have no place. Before anyone else West must learn this. In their greed for oil they do not hesitate in violating international law in invading these countries. UN had not sanctioned war against Iraq and US and UK attacked it and refused to wait for UN sanction. Such brazen violation of international law will only create chaos in the world. Even their excuse about weapons of mass destruction proved to be wrong. Then Bush and Blair started tackling of 'regime change'. Can one overthrow governments in other countries? Is it permitted by international law? Certainly not.

Mr. Engineer told his personal experience. Once during discussion an American official told me if it is political and not religious issue why these terrorists invoke Islam. I told him why President Bush invokes freedom and democracy every time to justify his invasion on Afghanistan and Iraq? He had no answer. Of course when we do something wrong we always invoke some legitimating ideology be it religion or be it some political values like freedom and democracy, the author comments.

To Engineer, violence will have no justification. Only love and peace can sustain humanity on this planet. Only greedy or angry people or those who believe in ideology of hate will resort to violence. "And as violence begets violence we should not counter-violence with violence. Buddha, Mahavir Jain, Christ, Prophet Muhammad (SAW) and Mahatma Gandhi in our own times have shown it is only love, peace and compassion which can effectively counter hatred and violence," the author borrows models from history to prove his argument.

Mr. Asghar Ali Engineer, then elaborates his views on the issue in plural perspective. In this globalized world all countries are multi-religious and multi-cultural. If few members of one community use violence against another community it can inflame situation and destroy the very spirit of multi-culturalism. This is precisely what has happened in UK and earlier in the US when on 9/11 New York towers were attacked. Thus it is very important for protecting multi-culturalism to maintain inter-religious and inter-cultural peace.

The author concludes that: "We need more Gandhis in the modern world to spread message of non-violence in politics." What is saddening is that even India experiences so much sectarian and communal violence, which happens to be land of Gandhi. Right wing politics of *Sangh Pariwar* preach ideology of hate to realise their own ambitions of power. In Pakistan the *jihadis* play in the hands of vested interests and right wing religious leaders to perpetrate violence in Pakistani society as well as in neighbouring India. "As I have pointed out in one of my articles earlier," the author finally remarks, "the world of Islam also needs a Gandhi to preach love and peace. In the past we had several Sufi saints like Maulana Rum to spread message of love and peace but in modern Islamic world Islam has not produced a towering figure like Gandhi or Khan Ghaffar Khan to give soothing message of peace and love. It needs one very badly."[11]

These apologist intellectuals have examined the case of Muslim involvement in terrorism as that of Islam and the Islamic fundamentals. Some of them evaluated the events without going into the details of the roots of terror, while others have tried to root this phenomenon into Islam and Islamic history itself. Self-assessment and reforming process is always appreciable if needed and is initiated with sincerity and honesty and within Islamic paradigm. The imported mentality and approach always worsens the situation. The reform and renovation if started from within by the authentic and reliable scholars and activists keeping in view the Islamic standards and contemporary requirements, prove always healthy and useful. The main stream Muslim community and committed scholars and loyal intellectuals have also examined the violence and terrorism committed on 7/7 but in the perspective of Muslim teachings and have rooted in the basic factors. Their approach represents that of the entire Muslim world and its real feelings and true reactions.

*****

NOTES AND REFERENCES

1. Shahid Malik, What the Leaders must do, The Hindu, July 25, 2005.
2. Tariq Ali, The Price of Occupation, *The Hindu*, July 9, 2005.
3. Salim Line, *The Hindu*, July 13, 2005.
4. Ziauddin Sardar, *Leader*, July 18, 2005 (Bombs with Lessons for us all). This article first appeared in the *New Statesman* U.K. For the latest in current and cultural affairs subscribe to the *New Statesman* print edition.
5. *New Statesman*, Sept. 17, 2001, entitled as 'Where is the hand of my God in this horror?"
6. For a detailed study of the author see his book *Desperately Seeking Paradise: Journey of a sceptical Muslim*, Granta Books. The article first appeared in the *New Statesman*, Sept. 13, 2004. For the latest in current and cultural affairs subscribe to the *New Statesman* print edition.
7. My *Fatwa* on the Fanatics, *The Observer*, Sept. 23, 2001.

   Ziauddin Sardar, travelling around several Muslim countries, finds that thinkers, activists, political leaders and ordinary Muslims across the globe are refusing to be defined by the ideology of violence and intolerance, but their responses are diverse.

   This has been a terrible year to be a Muslim.

   But, revolted by what is being perpetrated in the name of Islam, the Muslim world is bringing a whole range of new debates to the fore.

   For decades the core debate in the Muslim world was about establishing an ideological "Islamic state" and returning to the *Shariah*, the historical body of Islamic law.

   This debate, often led by so-called "Islamic movements", produced a narrow, intolerant, obscurantist, illiberal, brutal and confrontational interpretation of Islam. It is this interpretation that gave rise to what we now know as "Islamic fundamentalism".

   But the fixed simplistics of fundamentalists never were the whole of the debate – even though the fundamentalists shout the loudest and dominate the globe through violent expression.

   Now, fundamentalism is being challenged by emerging and alternative visions of Islam, each taking shape in different ways in different countries.

Pakistan was founded as the first modern Islamic state. But it was only in 1978 under the military regime of General Zia ul Haq that *Shariah* was made the law of the land.

What followed was a series of cases where the implementation of the law acquired a notorious reputation for practical injustice, especially towards women.

And it is women who are really standing up to this law.

The essence of the argument against the *Shariah* is much more than the fact that its interpretation and application is illiberal and contrary to contemporary ideas of human rights.

The fundamentalist position is that the *Qur'ān* is the source of all legislation in Islam and therefore the Sharia is an immutable body of sacred law.

It is concept itself that is now being challenged.

Shariah, it is being widely argued, is not divine but a "jurists' law", that was formulated and socially constructed during the early phase of Islamic history.

It can be changed, modified and reformulated – in its entirety.

Thus the *Shariah*, as an inherited body of rulings and precedent, is being reclaimed in Pakistan.

Muslim scholars are demanding the same right as their forebears to investigate the sources for alternative interpretations, new ways of framing and operating precepts and law.

We can see this activism not just in Pakistan but also in Morocco.

In Morocco an entirely recast family law aspect of Sharia has been produced by Islamic scholars.

It was promulgated by the King in response to widespread public demonstrations by women and, when published, became an instant best-seller.

What it has its opponents including women, its impeccable Islamic intellectual credentials-advancing the case for gender equality, poverty eradication, economic advancement and the development of free expression through civil society – are now the agenda of debate.

The irony is that neither Pakistan nor Morocco are democracies: one a thinly veiled military regime, the other a near-absolute monarchy.

But the activist proponents of this alternative interpretation of Islam are clear that it can never be fully realised without democracy; indeed that democracy is an essential hallmark of a genuine Islamic society.

Indonesia has the world's largest Muslim population.

Eight years ago, it threw off 30 years of dictatorship backed by the military. Democracy has led to a great outpouring of new thinking.

Established organisations such as Mohammadiyah and new civic society organisations such as the Liberal Islam Network-which have following in the tens of millions – are revising the conventional views of Islam and the state.

In seeking an interpretation of Islam that is both authentic and moderate, liberal, tolerant, open and democratic, they stress the importance of separation between religion and state.

And thus they come to a vision of modernity of Muslims that is rooted in, and inspired by, Islam, yet does not lay claim to being an infallible expression of religion and therefore closed to debate.

It is these agents of civil society that are setting the pace of change.

The demands they make on governments are producing a response. But it is no longer a case of seeking one solution.

There is a diversity of responses according to the particular circumstances of different countries, with different histories and different experiences of modernising and modernity.

The extremists have one all-embracing, all-constraining ideology.

But the reality of the Muslim world is its immense diversity.

The new ideas battling for the soul of Islam have a clear set of common principles but they are varied and must be heard in their own context and place.

A journey around the populous periphery of the Muslim world clearly demonstrates that the extremists are not only a minority but that the fossilised traditionalism from which they derive their legitimacy is also on the retreat.

There is a new air of optimism and confidence in many places that an Islam that is moderate, tolerant and democratic not only should – but will – actually be the future.

This new spirit, and the new ideas it is producing, is not tentative.

But it would be too soon to assert that the ideas are carrying all before them and have secured their dominance.

It is, however, beyond question that to understand the changes taking place in the Muslim world, and appreciate how Islam is being reformed, one has to listen to these voices from the edge.

Battle for Islam, was broadcast on BBC Two at 2100 BST on Monday, 5 September 2005.

8. Hasan Suroor, Beware the hype about a backlash, *The Hindu*, July 13, 2005.
9. Hasan Suroor, Lessons for Muslims from London Bombings, *The Hindu*, July 19, 2005.
10. Hasan Suroor, Who is a "moderate" Muslim and how? *The Hindu*, September 01, 2005. The author quotes Sir Syed Ahmad Khan and Dr. Zakir Hussain who were traditional modern leaders and were able "to separate religion from politics and more importantly they had a vision for the community which the present-day leaders lack. The author supports Mr. Rushdie who has dismissed Britain's Muslim leaders as a "joke" saying "nobody follows them" – a description that would fit most of the current crop of Muslim leaders the world over, says Mr. Suroor. But where is the alternative. The author then suggests the secular elite to get off its high pedestal and start engaging with ordinary Muslims – not as dispensers of wisdom lecturing them on their backwardness or problems with Islam but as partners.
11. Asghar Ali Engineer, London Bombings, Violence and Islam, *The Milli Gazette*, 1-15 August 2005, p. 16. Some scholars and journalists view that Britain's multiculturalism is responsible for London bombings in July 2005. Tariq Modood says, it rather needs to be extended to a "politics of equal respect" that includes Britain's Muslims in a new shared sense of national belonging. He writing on "Remaking multiculturalism after 7/7" says on September 29, 2005:

    In spring 2005, I published a book – Multicultural Politics: Racism, Ethnicity and Muslims in Britain – which argued that by making progress towards the goal of multicultural equality and acceptance, and embracing plural ways of belonging to Britain, we in Britain were developing a "multicultural Britishness".

    The flyer for the American edition claimed:

    "If an Islam-West divide is to be avoided in our time, Modood suggests, then Britain, with its relatively successful ethnic pluralism and its easygoing attitude toward religion, will provide a particularly revealing case and promising site for understanding".

    Such optimism would have struck some people as foolish at any time, but after the London bombings of 7 July and the abortive bombings of 21 July, it must strike many more as completely misguided. In particular, the fact that most of the individuals involved were born and/or brought up in Britain – a country that had given them or their parents of refuge from persecution, fear or poverty and guarantee of freedom of worship – has led many analysts, observers, intellectuals and opinion-formers to conclude that multiculturalism has failed; even worse, that it can be blamed for the bombings.

To take just four examples from a waterfall of commentary over the last ten-to-twelve weeks:

William Pfaff states that "these British bombers are a consequence of a misguided and catastrophic pursuit of multiculturalism" ("A monster of our own making", *Observer*, 21 August 2005).

Gilles Kepel observes that the bombers "were the children of Britain's own multicultural society" and that the bombings have "smashed" the implicit social consensus that produced multiculuralism "to smithereens" ("*Europe's answer to Londonistan*", open Democracy, 24 August 2005).

Martin Wolf concludes that multiculturalism's departure from the core political values that must underpin Britain's community "is dangerous because it destroys political community... (and) demeaning because it devalues citizenship. In this sense, at least, multiculturalism must be discarded as nonsense" ("When multiculturalism is a nonsense", *Financial Times*, 31 August 2005).

Trevor Phillips questions, in he context of a speech concerned with "a society... becoming more divided by race and religion", an "anything goes" multiculturalism... which leads to deeper division and inequality... In recent years we've focused far too much on the 'multi' and no enough on the common culture." ("After 7/7: Sleepwalking to segregation", *Commission for Racial Equality*, 22 September 2005).

Even those who don't directly regard multiculturalism as the cause of the bombings tend to believe that we need to review the concept, often concluding that it needs to be replaced by "integration". Indeed, this current of thinking predates 7/7 (and, for that matter, 9/11); it became prominent with David Blunkett's arrival at Britain's Home Office in June 2001 and his response to the riots in some northern English cities in the early summer that year.

Also in open Democracy on questions of British Muslims and British identity, citizenship and democracy, in the aftermath of the London bombs:

Mohammad Sajid, "The gap between us".
Maruf Khwaja, "Muslims in Britain: generations, experiences, futures".
"What happened? What changed? What now?" – a transcript of the 21 July meeting in London co-hosted by open Democracy and Q-News.
Sami Zubaida, "The London bombs: Iraq or the 'rage of Islam'?"
Ehsan Masood, "British Muslims must stop the war".
The argument against multiculturalism and for integration has, needless to say, an even longer lineage in critiques from both left and right in the 1970s. But its post-2001 manifestation was new in a crucial respect: it came from the pluralistic centre-left, and was articulated by people who previously rejected polarising models of race and class and were sympathetic to the "rainbow", coalitional politics of identity and the realignment and redefinition of progressive forces that it implied.

*****

5

ISLAMISTS' ARGUMENTS

Barbaric but not Unexpected

A veteran Arab-American journalist, Ramzy Baroud[1] who is the editor-in-chief of *Palestine chronicle.com* and the author of the newly published book "*A Force to be Reckoned with: Writings on the Second Palestinian Uprising* accepts the 7/7 attacks as barbaric. There is hardly any term that is capable of depicting the murder of over 50 people and the wounding of hundreds more during London's rush hour on July 7. Unexpected, however is the least relevant terms, the author says.

But why would "mass murder" an expression used fittingly by London's highly regarded mayor Ken Livingstone following the attcks become an "inevitable" event, is another dreadful component in this disastrous episode. It was Livingstone who warned in September 2002: "An assault on Iraq will inflame world opinion and jeopardize security and peace every where. London, as one of the major world cities, has a great deal to lose from war and a lot to gain from peace, international cooperation and global security". The mayor's words, says Ramzy Baroud, were poignant and ring true today more than ever before. However, they were of little consequence for British Prime Minister Tony Blair, so adamant in his quest for war, so incessant in maintaining his country's dangerous alliance with Washington's self serving and now debauched 'war on terror'.

Although Britain can only claim a small portion of the subsequent carnage in Afghanistan and Iraq, the writer claims, Blair was and remains an unyielding partner in both wars. He has, so pompously, overlooked untold atrocities against innocent civilians in both countries while maintaining an active role in ridding the world off evil farce, while continues to plague the world and increasingly, albeit misguidedly define the correlation between the west and the Muslim world.

It is quite a paradox that Blair was the first to infuse the term "barbaric" following the London carriage; a paradox because the barbarism in London had an undeniable Kinship with the years of barbarism in Iraq, which countries to unfold in full force. In May 2003, following protests from human rights groups regarding the British army's use of cluster bombs in and around the Iraqi city of Basra, British officials had nothing but unabashed rationalization as a response, Mr. Baroud explains.

Armed forces Minister Adam Ingram justified the use of cluster bombs in an interview with BBC radio, on military grounds, arguing: "Cluster bombs are not illegal. They are used in specific circumstances where there is a threat tour troops". Those "specific circumstances" according to British media, the author critically examines, compelled the dropping of 2,000 Israeli made cluster bombs on Basra and its surroundings in April 2003 alone. Richard Lloyd, Director of Landmine Action, asserted that he had seen maps – provided to the UN by the US military – showing cities that were almost completely masked by a heap of symbols indicating where cluster bombs had been used. "These weapons were used in and around virtually every built-up area where there was major fighting", Lloyd said. Hundreds of these bombs are still there, not yet detonated and just waiting to do off among hoards of scavenging children, a dreadful and recurring episode in both Afghanistan and Iraq; utterly barbaric indeed.

It is a catastrophe that innocent Londoners, who have fought so earnestly for the cause of justice from the very beginning, objecting so earnestly to the war, mass protesting and talk on their government like in no other capital in Europe, had to pay the profound price for Blair's reprehensible lies and forgeries – his groundless case for WMD and his unsubstantiated claims that regime change in Iraq means security for his country. But whoever said that barbarism subscribes to any rules of conduct, Mr. Baroud enquires into.

Terrorism is not random; it is a callous mirroring to an equally callous legacy of terror and violence, this time ensued in part by relentlessly arrogant and self-congratulating statesmen like Tony Blair, the author asserts. Commenting on the slaughter in London, Blair's response failed to abandon the highly predictable and self-observed rhetoric. "My opinion is that those people who kill the innocent and cause such bloodshed are solely responsible".

But is not the above so twisted an underlying principle? It is another cruel irony that following years of war in Afghanistan and Iraq with a human toll that has been put past the one hundred thousand mark and a price tag of hundreds if billions of dollars, to pin the sole responsibility on a few terrorists, who despite their reprehensible acts pale in comparison to the mega crimes of Bush and Blair against humanity, Mr. Baroud aggressively comments.

The critic goes on questioning; "Is it possible that we have not learned a single thing since the massacres of September 11, Jenin, Kandahar and Falluja? Such erroneous logic, the writer evaluates, will persist with pundits like Gerard Baker of *The Times* blaming" "14th century (Islamist) fanaticism" for the London bombings, while strongly rebuffing any linkage between group and state terrorism.

When will the Bush and Blair crowd wake up and swell the decomposed Iraqi bodies and forever quit utilizing the ever handy "we will not change our way of life" come back to terrorism, based on the fallacious conclusion that terrorists are blowing people up because they hate freedom? The reality that Blair conveniently wishes to neglect, the writer critically examines, is a plain as it is tragic. Terrorism and militancy is thriving all around, with Iraq as a base and cause. The Anglo-American war has wrought nothing but murder and mayhem, which crossed the borders of many countries and cities with London as its latest target. The intelligence failure that has led to war in Iraq is repeated with another disastrous failure that could not intercept a major bombing scheme that disabled a major city like London. This is yet another attestation of which neither sheer military strength nor superior intelligence holds the answer. "The answer", as Mr. Baroudi concludes, "lies in an immediate halt of all military aggressions perpetrated in the name of civilization and democratization by the super powers against vulnerable and defenseless countries. This void can only be filled by sensible diplomacy, cultural integration and dialogue to achieve what cluster bombs have utterly failed to deliver. Otherwise the "inevitable" attacks on London will go on with the same certainty as the promise of each new day".[2]

Wahhabism – Synonymous with all Evil?

Taqiuddin Malik, the freelance journalist explicitly condemns those western minded Muslims who fabricately, serving their vested interests, declare Islam and the holy Quran responsible for all kinds of terrorist activities while the entire Muslim world has multified the 7/7 atrocities in London and has criticized these explosions as against the teachings of Islam. It is very unfortunate the western media make these "pseudo-intellectuals" into torch-bearers of freedom. These "western" Muslim scholars also claim that as though the Muslim world is devoid of criminals save those inspired by "Wahhabism". They do not feel mass-murder enough to condemn the terrorism; they rather feel obliged to fabricate 'new reasons'. The author is stateforward to criticize these intellectuals and represents the true image of Islam. The full text of the article is quoted below:

To readers in the West: You are being manipulated.

Your own media are being used to drag you into a battle that has raged within Islam for many years. Your lack of familiarity with Islam has made you susceptible to this scheming and conniving, forcing you to unwittingly take sides in a battle you have nothing to do with. This is not a part of your war on terror.

After September 11, countless insta-pundits spoke and wrote prolifically on Islamic terrorism. But equally popular on the talk show circuits and in the left wing press were countless "Islamic scholars," many with questionable credentials, who in most cases were revered more for their moral relativism or their ability to draw large crowds of well-intentioned youth by twisting Islamic discourse to sound more like a flower-power inspired hippy rant about love and compassion, than for any actual academic qualification.

Ethnocentrism aside, many of those people acknowledged by the West as experts and scholars of Islam would not stand up to academic scrutiny by their peers in many other parts of the world. Some of these pseudo-scholars authored works during their time studying in the Middle East that reflected a completely flawed understanding of Islam, and were roundly and deservedly criticized. But once those scholars leave their academic institutions and head West, they style themselves as repressed intellectuals, ostracized for not toeing the party line, so to speak. Naturally, these individuals know how to present themselves to a Western audience; their discourse, even their appearance, seem calculated to sooth Western prejudices about what Muslims and terrorists look like. More power to them, then.

But so what if their stances on various issues are completely at odds with the consensus and traditions of Islam through the ages? As long as they espouse "freedom," "human rights," and make all the correct sympathetic noises about terrorism, they're guaranteed respect and good standing in Western academic, media, and even political circles. In other cases, they're made out to be torch-bearers of freedom, locked in an epic struggle to free the Muslim world from the strangle-hold of the bearded Mullahs.

Take for example, the inordinate amounts of media coverage granted fringe groups like Al-Fatiha, who espouse homosexual rights in Islam, or Irshad Manji, the "lesbian Muslim intellectual," or the unwholesome fascination and carnival-like atmosphere ("an event of historic proportions!") that surrounded a woman's insistence on leading prayers, making her out to be a sort of Muslim Rosa Parks.

Some maintain that it is intellectual terrorism, fascistic apparently, to claim that these people are incorrect in their beliefs, that they do not represent Islam. But it is no more unfair or fascistic than it would be to describe the Flat Earth Society as being unrepresentative of mainstream geology.

So, to return to our earlier point: These Muslim Flat Earth-ers are using your media as a platform to vent their spleens at their supposed oppressors, and to recruit you into supporting them as the underdog.

Distressingly, these pseudo-intellectuals have hijacked discourse on Islam. Wahhabism. in purely academic terms, is historically "a faith-based, political and reformist movement attributed to its founder Imam Muhammad ibn 'Abdul-Wahhab," (The Wahhabi Movement: History and Beliefs).

But, thanks to the successful demonization campaign being waged in the Western press by Muslim "intellectuals" with an axe to grind, coupled with the limitless opportunity provided by the misguided excesses of many Wahhabis, Wahhabism to the average Western reader is now synonymous with all that is evil and repressive about the Muslim world.

Someone blows up a bus full of children? Wahhabi bomber, obviously. Woman beaten and raped? Wahhabi misogynist, probably. And so on and so forth, ad museum. It is as though the entire Muslim world is devoid of criminals, save for those inspired by the teachings of Ibn Abdul-Wahhab.

You would be hard pressed to find an erudite Westerner who has not been brainwashed, through persistent media exposure, into believing this propagandistic load of hogwash.

Simultaneously, many of these sane Muslim spin doctors have also pushed hard to promote their own understanding of an esoteric "New Age" Islam, with allegedly ancient roots, in the West.

This has, of course, done wonders for intra-Islamic relations, and suspicion and hostility now abound.

Guess we can lay the blame squarely on Western journalists' and editors' shoulders. Or can we? On the one hand, maybe if they actually did the research to figure out who they're talking to, rather than speak to those most conveniently located, we'd have less of this mess. On the other hand, we can't expect them to know any better, given the sad state of affairs in the Muslim world, with even Muslim media taking the easy way out and referring to government appointees like Muhammad Sayyed Tantawi as the Grand Sheikh of "the highest seat of learning in the Sunni world."

A recent article by Ziauddin Sardar in the New Statesman is a good example of cheap opportunism masquerading as intellectual profundity. He cites the London bombings, a fatwa in India ordering a raped woman to divorce her husband, and the demolition of Islamic historic sites in Makkah. What is the common source of Evil with a capital E that binds these seemingly disparate events in Sardar's mind? You guessed it: Wahhabism.

For someone who rants bitterly about Wahhabism's ostensible penchant for decontextualizing events, Sardar is very apt at doing exactly the same thing.

He dedicates a good chunk of his article to providing his curiously warped perspective on Wahhabism, placing the ills of the world firmly at its door step; a trend that has become disturbingly prevalent as of late. According to Sardar, Wahhabism apparently "abhors history and drains it of all humanity," and "does not recognize, understand or appreciate a contrary view. Those who express an alternative opinion are seen as apostates, collaborators or worse." Ironically, many who subscribe to such farcically simplistic notions are quick to accuse their detractors of being reductionist and simplistic.

Sardar uses his over-dramatic prose to full effect, drawing on a vocabulary that makes him sound profound, while also playing on the readers' emotions-by conjuring up images of Wahhabis as criminally obtuse, malevolent atavisms of medieval barbarism, intent on stifling all dissent and brutally enforcing a faceless conformity on all. "No complaint or opposition is allowed... it does not recognize the diversity of Islam the humanist or rationalist tradition of Islam, or the great mystical tradition..." Of course, anything that opposes diversity or humanism must be foul, mustn't it?

Furthermore, Wahhabism, he asserts, is "aggressively self-righteous; and insists on imposing its notion of righteousness on others," a statement that immediately evokes images of Arthur Miller's *The Crucible,* prompting a near-Pavlovian reaction of moral outrage. As though Wahhabism has a monopoly on self-righteousness among all of Islam s schools of thought. Actually, unlike many of the new wave of Islamic "traditionalists," as they like to style themselves, Wahhabism utterly rejects the notion of compelling an individual to obey the precepts of a single madhhab, or school of jurisprudence, demonstrating a flexibility that many of those same "liberal" Muslim intellectuals and self-styled traditionalists, so popular with many young Western educated Muslims, would probably deride as a "heretical innovation." In fact, as far as abhorring history goes, did everyone lose sight of the fact that before Wahhabism, much of the Arabian peninsula's population had degenerated back into pagan, fetishistic adoration of graves, shrines, trees, and relics? That crime and vice was rampant? Or did that particular context for the rise of Wahhabism as a counter-weight to that *jahiliyah* [pre-Islamic ignorance] escape Sardar?

Sardar also makes the completely reprehensible and irresponsible suggestion that Wahhabism holds that "those who commit ṣin—that is, disagree or deviate—cannot be Muslims," linking Wahhabism to the Kharijites, the early Muslim sect who held that sin was a "contradiction for a true Muslim—it nullified the believer and demonstrated that inwardly he was an apostate who had turned against Islam," and that hence, "he could be put to death."

With that blatant and libelous falsity, Sardar deftly deals a killing blow to his already mortally-wounded credibility. Had he made a statement like that in front of a gathering of actual Islamic scholars, he'd have been jeered down from the podium, scorned for the Islamic Flat Earth-er he is. As it is, Sardar can publish falsehoods freely and with no fear of opprobrium or being exposed as, at best, a failed academic, or at worst, a cynical propagandist.

Wahhabis have nothing to do with Kharijites. Even a cursory reading of their sources demonstrates that Wahhabis have nothing but contempt for the deviated creeds of the Kharijites. The allegation is little more than a thinly-veiled slur to vilify Wahhabism by finking it to a notoriously deviated sect.

He then cranks up the slander a notch, asserting that Ibn Taymiyah, one of Islam's foremost scholars, and Muhammad Ibn Abd al-Wahhab, the founder of Wahhabism, are influenced by Kharijite thought. This is a curious (perhaps deliberate) oversight, given that Ibn Taymiyah made repeated references to hadiths describing the Kharijites as being renegades from Islam. Sardar also detects this alleged Kharijite influence in Sayyid Qutb, whom he helpfully describes as the "chief ideologue of the Muslim Brotherhood." These spurious allegations are, again, devoid of factual basis. Qutb was, if anything, very much a rogue element for the Brotherhood, a self-evident fact, given that the Brotherhood have sought peaceful, democratic change in Egypt for almost a half a century. Not very loyal to their "chief ideologue," apparently. And if Qutb advocated violence, it was certainly not, as Sardar suggests, because each and every citizen of society is an apostate worthy of death. The same applies to many of those groups inspired by Bin Laden. Perhaps Sardar thinks it is beneath him to read the writings that provide the intellectual foundations for these groups, but if so, perhaps he should be a little more cautious when making wild assertions about something he is unfamiliar with.

The point is, Muslim militants give Islamic scholars enough jurisprudential reason to condemn them. Why does Sardar feel obliged to fabricate new reasons? Mass-murder isn't enough for him? If he's out to undermine them intellectually, Islamic scholars have done so much more effectively, and apparently without feeling obliged to make things up to bolster their case as they go along.

A struggle for the soul of Islam, is the cliché he uses to describe it. "In that struggle, all Muslims have to examine their words, deeds, motivations and interpretations of Islam".

No, Sardar, Muslims should not engage in the knee-jerk, self-loathing, finger-pointing exercises that you and your disciples advocate under the euphemistic title of" self-criticism". We must not allow the actions of a few to force us to exist in a perpetual state of collective guilt, or to be consumed by mutual suspicion. We must not become another Germany, obliged to perpetually and publicly atone for and disavow crimes carried out in our names.[3]

Struggle for Survival

Zafar Bangash, a leading scholar on the contemporary Islam and Islamic movements has seen the post-7/7 developments in U.K. as an unending series of crusades against Islam. He asserts that there is a serious disconnected between Islam and the West undoubtedly; what is hotly contested is whose fault it is. Each side blames the other but, given that the western media dominate almost all discourse, Islam and Muslims are blamed for every thing that goes wrong in the world. There is little or no admission that much of the mayhem in the world is caused primarily by western policies that affect others in profoundly negative ways, Mr. Bangash argues.

The author first defines what does he mean by the west. It is neither a geographic entity nor has it to do merely with people. Many people living in North America and Europe, for example, are as much victims of Western policies as people living in Africa and Asia. Similarly most rulers in the Muslim world would come into category of belonging to the west. Thus it is more accurate to say, the author explains, "The west is an ideological construct that transcends physical boundaries. In this sense the west is global, but only in so far as others submit to its policies and advance its interests. It neither wishes to share the material benefits it enjoys nor wants others to acquire the rights as it claims for itself".

Mr. Bangash refers the cases of North America and Europe to prove his statement. These two areas are considered to be core of the west. Both are profligate, have a long history of dominating other societies and peoples and have exploited their resources without regards to the devastation it causes. Even today, other people's resources are plundered so that North America and Europe can maintain their rapacious life styles. Constituting a mere 25 percent of the world's population North Americans and Europeans consume more than 60 percent of its energy and food resources. At the same time, they also generate a disproportionate amount of pollution and cause massive environmental damage. The U.S. alone accounts for nearly 20 percent of the world's green house gas emissions. All the while, it stubbornly refuses to accept any responsibility for, or to improve, its behaviour, Mr. Zafar Bangash elaborates in detail.

Beyond the extravagant consumption lies the even more serious question of the violence that is directed against others, especially Muslims, explains the author assertively. Most wars in the last two decades, according to his analysis, have been waged against Muslims; naturally more than 90 percent of all victims of war have been Muslims, yet there is hardly any mention that this might be a reason that Muslims feel so angry. "There is an evil ideology", thunders Tony Blair of Britain; US President George Bush has made even more ludicrous assertions such as "they hate our freedoms". That's it; end of discussion. When state policies are based on such simplistic assertions, the writer explicitly evaluates, it is virtually impossible to have an informed dialogue.

"The west's attitude is clear enough: might is right and since they claim to have military might, they can dictate to others how they must behave", the writer seriously examines the west. "When there is resistance to such aggression, it is branded as "terrorism". Like Zionist Israel, other western states too claim the right to invade other countries and occupy their lands, as well as imposing pro-western rulers and supporting repressive dictators while proclaiming democracy. Then the western world is surprised that others do not find this acceptable", Mr. Bangash unveils the reality.

The learned analyst then exposes the crusading western behaviour which is deeply rooted in history; the entire colonial period can be considered in the light of the same mindset.[4] The crusades were launched by the Church on the false pretext that Christians were being "persecuted" by "heathens" (meaning Muslims) in Palestine.[5] The same assumptions guide today's policies: "others are uncivilized, and the west has the right to invade them. Talk of "evil ideology" springs from the same source, even if those uttering such words call themselves enlightened and secular. Likewise, the west can have nuclear weapons and even use them, but Muslims must not be permitted nuclear technology, even for peaceful purposes; US has the right to invade Afghanistan because of 9/11, but others have no right to retaliate against US or western aggression. The list goes on and on," the author enlists some of the apparent atrocities of the West.

Every anti-colonial struggle was demonized in its time, Mr. Bangash traces some popular cases. Nelson Mandela was branded a terrorist and spent 27 years in prison. When the African National congress called for sanctions against the apartheid regime, it was Margaret Thatcher, Britain's so-called Iron Lady, who claimed that they do not work. So why did she urge Bush Senior to attack Iraq in 1991, and then impose sanctions that were backed by Britain and France, leading to the deaths of some 1.5 million Iraqis? Iran has been subjected to similar sanctions regime. The answer is that apartheid South Africa, including sending hundreds of thousands of citizens to prop up the regime. Today a similar process is underway vis-à-vis the Zionist occupiers of Palestine. Sanctions, military assaults and aggression, evaluates the article, are reserved mainly for Muslims.

"Unless there is a significant shift in western policies especially toward Muslims", concludes Mr. Bangash, "there is likely to be more anger and violence, no matter how many pacifist *fatwas* are elicited from pliant *imams*. The struggle for survival is part of human nature, indeed of all living creatures. Muslims can hardly be expected to behave differently".[6]

New McCarthyism

Mr. Iqbal N. Siddiqui the editor-in-chief London-based *Crescent International*, the newsmagazine of the Islamic movement (all over the World) is of the firm view that the new McCarthyism in Britain actullay old chap, is a war on Islam. Since the bombings in July, 2005, police in London hae specifically targeted Muslims fro intrusive stop-and-searches, increasing the sense that all Muslims are being blamed and punished for the acts of a tiny minority, despite the fact that virtually all Muslims, and all Muslim organizations have condemned the bombings. The full text of the editorial written by Mr. Siddiqui is given below:

About fifteen years ago Muslims in Britain fought a long battle for the defence of Islam after the publication of Salman Rushdie's blasphemous novel *The Satanic Verses.* In the two months since the bomb-blasts in London on July 7, it has become increasingly clear that Muslim s in Britain face a similar battle now, as secular and liberal fundamentalists in Britain use the bombings as opportunity and justification for a much wider attack on the Muslim community in this country. Although it is entirely understandable that the British authorities should step up security precautions, and intensify investigations of those tiny and marginal groups among Muslims that espouse the sort of appalling violence that was seen on July 7, British politicians and many media and social commentators have turned the debate about the attacks of July 7 into a debate about Islam and Muslims in Britain and, in many cases, another full-scale offensive on Islam in this country.

One feature of the *Satanic Verses* controversy was what many Muslims regarded as a surprisingly hardline attitude on the part of Britain's liberal and secular intelligentsia, most of whom stubbornly refused to make any attempt to see the Muslim point of view, and revealed in the process a deep disdain, contempt and even hatred of many aspects of Islam and many of the Muslims' most valued religious and cultural practices. Behind the gentle, tolerant facade of British multiculturalism, many Muslims were shocked to find unreconstructed colonial attitudes towards Islam and Muslims as the eternal and irredeemable Other. These are the attitudes that have emerged yet again since the bombings last July.

On the face of it, Muslims might be regarded as having lost the *Satanic Verses* battle; the book remains in print and the author and his publishers remain unrepentant. But British Muslims and the establishment in Britain both learnt one thing: that Muslims living in a Western society are like square pegs in round holes. An accommodation of sorts is possible, but there are bound to be areas where the two cannot meet, as well as places where friction is inevitable; overall, the fit is bound to be imperfect. Although the British Muslim community consists largely of young people born and brought up in this country, speaking English as our first language, and more comfortable in many ways with local norms (or adaptations thereof) than with the culture and traditions of our parents' homelands, the fact is that our being Muslims involves an embodiment and assertion of values and principles thai appear alien to most of our fellow Britons.

Recognition of this reality does not preclude peaceful and harmonious co-existence, but it does demand understanding and accommodation on both sides, and an agreement to disagree. Muslims in Britain, like other minority communities, are accustomed to routinely making such accommodations, almost without noticing, in virtually every aspect of our daily lives. Of course we have our prickly, difficult, unreasonable and unruly elements, but then so does every community. We also have a tiny minority capable of acts of unbelievable inhumanity, as we saw on July 7; but then, so do other communities, be they Irish nationalists, British nationalists (as racists in Britain call themselves), animal-rights activists or, for that matter, government ministers. And it may well be that we have been blind to the threat that this minority poses to both wider British society and ourselves. But overall Muslims have made huge efforts to it into that society and to become a constructive and positive part of it. What we cannot accept are demands that we must integrate completely, setting aside major elements of our faith, worldview and way of life, in order to be accepted. Sooner or later wider British society is going to have to accept that Muslims in Britain are here to stay, and will stay as Muslims in the fullest sense of the word. Other British people are going to have to be as flexible and accommodating of us as we have long been of them.

In truth the July bombings are incidental to this debate; they have provided the opportunity for it to re-emerge, justifying attacks on Islam that only a couple of months ago would have been regarded as unacceptably Islamophobic, but the issue that has arisen since has nothing to do with the bombings. On the bombings, there is little difference of opinion or outlook; Muslims have been as shocked as everyone else in Britain, and condemned them as vociferously, if not more so; what goes without saying for others Muslims are obliged to repeat again and again. Nor is there any dispute about the right - indeed, responsibility - of the British authorities to take steps to prevent such tragedies from occurring again.

Where there is a difference is in understandings of the bombings' relevant context and ultimately the indirect blame for them. For most Muslims (and for many others), the bombings can only be understood in the context of British policy in the world, particularly its alliance with the US in its wars in Iraq and Afghanistan, as well as the longer history of Western support for tyrants in Muslim states and attacks on Muslim countries. There is ample evidence for this in terms of the targets that have been bombed in the past and the statements of some of the bombers and their supporters. Of course such a context does not justify what happened, but it is essential to understanding it.

But this is a reality that the British government cannot afford to except; desperation to deflect all attention from their own policies and from the fact that they provoked the bombings is no doubt one reason that British government ministers are so anxious to highlight anti-Western and pro-Islamic political opinion among British Muslims as die key that explains the bombings. This has combined with the permanent disquiet among many in the West, including many of the sane politicians, about Islamic political aspirations, social norms, and indeed many other elements of Islam. This is how the cruel and vicious stupidity of a few misguided Muslims has been turned into an onslaught initially against what Tony Blair called "extremist ideology", including in it notions of khilafah and jihad, and then extending it to include not only political activism, such as support for Islamic movements in Muslim countries, but also such fundamentals of Islam as shari'ah, hijab and Islamic education. What began as an anguished discourse about the roots of terror has become a witch-hunt in which all manner of Muslim community figures and organisations, many of them long regarded as "moderate", such as the Muslim Council of Britain and the Islamic Foundation, have been attacked for praising Maulana Maududi, describing Western society as morally decadent, condemning Israel or simply regarding Islam as superior to other religions. It is no exaggeration to suggest that Britain is in the grip of a new

McCarthyism, with Muslims the target and Islam the accusation.

As usual, whenever these episodes erupt, the immediate protest of the West is that the West has nothing against Islam; it is just the extremist misinterpretations of it that are the problem. In the current outbreak, the use of the phrase "war on Islam" has been cited as a defining characteristic of the extremism that supposedly gave rise to the London bombings. And, as usual, there are plenty of Muslims who are so cowed by the weight of the attack, or so desperate to be understood mid validated by non-Muslims, that they are happy to agree, arguing that they are free to practise Islam in Britain, so clearly it is not true that Britain is at war with Islam.

Unfortunately these arguments just won't wash any more. The key question is how we understand Islam. The liberal West would like us to see it in purely "religious" terms, as a matter of one's personal faith, spirituality and conduct; that they could accept, albeit grudgingly. But for most Muslims Islam is far more than that; it includes principles for collective and societal morality as well as the personal, and demands that we enjoin good in the broadest possible sense. That is why Muslims all over the world see Islam as central to their politics, and why Muslims in Britain sympathise with them, even as we recognise the limits of what we can do in that direction in Britain. That is why Muslims criticise Western societies - for many of the same ills that Westerners themselves highlight - in Islamic terms, and that is why Islam is invoked whenever and wherever Muslims fight against aggression and oppression; which usually means, in the modern world, against Western governments or their allies, or both. This broader, more complete understanding of Islam is what the West is most definitely at war with; both because Westerners are at war with anything that stands in the way of heir hegemony and interests, and because of the deep-seated and irrational hatred for Islam that many secular Westerners harbour.

Muslims in Britain cannot afford to delude themselves: Islam is under attack in Britain, as just one part of a global war on Islam. For British Muslims it is not yet a military war, but it is a social war and a political war for the right to practice Islam fully in Britain, which includes both the way we live as a community in this country and the way in which we identify with our brothers and sisters elsewhere in the world.

This is a war we will have to fight again and again; it may be one that, given the wider historical and geopolitical situation, we cannot win. It is certainly one that we cannot afford to lose if we and our future generations are to survive as Muslims in this country.[7]

Facing Islamophobic Witch Hunt

The noted journalist of U.K. Mr. Ahmad Musa speaks of the aftermath of July, 7, in Great Britain and tells us the "Islamophobic witch hunt" that is being faced by the Muslims and Muslim organizations in U.K. He finds that despite widespread Muslim condemnation of the bombings. British politicians and authorities have turned the investigations into bombings into an attack on the Muslims community as a whole, with Prime Minister blaming the bombings on the "evil ideology" of political Muslim "Extremism". The full paper is quoted below:

On August 24/the British government announced derails of new measures to be taken against foreign Muslims living in Britain. Foreign Muslims will be deported from Britain, or not permitted to enter the country in the first place, if they are considered by the government to be "fostering hatred or fomenting, or glorifying terrorist violence". In the past Britain has not usually deported people to countries where they may be tortured; this may be changed, provided that the countries involved promise not to mistreat deportees. The government also pledged to amend its human-rights legislation in order to prevent people from using it to circumvent the new rules. The British government will also automatically consider deporting any foreigner who is suspected of "seeking to provoke terrorist acts", fomenting other serious criminal activity or fostering hatred that might lead to inter-community violence.

The British government will also draw up a new database of Muslims anywhere in the world who are thought to have links with terrorism. These will be prevented from entering the UK at alt. The database will include those accused of any acts included on a list of "unacceptable behaviour", including "radical preaching" and publishing websites and articles intended to foment terrorism. The new rules will he retroactive, including statements, speeches and articles published in the past.

Clarke also said, announcing the new measures, that the first deportation orders under them would come very quickly, possibly within days. He had already said that Omar Bakri Muhammad, the former leader of the al-Muhajirun group, would not be allowed back into the country after he left for a visit to Lebanon. Others like to he targeted include Dr Muhammad al-Massari, the Saudi dissident who has been the target of a media campaign, and other Arab Islamic activists in London, some of whom are currently on police bail, having been released from imprisonment without charge on the orders of the high court earlier this year.

The British government's deportation plans have been criticised by human-rights groups because the government seems to be determined to send Muslims back to countries where the torture and persecution of polilical dissidents is known to occur. The government has said that it will only deport people after obtaining assurances that they will not be mistreated, but human-rights groups point out that the assurances of governments that routinely use torture are worthless. The government already has an agreement from Jordan not to mistreat deportees, anil is seeking similar assurances from other countries, including Algeria and Saudi Arabia.

The measures have also been criticised as being political moves designed to appease public opinion and the rightwing press in Britain in the aftermath of the bombings in July, rather than being genuinely necessary for security reasons. The Islamic Human Rights Commission, the main Muslim community advocacy group in Britain, has issued a statement saying that "The 1HRC views the new grounds for deportation as the criminalization of thought, conscience and belief... The IHRC further notes that much of the reasoning behind the new grounds is based on fallacy rather than fact. The idea that foreign preachers who don't speak English are radicalizing British youth who speak nothing but English is absurd."

Although the measures, announced by home secretary Charles Clarke, focused on foreign Muslims, they are expected to be followed by new measures aimed at British Muslims. On August 5, when Tony Blair announced two-week consultation period for the proposals that became the measures announced on August 24, a number of measures targeting British Muslims were also included. These included expanding the use of control orders against British Muslims suspected of possible involvement in terrorism, and possibly giving the police greater powers to arrest and hold such suspects before having to charge them.

However, the main measure announced by Blair on August 5 totally exposed the reality that these measures are more about being seen to be doing something, because of the public's anger that Blair's foreign policy has brought these bombings on London, than about genuinely addressing a real problem. This measure was the decision to ban the Hizb al-Tahrir, an Islamic group that espouses peaceful political change in Muslim countries in order to establish khilafah in the Muslim world.

The Hizb al-Tahrir takes a primarily intellectual and educational approach to political change, and has never been implicated in espousing or justifying violence, However, because of its popularity among university students, and its opposition to Israel, it has been targeted by Jewish groups and accused of anti-semitism. This has made it the target of Britain's right-wing tabloid media and given it a higher profile than most other Islamic groups in the country. The government's decision to ban it evidently owes more to its profile, and the government's need to be seen to be doing something, than anything it says or does. The government's problem is that the few people and groups who have praised or justified terrorist activities are so small and marginal that measures against them would not be sufficient for its purpose. The result is that a peaceful and respected Islamic group has been targeted for no fault of its own.

The ban on Hizb al-Tahrir reflects the fact that the campaign against Muslims since July 7 goes far beyond security measures, which most Muslims would understand and support. The tone of this campaign was set by Blair on July 16, when he linked the bombings to the "evil ideology" of political Islam, which he grossly misrepresented as aiming for (lie expulsion all non-Muslims from Muslim countries, the elimination of Israel, the establishment of Taliban-style states, The imposition of Shari'ah law in the Arab world, and the establishment of one "caliphate" of all Muslim countries.

This is a catch-all description that takes in far more than just terrorism; while no Muslim demands the expulsion of all non-Muslims from Muslim countries, which is a sheer fabrication, many oppose Israel and aspire to the establishment of Shari 'ah and a khilafah without meaning violence of any kind, let alone terrorism.

This speech, regarded as a masterpiece by political commentators in the West, and praised also by some "moderate" Muslims who are keen to curry favour with the powers that be, set the tone for the subsequent debate in the British media about the terrorist attacks and their causes. Instead of focusing on the fact of Britain's unquestioning support for US policies in the Muslim world, including its wars in Afghanistan and Iraq, which polls show most British people regard as a major reason for the bombings, the media are concentrating on which some have called "the Muslim problem" or "the problem of Islam", arguing, that the bombings happened because British Muslims have failed to integrate properly into British society or adopt British values and ways of life.

Despite the fact that Muslims have a long record of largely peaceful community life in Britain, the entire community is now under attack for its supposed implication in the terrorist acts perpetrated by a few individuals. At the same time, there has been a wave of Islamophobic attacks on Muslim individuals, mosques and institutions. It is difficult to avoid the conclusion that Blair and his government have deliberately turned the flak onto the Muslim community in order to distract attention from their own policies.

At the same time, they have found many in Britain's media happy to join in a campaign against Muslims that goes far beyond concern over terrorism. Muslim schools, *halal* meat, *hijab* and the fact that many second-generation Muslims in Britain Pakistan or Bangladesh in cricket, rather than England, have all become grounds for attacking Muslims. Even at the serious end of the media spectrum, a deep anti-Islamic bias has been revealed, in a documentary broadcast under its prestigious Panorama title on August 21, the BBC accused the Muslim Council of Britain - usually regarded as a moderate body - of fostering extremism. In the process, the programme attacked many key aspects of Islam, from the aspiration for *shari'ah* to women's desire to wear Islamic dress. Among the things characterised as "extremist" in the programme were believing Islam to be superior to other faiths, women wearing *hijab* and *niqab,* and support for Palestinians, Chechnyans and Kashmiris.

Massoud Shadjareh, chairman of the IHRC, said after the broadcast of the Panorama documentary that the campaign is in danger of making simply being a Muslim an extremist act. "If this phase in community relations does not pass quickly, irreparable damage may be done," he warned. [8]

Terrorism is double-edged

Dr. Zafarul Islam Khan, the editor of Delhi-based *the Milli-Gazdette* talks about the terrorism, as a double-edged phenomenon. He expresses his doubts about those committed whether they were Al-Qaeda workers or these blasts were executed or facilitated by Britain's ruthless M16. The author admits there is no doubt that there is anger in the Muslim communities worldwide against the American – British brutal occupation of Iraq and blind support of Zionist crimes in Palestine. "Backlash" or "blowback" was expected and indeed many warned against it. No power should think that its crimes will go unpunished. Victims will fight back with whatever they can. "They may not have Stealth aircraft and patriot missiles but they have their own bodies to below if driven to the wall and this is what they are doing in Iraq and Palestine. No doubt Americans and Britishers too will resort to similar tactics if their countries are occupied by a foreign power", the author firmly asserts.

The scholar incompromisingly declares that the Americans and their lackies should realize that there is a limit to what others may accept and lump. The sooner they rectify their mistakes and review their grandiose plans to control world resources the better. If they fail to learn, blow back will only intensify and the tormentors will feel the heat on their own streets and undergrounds.

Resistance in Iraq and Palestine is fully justified under Islamic and international laws as every occupied nation and country is fully entitled to resist foreign occupations in whatever way it can in order to drive away the invaders, the author asserts. But people living in countries like the US and

UK, as citizens or guests with visas, are not allowed at all to indulge in such criminal activities which are against the covenant they have willingly accepted when applying for citizenship or seeking visas. "If they feel strongly about the injustice, they should go to Iraq and Palestine and any other similarly occupied country and fight there. They will be fully justified under Islam and international law to do so, while their treacherous and terrorist acts against their host societies are clearly abhorred by Islam which does not tolerate treachery. Even a Muslim state is not allowed to declare war against another state without first abolishing treaties with that country", Dr. Khan explicitly issues the verdict.[9]

Dr. Gayasuddin Siddiqui, leader of the Muslim Parliament UK told a Muslim conference in Birmingham, attended by over 3000 people, that they must confront extremism within their ranks if they wished to live in peace in Britain. He told the audience that both the Muslim community and our secret services must end "denial" of their role in creating conditions leading up to bombings in London on 7 July. He said first generation of explosives experts among the *jehadists* were trained by the CIA and our secret services in Afghanistan in the wake of the soviet invasion in 1979. These jehadists are now acting as masterminds for the current generation of suicide bombers. The conference organized by *Jamaat Ahl al-Sunnah* also issued a *fatwa* declaring suicide bombing a crime and an un-Islamic act.[10] Following is the text of his speech:

Muslims need to reclaim Islam from the extremists. Islam is about social justice, tolerance and equality. It seeks to establish a just, enlightened and egalitarian society in which all human beings are equal to God and under the law. It was this Islam that created one of the most dynamic societies in history, the achievement of which gave rise to what is known in Europe as the Renaissance. Intolerant Islam, which shows no respect for any of these qualities and is a negation of Islam's own civilisational record, is a phenomenon peculiar to our times and arose as a consequence of the convergence between salafist/wahabist teachings and the nefarious aims of the British and the American secret services in the wake of the Soviet invasion of Afghanistan in 1979.

For far too long Muslims tolerated presence of this movement within their ranks. Now four British-born young men have been found to be involved in the London bombings. The time has come to go beyond the 'denial'. We must challenge this evil theology, which motivates and inspires young people to become suicide bombers. We must reject any ideology ,which does not respect human life, honour and dignity. We must condemn suicide bombing as a weapon of resistance or revenge under any circumstances. Two things must be happened simultaneously:

Our security services must come clean. They must acknowledge that they were involved in the training of earlier generations of 'holy warriors'. These 'holy warriors' were trained in sabotage techniques and how to make explosives from household items. The old hats are now the trainers, planners and masterminds of the current generation of suicide bombers. With such acknowledgements and information of training by our security services the total picture of the problem will always remain obscure.

We must identify all those Islamic groups who supported and participated in the 'Afghan jihad' and trace their links in Britain their identification and linage is important to know who the promoters of 'jihadist' ideology are in Britain. Many of these groups will be found to be in control of many mosques and Islamic centres. These groups hold conferences in Britain and invite clerics who have supported jihadist activities in Afghanistan and beyond.

Most mosques are not equipped to deal with young people (many mosques still do not allow women to use mosque facilities). They do not have the staff equipped with

Islamic knowledge, experience and professionalism. Young people have drifted away either because they were banned to discuss controversial issues in the mosque or found nothing inspiring on offer there. Our mosques are largely tribal and controlled by old men on the dole with no understanding of the changing world around them. Expansion of mosque activities could have provide the opportunity to many young men and women to become involved in youth projects. The unwelcoming and suffocating atmosphere within mosques did not allow this to happen. Many radical and active young people began drifting away organizing themselves outside the influence of the mosque structure. Some regrettably came under the influence of those promoting 'wahabist/jihadist ideology. Muslim youth have nowhere to go to learn, discuss or get professional advice on issues relating to growing up. To meet some of these challenges we need to take some immediate measures:

All mosques committees should be reorganized bringing in young people in their management committees as a matter of urgency. 40% of committee composition should got to under 30 years within one year. This could include women. Muslim schools should take non-Muslim pupils, to create a semblance of a multi-cultural and multi-faith mix that exists in the society. Muslim charities should change their funding priorities. Henceforth 60% of the charitable funds should be allocated to causes in Britain like arts, theatre, and supporting students taking up careers in journalism.[11]

Egyptian-born Professor Tariq Ramadan emphasized upon Britain of all races to pull together promote a common understanding. He said only a shared dialogue between Britain's different communities could isolate extremists. He told *The Guardian* that he intended to press ahead with his lecture visit to London and Birmingham despite calls on Tuesday from *The Sun* newspaper for him to be banned from the country. The newspaper claimed that Prof. Ramadan, acclaimed by *Time magazine* as one of the 21st century's most likely innovators, had sought to justify suicide bombings and was banned in the U.S. and France for links to terrorists. It pointed out that the London conference had been partly funded by the capital's Metropolitan Police (MET) and the Association of Chief Police Officers (ACPO). Prof. Ramadan acknowledged that he had been banned from working in the U.S. but said he was also invited to reapply for a visa. He said the ban in France was successfully challenged in the courts. He is a Swiss citizen but has an office in Paris.

"To be targeted as a danger is ridiculous", he said, "My point to young Muslims is to say know who you are and assert your identity but at the same time you should promote an inter-community debate and a critical attitude towards people who are promoting hatred and killing innocent people. I always speak of the middle path and the need to build bridges ... I have never said that bombing was justified. What I said was when we are dealing with a specific environment and a history of oppression, we can understand why people use other means. But that does not justify it".[12]

Weaving Terror

Mr. Ejaz Ahamd Aslam editor of Delhi-based *Radiance* viewsweekly and also the secretary of 'Jamaat Islami of India sees the whole episode of 'War on terror' in the perspective of actually weaving the terror. The writer in one of the editorials demonstrates his sorrow and anger how unsafe the world stands today can be gauged from the fact that public places can be struck anywhere, any thing, killing civilians like rats. At least the grisly random attacks in London and Sharm al-Sheikh in recent days make us believe this. "Our heart bleeds", the editorial comments, and so does the heart of every peace – and justice-loving person, at the sad spectacle of such gory incidents. For killing of innocent lives is highly condemnable. Yes, in the strongest of terms – whoever the perpetrators. And for, killing one innocent person is in fact the killing of entire humanity".

The editor goes into the causes and motives of terror and asks surprisingly: then, what is the root cause of trading terror, mindless and inhuman? Why some disgruntled and radically disaffected youth end their lives – after all precious – in suicide attacks? What do they aim at? And what do they get in return? Pat comes the reply through media that this is no terrorism! Really? Then what? They say they do so to retaliate against grave injustices done to them elsewhere and to be revenged on the perpetrators. And thereby they perhaps think they might be able to pressurize the powers- that-be to do justice in future.

The horror and chaos, destruction and devastation, the now infamous war on terror has caused in Afghanistan and Iraq – leave aside the Vietnams – and the horrendous things Israel has inflicted upon the Palestinians border, without any shred of doubt, on crimes against humanity, the editor aggressively talks against the crimes of the West: "It is really unacceptable that Israel goes on indiscriminately destroying Palestinian homes simply because a bomber came from that area. Equally unacceptable is that Bush and Blair go on attacking any land in the name of "pre-emptive" war and of course without any justification".

"Do you think brutal killings of innocent men, women and children would go with impurity"? The editor puts very relevant and agitating questions: "Do you assue shameful humiliation and harassment of prisoners in Guantanamo and Abu Gharib would go hus-hush? Do you feel leveling of sovereign states would go unmoved? Do you consider desecration of the Holy Book of Islam would go without retaliation? Do you think occupation of the Palestinian Land, building Israel settlements in Palestine lands and killing Palestinian leaders and civilians would go unpunished? Do you think the blood running in the veins of Muslims is not that red? The warmanagers of Bush, Blair and Sharon owe cogent replies".

The writer firmly asserts that it seems to be a grim remainder of the fact that Bush-Blair war on terror is yielding to bitter a result, and that their extended misventure from Afghanistan to Iraq has come home to roost. "This seems to be the natural corollary of their ill-conceived policy and their weaving terror via war on terror, and they can not escape from it however massive their preparation to avert it. At least the July 21 repeated blasts in London, though no casualty, tell this bitter fact right in the face".

"The irony of ironies", says the editor, "is that whenever such blasts rock the world, attempts are made to associate Islam and Muslims with terrorism – even before making any investigation and without any solid proof." Some Muslim youth may or many not do such acts. When the Timothy Mc Veighs, the Ted Kacznskis and the Eric Rudolphs are named after due investigation, the writer painstakingly is surprised, no one calls them Christian or Jew terrorists. "But it is assumed rather demanded that Muslims some how answer for any terrorist act anywhere in the world. This is simply double-dealing and cross Islamophobia".

The need of the hour is that the big bowers take up the issue of terrorism seriously but coolly – without any bias and assumption and of course in its face value – cast insight into human consequences of the US-led war on terror, recast their attitude towards Islam and Muslims, try to understand the message of the Holy Quran in order to ascertain whether it teaches peace or terrorism, and above all need to revise their foreign policy. And all this to conquer peace and make this planet worth living", the writer concludes.[13]

Occupational Terrors

Mr. Jawed Anwar, the editor-in-chief of *Muslims Weekly* U.S.A. has discussed the issue of war on terror in terms of desired Muslim stand. The 9/11 tragedy on the surface of America was the historical and turning point of the modern history of war, occupation and terrorism. However, before

9/11, more than 120 million human beings were killed, bombed and slaughtered after two world wars and the cold war with the Soviet Union. Unfortunately America, was directly or indirectly involved in most of these wars and deaths, the writer provides a data of war crimes committed by the west in pre-9/11 period. Before 9/11, 14 million people were killed and several nations were destroyed in World War I under the occupation of Great Britain and France. Before 9/11, 60 million people were butchered in World War II. Before 9/11, two cities of Japan were nuked and completely wiped off the map of the world. Before 9/11 Jews suffered ethnic – cleaning and the holocaust in Germany. Before 9/11, most of the killings, massacres, ethnic cleansing and destructions were plotted in Asia and Africa. Before 9/11, in one day of the Korean war 100,000 people were slaughtered. Before 9/11 250, 000 Palestinians were killed, eight million were occupied or dispersed to all four corners of the world, and four million were put into camps; a third generation is growing up in the camps. This is the largest and bloodiest ethnic cleansing after World War II, perpetuated by Zionists and supported by Britain and the U.S. . Before 9/11 three million human beings were butchered in Vietnam. Before 9/11 Bosnia and Cosovo paid the price in the form of their 'ethnic cleansing" to extend the American empire to the Balkans. Hundreds of thousands of men and boys were killed, and hundreds of thousands of girls and women were mass-raped in Bosnia and Kosovo. Before 9/11, Chechnya was bombed to ground zero, and hundreds of thousands of people were killed and forced to uproot from the country. Before 9/11, the Cold War, the bloodiest war fought in human history, had already left its ruins.

Before 9/11, nations were the war victim of our covert and overt operations all over Africa, Asia and Latin America. Before 9/11, there was a big game in Africa; consider the wastelands of Somalia, Ethiopia, Congo, Rawanda. You can't name one African nation which came out of the Cold war unscathed. There are 49 major wars plotted in African and Asian nations. Before 9/11 1.5 million people died in the plot of Iran- Iraq war with one trillion dollar losses. Before 9/11, hundreds of thousands of Muslims were killed in the thousands of anti-Muslim riots in India after independence from the British Raj. Before 9/11, one million children died in Iraq due to the sanction against Iraq in a " suspicion" that Iraq might build weapons of mass destruction that might be used against our "beloved" Israel. Before 9/11, there were 14 million refugees, mostly Muslims, displaced from their homes. Millions of them are still living in the campus.

When 9/11 happened, Mr. Jawed Anwar continues, 3000+people were dead in the Twin Towers; dead ones belonged to various races, colours and religions. Several of our Muslim brothers and sisters from our neighborhoods died in the Twin Towers. Every Muslim organization and leader condemned the act of terrorism and helped the government in its critical junction. But in the aftermath of the tragedy, Muslims were the only victims of profiling, special registration and deportation. Thousands of Muslims who have been here for decades, but had no legal papers and were contributing to the American economy by their hard work, were deported after 9/11. Our government multiplied the suffering and pain of the public in general and Muslims in particular after 9/11. Various independent sources, inquires, and researches are now showing and proving that 9/11 plot was an "internal plot" because the tragedy had to be used as a smoke-screen to enhance imperialism and occupy the land and resources of the Muslim World, the write up explains in detail.

Now we are facing the tragedy of 7/7 in the London subway and bus bombings. Fifty-nine civilians including children were killed. Naturally, Muslims all over the world are condemning the act. Muslims are very clear in what in terror, and what is jihad and what is fasad (chaos), the writer explicitly states.

Will this attack provide another excuse to attack Iraq and Syria, he initiates a provoking question. Then the author enlists some atrocities committed by the west in the pre-7/7 tragedy. Before 7/7, Afghanistan was leveled, and the US government used the most powerful and destructive bombs from the sky, and then occupied the Land. Before 7/7, 100,000 people were killed in Afghanistan, now ruled by a puppet Hamid Karzai, whose job is killing his opponents and he has been given a free hand to do anything. He is allowing opium poppy cultivation and Afghanistan is becoming the largest producer of opium in the world. We will find heroine and refined opium in our neighborhoods in America, the largest consumer of the drug. Before 7/7, Iraq was attacked and air-bombed by the US. Britain and other allied forces and then occupied. Before 7/7, 120,000 were dead in post-occupied Iraq. Before 7/7, the prisoners in Guantanamo Bay and Abu Gharib camps were humiliated, abused and tortured in the most brutal way. Before 7/7, the Holy Quran was desecrated in Guantanamo Bay; that hit and broke the hearts of 1.2 billion Muslims worldwide. Before 7/7, Iraq was still bleeding and the daily casualty is more than the total casualty of London bombings, the author goes on.

Everyone understands the difference between the value attributed to Muslim blood and the value of others' blood, Mr. Jawed Anwar sorrowfully compares. Muslim blood is now cheap and expendable. Muslim organizations in America condemned the London bombings and all acts of terrorism. But still no one from the government and media is even listening to the organizations. The government and media compelled Muslims to speak out against terrorism but keep silent on occupation and government-sponsored terrorism. Muslim organizations compete with each other in speaking out against the terrorists' attacks but their proclamations have gotten little attention, or have not been taken seriously, and the organizations have been timid about seeking and proclaiming the real picture. "If we lose the 'colour of Allah" by telling lies or by mixing truth with lies, no other's colour will protect Muslims," the author as a true believer asserts.

Mr. Jawed Anwar then starts asking the questions, very simple questions:

Who are the real culprits?

Who said, 'Level Iraq'?

Who said, 'Missile Sudan and Afghanistan?

Who said, 'Clinton has used a hammer; we should use A sledge hammer?'

It was definitely not Muslims, but the criminals sitting in government positions, the writer responds confidently. These were the real traitors who brought confrontation between Muslims and Americans.

"What is the solution for ending terrorism in the world"? Mr. Anwar touches the most sensitive question, the stateforward and honest response of which is not given by most of the analysts and scholars. But to the present writer every sane person of the world will say the same thing: "End the occupation to end the terrorism, and establish justice to bring peace in the world. The solution is very simple, practical and quick."

So the question is: why are Muslim organizations not speaking the truth? The author unveils the untold truth: "I will say that Muslim leadership in America is the most depoliticized and disoriented leadership. They do no have any clear-cut vision of world politics and enough knowledge (political) of the Quran to interpret and make a decision and stand in the right direction."

"Saying that "killing one person is like killing the whole of mankind" and preaching war ethics of Quran that protect children and civilians in the war, are not going to influence those people who are occupied and become slaves and who are taking and asking for "revenge" (if it is proved that they belong to any Muslim group)," Mr. Anwar argues the other side of the picture strongly. "They have their own set of arguments. When we say that civilians, women, children should be protected in all circumstances and in all conditions, the victim of occupation say, 'we have already tried by attacking military and government targets to end the occupation, but the big powers did not move out; but now our killing of a few civilians has built an enormous public pressure on governments to withdraw their forces from our lands'. Withdrawal of Spain's military from Iraq and change of the government in Spain was a success story for them. When we say "suicide bombing" is *haram* and unlawful in Islam, the occupied, uprooted citizens say, 'Give us a land, military arsenals, F 16_s , and other arms and ammunitions, and we vow that we will never again attack by suicide bombings. The desperate and oppressed people have their own logic and perception. They are not going to listen to the preaching, *nasihah*, and arguments of affluent Muslims of America," Mr. Jawed Anwar unhesitatingly explains in detail the thinking and argument of the new anger generation.

What should we do? The author clearly responds and offers the honest suggestion that they should speak out truth and stand on justice in every circumstance. As a 'witness' of humankind and torchbearer of justice their stand should be very clear, non-apologetic, free from any pressure, related to the real circumstances, and according to the holy Quran and Sunnah.

Historically speaking, the writer honestly admits, Muslims have always been beneficent, supportive and providing for America. In the entire history of America, Muslims never, ever worked against American national interest. They were with America in World War I, World War II, in the Cold War, and now in the present war against terror. Pakistan, Iran and Turkey were the frontline states against Soviet Union, defending America. Muslim hearts were beating with America even in the British occupation. Saddam Hussein, a nationalist leader of Iraq, was once forced to pack out Great Britain and welcome America. Libya ousted a pro-European king and welcomed America. Syrians ousted the French and welcomed Americans.

But what did they get in return?- humiliation, sanction, death and destruction, Why ? Reason: Anti- American, anti-Muslims forces desired it and got it, the author's response is stateforward and explicit.

"So I request the Muslim leadership at large", Mr. Jawed Anwar suggests honestly in his concluding remarks, "instead of apologizing, tell the truth; you will be more patriotic and loyal in serving America in its critical junction of history. To be sincere and honest citizens, we should not hide the truth. The truth is, bloodshed is counter productive. Fair-minded Americans have already reached the conclusion. They are saying 'violence breeds violence' and 'If we will kill one terrorist we will breed three terrorists'. Muslim leadership should at least align with this pitch with their stand and arguments based on truth."[14]

Why WOT Counter-Productive?

Dr. S. Ausaf Saied Wasfi, a Delhi-based senior columnist and writer says that 7/7 did not learn lesson from 9/11. The western powers first author a cause. When the mischief creates its natural reaction, they dub the protest terror. The problem is they neither learn nor un-learn any lesson from history. The writer is of firm view that unless and until the west stops inflicting hot and cold violence on the defenseless Muslim world, there seems no hope of peace here or anywhere. As the first step, the U.S. must ease its grip over Saudi Arabia, the nerve-centre of Islam, quit Afghanistan, vacate Iraq and allow the Palestinians to live in their homeland like a sovereign nation. The writer astonishingly asks, "why do the aggressors not reconcile with the fact the

Muslim blood, be it Afghani or Iraqi, is as red and thick as theirs ?" "Add to this," says Dr. Wasfi, "that their case is morally strong and legally legitimate. And the Muslim antagonists have no case at all."[15]

Dr. Wasfi discusses why the much-typed war on terror has proved counter-production and suggests measures to deal with the situation. Through the new slogan of 'global struggle against violent extremism" the Bush administration seeks to push the idea that the long-term struggle against Islam is as much an ideological battle as a military mission. Gen. Richard B. Myers, Chairman of the joint chiefs of staff, told the national press club in Washington that although the military was heavily engaged in the mission now, future efforts require "all instruments of our national power, all instruments of international communities' national power." The solution was "more diplomatic, more economic, more political than it is military." This refers the multi-dimensional onslaught on Islam and Muslims, de-Islamization of Muslims through media, public opinion and guns.

Dr. Wasfi quotes Mr. Rumsfeld, senior national adviser to President Bush: 'It would be a global struggle against the enemies of freedom and the enemies of civilization'. The US President has, of late, been using the expression "worldwide clash of ideas". Till now the manner in which these civilized from the West have used the word 'terrorist' inevitably created the impression that in their view-for example-the demand of the Palestinian dispossessed is synonymous with the demands of Carlos the Jackal, the world's most notorious terrorist, or Germany's Baader Meinhof Gang or Itlay's Red Brigade. Can you recall that Mr. Leonid Brezhnev the erstwhile USSR chief had described the Afghan Mujahideen as 'dacoits' and 'thugs'? And not long ago, the Italian Prime Minister. Mr. Silvio Berlusconi tried to distract focus from the real irritations by asserting that the "western civilization was superior to Islam". Taking a cue from him, says Dr. Wasfi, his cabinet colleague Mr. Roberto Galderoli said on

July 27, 2005 that the terrorist bombings in London were a clash between "a civilization and a non-civilization." Need the victims of Palestine, Afghanistan and Iraq tell these wiseacres at the top of their voice that civilization is not the point at issue. The point at issue is the redress of the grievances of the decapitated, dishonored and dispossessed, the writer clearly states.

America has a history of aggressions on unarmed, smaller Muslim nation-states. During the hey-day of Mr. Clinton, a pharmaceutical laboratory in Sudan was flattened by the US bombings. A US air strike at the residence of Col. Moammar Gaddafi killed his daughter. Several marriage processions were turned into funeral processions in Afghanistan and Iraq by US fighter pilots and Washington never said sorry for its blunders.

The American critics of Mr. Bush and Mr. Blair ask: Have the security cameras all over London and in much of America deterred the terrorists? Has holding the prisoners with no access to legal counsels in Abu Gharib and Gitmo deterred the terrorists? Could the use of torture to extract information from the prisoners stop bombers in London? The western media has alleged that bombing in London which claimed several lives were "well-coordinated" and obviously "planned in advance", Dr. Wasfi expressed his suspicion.

At the risk of repetition of a known fact, the terrorists, in October 2002 sniffed off 202 persons in Bali. It was retaliation against the role that Australia played in the post-9/11. In March 2004, they killed 191 in Madrid train blasts for the role Jose Maria Aznar of Spain chose to play during Iraq war. Tony Blair is facing the music for blind support to Bush. In 7/7 dozens were killed. The toll in Sharm al-Sheikh is 88 while earlier October they had killed 34 at Taba and Ras Shiran. Mr. Hosni Mubarak is paying the price for his proximity with Mr. Bush. For similar reasons Gulf monarchs are facing public anger. For his obvious tilt towards Washington, President Musharraf of Pakistan has come face to face with death four times, Dr. Wasfi counts few terrorist activities and their motives to illustrate his point of view.

The US critics of Mr. Bush's policy towards the Islamic World say today between 20,000 and 30,000 insurgents launch some 50 attacks each day, analyses the writer. There are at least six smaller terrorist groups that mount attacks against the US and its allies' interests. The Islamic websites claim they come from Saudi Arabia, Kuwait, Syria, Jordan, Libya, Algeria and European countries. According to the Western media, the terrorists are now threatening with the use of biological and chemical weapons and what they call "dirty nuke."

"Instead of behaving like the proverbial poor village school master, who though vanquished, would continue arguing his non-case, Mr. Bush and Mr. Blair," concludes Dr. Wasfi, "should first, sincerely and honestly, apologise to the Islamic world for the savage destruction they have caused to their victims and their religious and cultural heritage. It should be followed by immediate and complete pullout from Afghanistan and Iraq and casing of their grip over Gulf sheikhdoms, particularly Egypt. Following this, they must enter into a constructive dialogue with their victims' leadership, not toadies."[16]

The Present-day Crusaders

Dr. Abdul Haq Ansari, *Ameer* , *'Jama'at Islami* of India, also a distinguished scholar of Islamic ethics, philosophy and tasawwuf_expressed his grief over the silence Pope Benedict XVI maintained about the root causes of terrorism while elaborating on the menace of terrorism in meeting with Muslim leaders.

On first foreign trip of his pontificate, the Pope met a 20-member delegation of Muslim leaders of Germany in Cologne on August 20, 2005 and urged them to help defeat terrorism which he said aims at poisoning ties between Christians and Muslims. 'Terrorist activities are continually recurring in various parts of the World, sowing death and destructions, and plunging many of our brothers and sisters into grief and despair. Those who instigate and plan these attacks evidently wish to poison our relations, making use of all means, including religion, to oppose every attempt to build a peaceful, fair and serene life together', said the 78-year-old pontiff in the prepared text of his address to the Muslim leaders.

Reacting to his statement, Dr. Ansari said that the Pope conveniently forgot to mention the actual reasons behind the eruption of violence. He termed his silence to be against his high stature. While appreciating his call for dialogue between Muslims and Christians, Dr. Ansari asked the Pope to instruct his own followers to stop state terrorism. He should ask them to maintain human rights, peace and sovereignty of independent nations. "His silence, that is unjust and against religious spirit, over such issues will help the Christian forces to justify their brutal acts and violence,' the Ameer said.

Acknowledging that Christians too had killed God's name in the past – a reference to the Crusades- the Pope said both Christians and Muslims had to learn from their past conflicts. ' How many pages in history record battles and even wars that have been waged, with both sides invoking the name of God, as if fighting and killing the enemy could be pleasing to Him,' the Pope said. 'The recollection of these sad events should fill us with shame, for we know only too well what atrocities have been committed in the name of religion,' he said.

But once again the Pope did not mention the present-day Crusaders-America, Britain and allied forces-who are attacking, plundering and capturing Muslim countries one-by-one. 'If a Muslim country had adopted the same policy against the Christian or Jewish community, wouldn't it have retaliated ? And would you label the retaliation as terrorism?' the Ameer asked the pontiff. Dr. Ansari said 'If the reverend Pope has a glimpse at the recent world history and events, he would have known that it is the armies of the Christian states who occupied the Palestinian Land 50 years ago, massacred thousand of Muslim natives and forced millions to leave their home. Israel with the help of Christian world is still killing innocent Palestinians. If the Christian powers, who are patronizing Israel, had pressurized it to vacate the occupied Palestine Land 25-30 years ago, Palestinians would not have been killed nor forced to take up the eudgels to protect themselves,' he said.

The Pope told the Muslim leaders that all believers had to do their part in condemning terror. 'If together we can succeed in eliminating from hearts any trace of rancour, in resisting every form of intolerance and in opposing every manifestation of violence, we will turn back the wave of cruel fanaticism that endangers the lives of so many people and hinders progress towards world peace' said the pontiff. He went on: 'We must seek paths of reconciliation and learn to live with respect for each other's identity'.

Dr. Ansari, however, appealed to the Pope to support truth and justice to save the sanctity of his position. He also hoped the Pope to instruct the rulers of Christian world to give up their injust and brutal policy against the Muslim world so that peace and prosperity could be restored in the world.[17]

Notes & References:

1. The author may be contacted at Ramzybaroud @homail.com.
2. Ramzy Baroud, Barbaric But not Unexpected. *The Milli Gazette*, 1-5, August 2005, p. 27.
3. Taqiuddin Malik, The Source of All Evil updated on July 25.05. The author is an Egyptian free lance writer. He can be emailed at taqiuddin malik@hotmail.com.The wors cited in the article are:
   - Sardar, Ziauddin"The struggle for Islam's soul, "*The New Statesman*. July 18, 2005. Accessed: July 20, 2005.
   - "*The Wahhabi Movement: History and Beliefs*," IslamOnline.net. February 9, 2004. Accessed: July 20, 2005.
4. The same crusading mentality of the West against Islam and Muslims has been studied by the Swiss experts even in recent days. According to a Swiss scholar in Geneva "The West has misjudged Islam and done it injustice largely because of shallow knowledge of Muslim faith driven from the distorted writings of early orientalists". The expert further says, "Rising Islamophobia is the result of the West's shallow dealing with and misunderstanding of Islam". Arnold Hottinger, who spend 50 years in the Middle Esast reporting for the leading *Neue Zurcher Zeitung* newspaper, told a day-long seminar organized by the Paulus Akademie. Hottinger, a fluent Arabic speaker, faulted the West of portraying Muslims as the terriflying neighbour for long centruries. "Early orientalists and churchmen only portrayed Islam as a religion of violence and wars", he told his attentive audience. "This image found its way into text books turning the Muslim world to a terrifying neighbour, which is a major injustice to Islam". Hottinger has authored a number of books about the Muslim world in addition to writing many articles and giving lectures. The Swiss expert said Islam is a melting pot for people of different ethnic and cultural background, a fact, he said, that is hard for the West to conceive. "No textbook in the West explains how Islam rapidly grew in Asia, which is home to the majority of Muslims worldwide." Hottinger said, "When the Muslim immigrants came to Europe, a negative miage of Islam was already deeply-rooted". The Swiss expert also shed light on

Europe's bad history of imperialism and colonicalism in Arab and Muslim countries. He cited Europe's role in the dissolution of the ottoman Empire, causing many ethnic and border conflicts still raving in several Arab and Muslim countries. When the First world War (1914-18) broke out, the Ottoman Empire broke neutrality and fought on the side of the Central Powers. The Ottomans were eventually defeated by the Allies in the Balkans Thrace, Syria, Palestine and Iraq and its territories were colonized by the Victors. On Turkey's bid to join the European Union, Hottinger said refusal to allow the admission of Muslim but secular Turkey would be a 'big mistake". He cautioned that such a position would have major consequence as it would prove the view of "Muslim extremists" that the West is not willing to make any rapprochement with Islam and Muslims. "It will also prove that Europe is a Christians-only continent and will cast doubts on efforts to bridge the gaps between the two sides". Last December (2004) the European Union agreed to open membership talks with turkey to join the 25-nation bloc. *The MilliGazette*, 16-31 July 2005, p. 25.

5. The Crusades started in November 1095 when Pope Urban II granted remission of all sins to anyone who joined the war against Muslims. The first Crusades, in which more than 10000 Muslims were slaughtered in Masjid al-Aqsa, was won by the Christians. In the next two crusades the Muslims extracted revenge, winning under the leadership of Salahuddin Ayyubi (1138-1193AD). The second round of battles started when Chatillon attacked pilgrims going for Hajj in 1187. Salahuddin's forces won the day. While Chatillon paid the price with his head, King Guy was raised his knees by Salahuddin, and told to act in a manner befitting a king. Remarkably, Salahuddin issued instructions not to convert any church into a mosque or hurt the Christians. Widows were spared and many slaves were freed by him. Of course, the soldiers on the ground did not always live up to the ideals of the ruler. Incidentally in this battle, Salahuddin entered Jerusalem on October 2, 1187, the day on which Muslims celebrated too the ascension of the Prophet to heaven. The third round brought Richard. The Lionheart face to face with Salahuddin. While Ricahrd saved his lie with his customary valour, he could not

prolong the Christian occupation of the Holy Land. Incidentally Salahuddin and Richard were engaged in a direct combat too, with the former of horseback as befitted his royal stature.

6. Zafar Bangash, the Trouble with the West, *Crete scent International*, Vol. 34, No. 7, Rajab-Shaban 1426/ September 2005, p. 2.
7. Iqbal N. Siddiqui, *Crescent International*, *Ibid*, pp. 3-4.
8. Ahmad Musa, Muslims and Muslims Organizations facing an Islamophobic witch hunt in Britain, *Ibid.*, pp. 9-10.
9. Dr. Zafarul Islam Khan, *The Milli Gazette*, 1-15, August 2005, p. 01.
10. Britain's largest sunni group on Monday issued a *fatwa* condemning the July 7 terror bombings in London. Jamaat *Ahl-e-Sunnat*, or the Sunni Council said in Birmingam, the bombings were against Islam, adding that any kind of suicide attack was against the Quran. "Leaving aside the atrocities being committed in Palestine and Iraq, the attacks in London have no Islamic justification, are totally condemned and we equally condmen those who may have been behind the masterminding of these acts, those who incited these youths in order to further their own perverted ideology", the groups' *fatwa* said. "We wish to clarify again and to categorically condemn all forms of terrorism, be it state terrorism or otherwise". More than 200 Sunni clerics, scholars and community leaders attended he meeting, which was scheduled before the July 7 bombings. "Who has given anyone the right to kill others? It is a sin. Anyone who commits suicide will be sent to hell. "said Mufti Muhammad Gul Rahman Qadri, the council's chairman. *The Times of India*, July 19, 2005, p. 13. According to another news published in The Hindu (December, 9, 2005). Muslim leaders from across the globe agreed on December 8, 2005, on measures to combat terrorism and defend the image of Islam at a summit in the holy city of Makkah. The leaders organised a two-day summit of the Organization of Islamic Conference (OIC) pledging to "update national laws to criminalize all acts of terrorism as well as its financing and incitement." In a Makkah Declaration read out in a final session, they also called upon their peoples to "combat forcefully the preachers of sedition and deviation, who aim to distort the peaceful principles of Islam". Saudi foreign

Minister Saud al-Faisal said later on Wednesday on 7, 2005, that Muslim leaders who met in Makkah, western Saudi Arabia, they agreed to "combat terrorism and extremism and stressed the moderate nature of Islam". They stressed the need to stop blaming outside forces for problems in the Muslim world and focus on cooperation", he said. They agreed "on stressing the importance of cooperation between Muslims and putting an end to complaints of foreign conspiracies and concentrating on common efforts to face development challenges". The summit opened with a cell from regional powerhouse Saudi Arabia for moderation and tolerance and a rejection of extremist violence".

North American Muslims also issued a *fatwa* (religious edict) in Phoenix against extremism and terrorism in order to prevent disgruntled Muslims who might be tempted to use their religion to justify violence. It has been signed by representatives of more than 250 mosques and Islamic centres and endorsed by over 170 Muslim group leaders and institutions. This American *fatwa* followed the one issued in March 2005 by the Islamic Commission of Spain, which declared Osama bin Laden an 'apostate" and urged other Muslims to denounce the Al-Qaeda leader. The Spanish ruling marked the first time Muslim clerics had (collectively) denounced terrorism in religious vocabulary, invoking Islamic instruments such as *fatwa* and apostasy, instead of qualified condemnation as in the past. The London attacks also prompted a number of Muslim organizations to issue a fatwa denouncing violence-UNI (*The Hindu* September 25, 2005).

11. Dr. Gayasuddin Siddiqui, *The Milli Gazette*, 16 August, 15 September, 2005, p. 26.
12. Hugh Miur, *The Hindu*, July 14, 2005. Leading Muslim scholars meeting in a three-day conference in Amman from 4 to 6 July 2005, banned killing in the name of Islam and urged respect for other opinions in the Muslim world. "We condemn the principle of accusation of apostasy and the legalization of the assassination of Muslims for religious reasons", 180 scholars said Wednesday at the end of the first International Islamic Conference in Jordan. The statement was based on religious edicts or fatwas issued by Sheikh Mohamamd Sayyed Tantawi of Al-Azhar in Cairo, the highest Muslim Sunni authority, Ayatollah Ali Sistani,

shiete leader based in Iraq, and Egypts *Mufti* Sheikh Ali Juma'ah as well as other senior leaders in Saudi Arabia, Turkey and Jordan. At the beginning of the conference, Jordan's King Abdullah II denounced all kinds of religious extremists. He also urged Muslim states to harmonize their schools of jurisprudence. "Divisions within the global Islamic community, acts of violence and terrorism and accusations of apostasy and the killing of Muslims in the name of Islam violate the spirit of Islam," he said in an address. Muslim scholars also agreed *fatwas* (religious edicts) on labeling other Muslims as "apostate" should be limited to scholars with religious authority, urging to unify the words and stances of Muslims to highlight the Islamic teachings of moderation, tolerance and respect for other. Wrapping up their meeting in the Jordanian capital Amman Wednesday, July 6, 2005 the 170 Muslim scholars from 40 countries also proposed to form an "Islamic-Christian Alliance" to clear misconceptions about Islam, Reuters said, "Declaring that person an apostate is impossible, verily his or her blood, honour and property are sacrosanct" said the final statement of International Islamic Conference.

"The issuance of religious edicts is limited to qualified Muslim scholars in the eight schools of jurisprudence," added the statements read out by Jordanian Religious Affairs Minister Abdul Salam Al-Abadi. The Islamic Conference titled "the True Islam and its Role in Modern Society "was opened by King Abdullah II Monday to discuss the challenges encountering Muslims and Obstacles facing Islam. "The meeting, organized by the Jordanian ministry of religious affairs, also tackled Islam's stance on extremism, terrorism, reform and human rights. King Abdullah condemned what he termed: religious extremism." The meeting called for "casting aside disagreement between Muslims and unifying their words and stances.

The conference's final statement was based on fatwas issued by 10 top Muslim scholars-including Al-Azhar Grand Imam sheikh Mohammad Sayyed Tantawi, Iraq's Grand Ayatollah Ali al-Sistani, Egypt's mufti sheikh Ali al-Juma'ah-that fatwas must only be in the hands of qualified scholars recognized by the eight Islamic schools of thought. The Islamic Conference was also attended by a host of Christian clergymen who proposed the set-up of an "Islamic-Christian

Alliance". "We should form an alliance between the Arab and Muslim nation" said bishop Nabil Haddad, director of the Jordanian Centre for Religious Co-existence Research. "This alliance will be tasked with showing that Islam is religion of moderation, peace and tolerance. "the cancer of Islamophobia has spread across the United States and Europe since the 9/11 attacks. A recent report released by the International Helsinki Federation for Human Rights (IHF) said Muslim minorities across Europe have been experiencing growing distrust, hostility and discrimination since the 2001 attacks. The United Nations commission on Human Rights adopted on April 12 a resolution calling for combating defamation campaigns against Islam and Muslims in the West.

Sheikh Mohammad Sayyid Tantawi, the Grand Sheikh of Al-Azhar, has affirmed that it is not permissible to declare those who follow other Islamic sects as heretics as long as they are in agreement on articles of faith and its pillars, regardless of the differences in implementing the requirements of those pillars. This was contained in a letter which the Grand Shiekh has addressed to Prince Ghazy bin Mohammad, Advisor to the Jordanian monarch King Abdullah II. The memorandum contains mostly fatwas on various matters of faith which the Advisor had asked for, particularly those focusing on declaring followers of other sects such Ibadhis, dhahiriyah, Jafariyah, Zaidiyah, Ashariyyah and Sufism as heretics. In his letter the Grand Sheidkh said that it is not permissible for one to refer to another as denier of truth, except if the person referred to has decried what has come in the Islamic Shariah, such as the basic articles of faith in Allah, His prophets, the angels, His books, and sincere worship of Allah. *The Milli Gazette*, 16-31 July 2005, p. 27. These *fatwa* are issued in the context of jurisprudential differences within the Muslim community but their implications and applications are based upon certain principles and include the non Muslims also who enjoy full rights and guarantees in Islam.

13. Ejaz Ahmad Aslam. Editorial, *Radiance* Vewsweekly. Xe. XL, No 12, July 31-August 6, 2005, Pos.
14. Jawed Anwar, Occupation vs. Terrorism: what should be out stand? Radiance Views Weekly. Vol.XL, No12.July 31-August 6.2005, pp.18-19.

15. Dr. S. Ausaf Saied Wasfi, 7/7 did not learn lesson from 9/11. *Radiance* Views Weekly. Vol.XI. No 11.24-30 July 2005, pp.10-11. the All India Muslim Majlis Mushawarat (AIMMM)On July 8. 2005 strongly condemned the July 7terrorist attacks in London. 'it is particularly deplorable because it took place at a time when the leading economic powers of the world had gathered on the British soil it to plan for the elimination of global poverty and rising indebtedness of the developing countries from the face of planet', it's president Syed Shahabuddin said. We offer our deep condolences to the next-of kin of those killed and sympathy to those who have been injured he said. He reiterated his absolute and unconditional rejection of such violent acts committed in the name of Islam. *Ibid*,p.10.
16. Dr. S. Ausaf Saied Wasfi, why 'war on Terror' has proved counter productive? Radiance Viewsweekly, vol. xl. No13. 7-13 August, 2005,pp.22-23.
17. Radiance Views Weekly. Vol. XL. No 18, 11-17 September, 2005,p.24. (Pope's Silence is Unjust, Against Religious Spirit.)

6

ISLAMIC JUSTIFICATIONS EXAMINED

Official Otherworldliness

It is unfortunate that most of the western writers, analysts and intellectuals have no urge to know the real motives, concepts and ideologies of the suicide bombers. They start talking on the terror, violence, hijacking and bombing in terms of crusades and do not feel any need to understand the psychology of these people involved in these acts. Mr. Seumas Milne is surprised to see that when British M.P. George Galloway, having overturned a substantial Labour majority over Iraq in a London constituency with a large Muslim population, declared that Londoners had paid the price of a "despicable act" for the Government's failure to heed the warnings of Al-Qaeda, he was accused by Defence Minister Adam Ingram of "dipping his poisonous tongue in a pool of blood".

The question arises whose tongue is poisonous? Of those who speak the truth and sincerely talk on the issues; who do not believe in Ostrich-policy and face the challenges openeyedly or those who are disloyal to the issues and serve their vested interests? What is the criteria of being poisonous? And how the British Defence Minister charges one as poisonous and on what basis? It was with this mentality of accusations without any scrutiny that Mr. Bush blames an "Evil ideology" being responsible for 7/7 attacks. The same attitude was adopted after 9/11 blasts in the United States when the champions of occupations of Iraq and Afghanistan had claimed that "Al-Qaeda and its supporters had basically no demands that could possibly be met or negotiated over; that they were really motivated by a hatred of western freedoms and way of life; and that their Islamist ideology aimed at global domination". The reality was neatly summed up this week in a radio exchange between the BBC's political editor Andrew Marr, and its security correspondent Frank Gardner, who was left disabled by an Al-Qaeda attack in Saudi Arabia last year. Was it the "very diversity that melting pot aspect of London" that Islamist extremists found so offensive that they wanted to kill innocent civilians in Britain's capital. Mr. Marr wondered. "No, it is not that", replied Mr. Gardner briskly, who is better acquainted with Al-Qaeda thinking than most. "What they find offensive are the policies of western governments and specifically the presence of western troops in Muslim lands notably Iraq and Afghanistan".[1]

Mr. Seumas Milne is a severe critic to the analyses made by the western media and politicians while examining the 7/7 blasts. He condemned 'the bulk of Britain's' political class and media' distinguishing itself by a 'willful and dangerous refusal to face up the reality'. The entire foreign policy of the country is based upon the 'disinformations' that is entitled by him as 'official otherworldliness".

Mr. Javed Anwar [2] in the United States is angry and outspoken about the Muslim leadership that it is not speaking the truth; it is rather apologizing for these attacks and does not stand for justice. The Muslim leadership also following the "official otherworldliness" is hiding the realities not only in the western countries but across the world. It is an unjust treatment with the issue and is against the academic sincerity and intellectual honesty as well as this does not solve the problem and goes against the loyalty and patriotism also.

The Only Method Survived

"How the bombers feel?

Saying that "killing one person is like killing the whole of mankind[3]" and preaching war ethics of the Quran that protect children and civilians in the war, are not going to influence those people who are occupied and have become slaves and who are taking and asking for revenge. They have their own set of arguments. When we say that civilians, women, children should be protected in all circumstances and in all conditions, the victims of occupation say 'we have already tried by attacking military and government targets to end the occupation, but the big powers did not move out; but now our killing of a few civilians has built an enormous public pressure on governments to withdraw their forces from our lands.' Withdrawal of Spain's military from Iraq and change of the government in Spain was a success story for them. When we say "suicide bombing is *haram* and unlawful in Islam, the occupied, uprooted citizens say, 'Give us a land, military arsenals, F-16s, and other arms and ammunitions, and we vow that we will never again attack by suicide bombings'. The desperate and oppressed people have their own logic and perception. They are not going to listen to the preaching, *nasihah* and arguments of affluent Muslims of America".[4]

Well! The bombers are not ready to listen the Quranic ethics of war. It is true that Islam is not a 'pacifist religion' and Muslims are expected to fight aggressors and oppressors, and to establish justice in the world. In the case of the US and Britain, it is understandable that Islamic activists may consider it legitimate to fight back, just as Iraqis are fighting back in their own country. However, says Mr. Iqbal N. Sddiqui, "Iraq and Palestine demonstrate that even within *jihad* there are distinctions to be drawn, between legitimate and illegitimate targets. This is true also of struggle underway against oppressive governments in Muslim countries and against non-Muslim states that are at war with Muslim countries".

Mr. Siddiqui well argues that repeated experiences in Muslim countries indicate that militant jihad seldom succeeds in achieving political change. When Islamic movements are pushed into militancy, often by the suppression of nonviolent Islamic activism, it provokes government repression and erodes popular support, thus playing in the hands of the political powers that already dominate the Muslims. Egypt and Algeria both give examples of popular Islamic movements that lost credibility and support in this way.

It is clear that armed struggle by small militant groups, Mr. Siddiqui further explains, can not overthrow established political orders ; the example of Iran indicated that a political movement that mobilizes large scale popular support is far more likely to succeed. It is to prevent precisely this development that governments put pressure on peaceful movements, aiming to discredit them either by drawing them into established political institutions (thus blunting their opposition) or by forcing them into violence that then justifies repression. It is for this reason that, a part from the misguided few responsible for such bombings, the only to welcome them are the powers that they are supposed to challenge.

The same is true of terrorism in Western countries or against Western targets in Muslim countries, says with arguments Mr. Siddiqui. George Bush and Tony Blair must be drawing much satisfaction from the fact that Muslims have provided them with justification for their "war on terror". The best excuses for one's crimes are those that are convincing and believable; the London bombers have provided evidence for the West's claim that its own aggression against Muslim countries is necessary to fight terrorism. A large proportion of British population is opposed to the war in Iraq and wholly distrusts Bush and, to lesser extent, Blair. A large part of the British Muslim community has much sympathy with the *mujahideen* fighting against Western troops in Iraq and Afghanistan and opposing pro-western regimes elsewhere. But bombings like those in London serve only to alienate people in Britain, both Muslims and non-Muslims, who are appalled by the violent deaths of ordinary people.

Mr. Siddiqui clearly declares that "the fact the western governments have no concern for Muslim lives does not justify Muslims' cold-blooded brutality against either Muslim or western civilians. However brutal and two-faced western politicians and their allies in the Muslim world may be, Muslims must work according to high standards...there can be no question that attacks on civilian targets, in office buildings or other public spaces, even in response to the deaths of thousands of Muslim civilians at the West's hands, is utterly unjustifiable and unacceptable by Islamic standards." "One reason for the retreate from the violence of Islamic movements in Algeria and Egypt," concludes Mr. Siddiqui, was the realization that the conflict was creating a generation of brutalized and embittered young Muslims, endangering their souls and *akhirah*. The same consideration should now guide Muslims' responses to misguided and unacceptable violence from Muslims around the world, and help us to find other ways to fight our enemies and pressure our legitimate objectives." [5]

Sayyid Abul Ala Maududi (1903-1979) the champion of Islamic revivalism in the modern world and the most targeted Islamic figure by the West was not convinced with any terrorist activity. He went to London for medical treatment in the winter of 1969, Ziauddin Sardar reports[6] Sardar alongwith thousands of students went to Heathrow Airport to welcome him. Maududi was interviewed at length for *The_Muslim*, the Federation of Students Islamic Scoiety (FOSIS) magazine. Many questions were answered, most important of all was about armed revolt. "Do you think that the Islamic state can be established by an armed revolt ? " "I do not think this is the right road for us to pursue," he replied without a moment's hesitation. "Such a policy, instead of producing any good, may prove to be highly harmful." Maududi elaborated," Even if we establish an Islamic state through armed revolution, it would not be possible to run the state and carry on its affairs in accordance with the Islamic way, for the simple reason that society and its different sections have not been properly prepared for the moral transformation that Islam wants. Armed revolution as a means to power is open to others as well as-so there is a danger that Muslim countries will become ensnared in vicious circle of revolutions and counter-revolutions and of conspiracies and counter-conspiracies. More over to bring about an armed revolution, you have to organize your movement on the pattern of secret societies. These have a temperament of their own. They admit to no dissent and disagreement. The voice of criticism is silenced, and free, fair and frank discussions become conspicuous by their absence. Another demand of the inner logic of secret societies is to permit workers to resort to deceit, lies, forgeries, frauds, bloodshed and many other things, which are for bidden in Islam. It is also in the nature of revolutions brought about by bullet that they can be maintained only through the bullet. This produces a climate where peaceful switch-over towards an Islamic order virtually becomes impossible."[7]

Maududi's stand against unconstitutional and underground activities had undergone no slighter change even when *Jamā'at* Islami under his leadership was pushed out of politics by the President Ayyub Khan and its members and followers were harassed and tortured. He publicly announced his conviction: "I am in principle opposed to all unlawful, unconstitutional and underground activities. I did not come to this opinion out of consideration of any expediency or in response to any challenge. My opinion is rather the product of contemplation and studying....Respect for law is the basic tenet for a civilized society....Covert activity is a greater menace to society than the one it seeks to remove.[8]

Sacrificing one for the Faith

An strong theological and juristic justification was provided by Shaykh Yousuf al-Qaradhawi, a distinguished Islamic scholar equally respected and followed by both the moderate and extremist Islamic groups across the Muslim world. He discussed the issue of suicide bombing in Islamic perspective especially in the context of Palestinians. His lengthy statement in the form of a writeup was published in Arabic monthly *Filistin al-Muslimah* (The Muslim Palestine) in its issue of Rabi al-Thani 1417 AH./September 1996 (pp. 51-52). Shaykh al-Qaradhawi declared the suicide bombing a noble method of jihad that is basically included in the Shariah obligation of militarily preparation in order to terrorize the enemies of Allah, which is explicitly prescribed in the holy Quran:

> Against them make ready
> Your strength to the utmost
> Of your power, including
> Steeds of war, to strike terror
> In to (the hearts of) the enemies,
> Of God and your enemies,
> And others, besides, whom
> Ye may not know, but whom,
> God doth know. (al-Anfal : 8)

Shaykh Qaradhawi says that this kind of jihad has no concern with the suicide. Labelling it suicide is wrong and misleading. The psychology of one who intentionally performs it is for from and opposed to the psychology of a suiciding man. He further says:

"A person who commits suicide originally kills himself in order to rescue his personal sufferings and hardships. But a warrior, *(mujahid)* sacrifices himself for the domination of his faith and of *Ummah*. A suicider has given up all the hopes and expectations in God and has lost his confidence while a warrior has total faith and reliance on God. A suicider seeks or tries to seek deliverance by killing himself but a *mujahid* does battle with his enemy and the enemy of God with his novel weapon which Providence has put up in the hands of the weak, so that he should be in a position to fight the powerful and arrogant. The *mujahid* becomes a living bomb who decides when and where the explosion will take place in the enemies' midst; the enemies find themselves helpless in the face of the brave martyr who has sold his soul to Allah, and who has sought out martyrdom for God's sake."

Shaykh Qaradhawi is not convinced with calling these warriors the suiciders. "They are actually the martyrs who have sacrificed their lives eagerly in the way of Allah." "The thing only considerable is that whether his intention was exclusively to please Allah and whether these sacrificing warriors have any other option to terrorize the enemies of God or not. These youths are neither suiciders nor terrorists; they are basically the defenders of their faith and nation and they have performed their duties towards their belongings. The sanction is provided by their religion that has made incumbent upon them to defend their resources, dignity and honour and has not allowed to withdraw from their land and country which is the part of the Muslim world."

Shaykh Qaradhawi further says that the Quranic verse:

> "And make not your own hands
> Contribute to (your) destruction
> (*Al-Baqarah* : 195)

does not apply to these *mujahids*; they are not contributing to their *tahlukah* (destruction); their motive lies in terrorizing the enemies and also in encouraging and assisting their oppressed and persecuted helpless people. They are fighting Israel every male and female which is combatant and a soldier of its army who may be called to join the military at any time. Consequently it is not the killing of innocents, though the possibility of killing mistakenly some boys and old-age people or harming them may not be overlooked. It however, comes under the category of unavoidables of a war".[9]

Qaradhawi Cities the Exegesists

While explaining the above-quoted verse No.195 of the Quranic chapter *Al-Baqarah* that forbids Muslims to contribute to their destruction (*tahlukah*) Shaykh Qaradhawi refers the classical commentators of the Quran to prove his argument. Since the theological opponents while criticising the suicide bombers concentrate on the same verse and issue the verdict mullifying the selfless destruction and suicide whatever the intention was motivating, Shaykh's discussion basically revolves around the explanation of the same verse.

Ahmad bin Ali Abu Bakr Jassas (305-370 AH/917-980 AD) the hanafid jurist as well as the *mufassir* elaborates the verse under discussion in his *Ahkam Al-Quran* (Ordinances of the Quran) referring Abu Ayyub Ansari the famous companion who interprets that it meant we the Muslims were checked to avoid jihad and take care exclusively of our properties staying permanently in Madinah. Abu Imran, the narrator says that Abu Ayyub Ansari was engaged in waging Jihad the whole life and passed away and was buried near the wall of Constantinople in fighting against the Byzantines.[10]

Jassas quotes Muhammad bin al-Hassan al-Shaybani (131-189 AH/748-804 AD) the prominent hanafid jurist who analyses the case in detail in his book *Kitab al-Siyar-al-Kabeer*. To this juristic opinion in case a Muslim alone attacks a group of one thousand it is justified in law provided he would scape safely presumably or he would harm the enemy utmost and if there are no such chances, I personally dislike this attempt that put him into destruction and death without having take care to achieve a considerable advantage in favour of Muslims. Jassas comments on it by adding if there is a possibility to gain for the faith in this attack, it should be counted the pleasant tidings mentioned in the holy Quran as Allah explicitly announces:

> God has purchased of the Believers
> Their persons and their goods;
> For theirs (in return)
> Is the garden (of paradise):
> They fight in His cause,
> And slay and are slain.[11]

> Think not of those
> Who are slain in God's way
> As dead. Nay, they live,
> Finding their sustenance
> In the presence of their Lord.[12]

> And there is a type a man
> Who gives his life
> To earn the pleasure of God.[13]

Jassas further argues that the following Islamic texts and their implications also are applied in such cases:

> Enjoin what is just
> And forbid what is wrong
> And bear with patient constancy
> Whatever belide thee; for this
> Is firmness (of purpose)
> In (the conduct of) affairs.[14]

Ikramah has quoted a narration being ascribed to Abdullah Ibn Abbas who has narrated the Prophet is reported to have said:

> Most virtuous among the martyrs is Hamzah Ibn Abdul Muttalib and the man killed in response to proclaiming a truth before a tyrant ruler."[15]

Another hadith of the same meaning is narrated by Abu Said Khudri, according to which the Prophet said:

> "The noblest jihad is uttering a true word to a tyrant ruler."[16]

Jassas then refers a *marfu hadith* ascribed to Abu Hurayrah that follows:

> "The worst habit of a man is his excessive greed and insulting cowardice."[17]

And concludes that the nullification of cowardice itself approves and authenticates such a dangerous initiating that results in the gain for the faith and that forecasts confidently the ruin and destruction of man in action.[18]

Shaykh Qaradhawi refers Muhammad bin Ahmad Qurtubi (d.671 AH- 1273 AD) the malikid jurist also who expresses his views in his *tafsir Al-Jami li Ahkam al-Quran* and supports al-Shaybani, He cites the malikid scholars and Theologians in this regard like al-Qasim bin Muhammad, al-Qasim bin Fuhaymarah, Abdul Malik, Ibn Khuwaz Mandad etc. as well as several other traditions of the Prophet. All these sources qualify a Muslim to attack alone on a huge troop if he is capable and follows sincerely the will of God.[19]

Imam Muhamamd bin Umar Fakhruddin Razi (554-606 A.H./1150-1210 AD) the shafi'ite jurist and theologian has interpreted the verse in the terms that jumping in the battle without hoping any gain except the death of his own is forbidden. Contributing to one's own destruction in the battlefield is legally obligatory only when it bears the possibility of heavy casualties of the enemies. If the chances of hitting the targets are not so clear and there is a maximum possibility of being slain, the attack remains no more justified.[20]

Al-Hafiz Ismail bin Umar bin Kathir (701-774 AH/ 1302-1373 A.D.) has traced a narration in his *Tafsir al-*

Quran al-Karim that a man asked Al-Bara bin Adhib Ansari, the companion: I attack the troop of enemies who might have killed me whether I suppose myself as one who contributes to his own destruction (*tahlukah* as referred in the Quran)? "No", the companion replied", because Allah has said in the Quran addressing his Prophet:

> Then fight in God's cause
> You are held responsible
> Only for yourself.[21]

The holy verse consisting of 'destructing oneself' (*tahlukah)* initially warns those who are reluctant to spend their wealth in the noble cause of jihad.[22] Imam Muhammad Ibn Jarir Tabari (224-310 AH/839-913 AD) also holds the same view.[23]

Shaykhul Islam Ahmad bin Abdul Halim Ibn Taimiyah (661-728AH/ 1262-1328AD) has taken the same line in his famous *Fatawa* arguing by the narration of Imam Muslim in his *Al-Jami Al-Sahih*. It is discussed in the context of the story of the makers of the pit of fire" (*Ashab al-Ukhdud)*[24]. According to the legend the courageous young boy for the sake of faith tells his fellows of a tactics to hit with the arrow proclaiming by the name of Allah, the Lrod of the boy *(bismillah e Rabb al-ghulam*). Ibn Taimiyah issues the verdict saying, ... That is why all the four juristic *Imams* have given the sanction to a Muslim who unhesitatingly jumps into troops of the enemies though the possibility of his being slain is proportionally lies more.[25]

Imam Muhammad bin Ali al-Shawkani (1173-1250AH/1760-1834) basing his argument on the verse under discussion derives his conclusion in a logical way. To him the generality of a word is to be considered; not any specific reason working behind should be treated as a specific condition. Every aspect covering the destruction in the realm of both the religion and the worldly affair, naturally comes under the jurisdiction of the verse. Consequently include the implications of the verse also a man who suddenly jumps in the battlefield and attacks offensively a grand military troop though he had no scope to return safe nor had any far-reaching consequence in favour of the *mujahidin*. It implies that if such an offense has any chance to gain for the warriors of Islam that will not be included in destruction of one self (*tahlukah*).[26]

Muhammad Rashid Rida (1282-1354 AH./1865-1935) the modern reformist scholar and activist has included in the prohibited acts-quoted in the Chapter 2: 195- the issue of a man who without having fully acquainted with the war tactics and methods, penetrates in the battlefield and also all illegal and unIslamic initiatives to be taken by as a man initiates it for the sake of his self not for the sake of supporting the truth. It implies that a well-planned Islamic offensive-aimed at terrorizing the enemy and strengthening the noble truth-is out of any questioning.[27]

Shaykh Qaradhawi after quoting the classical and modern jurists and exegesists strongly condemns those who defame the sacrificing warriors. "Those martyrs," says the Shaykh, "are originally the faithful who sold themselves for the cause of Allah and were slain in His way. These are the living elements who are the spokesmen of the activism and dynamism inherent in the Ummah; they insist on the combat against the occupying Jews and are not ready for any compromise or withdrawal."

"Our request in this regard", says the Shaykh, is to initiate, if unavoidable, such a sacrificing and martyrous activities only after a due consideration and careful examination of minus and plus points. Rather better is to launch such operations after collective thinking and evaluation of sincere and loyal Muslims relying upon Allah," he concludes.[28]

It is interesting to note that Shaykh Qaradhawi's individual opinion-as against the consensus in Islamic history as well as in the contemporary world-is mainly based on the Islamic texts very general in nature. These texts-quoted above-communicate no clear-cut opinion on the suicide bombing under discussion. Contrary to it *Al-Jami Al-Sahih* of Imam Bukhari and other authentic collections are full of Prophetic traditions in opposition to suicide. Death brought about by one's own hands was unambiguously condemned by the Ulama in history and in the modern period as well.

The Classical stand

The Quranic verses and the traditions of the Prophet cited by Shaykh Qaradhawi do not reveal any explicit message in this context. These do not suffice to prove the views of the Shaykh. The verse pertaining a negation of destruction by one's own hands (*tahlukah*) (*Al-Baqarah:* 195) apparently condemns the suicide operations. Other verses and traditions are basically the motivating and inspiring one to wage jihad against combatants. These texts therefore, are understood and interpreted by all the jurists and scholars in terms of an official Jihad to be waged by the Islamic state after it has already fulfilled all the prerequisites. While commenting on the underlying reasons which form the basis of state authority for *Jihad* Maulana Amin Ahsan Islahi explicitly writes:

"The first reason for this condition is that God Almighty does not like dissolution and disintegration of an evil system until a strong probability exists that those who are out to disintegrate the system will provide people with an alternative and righteous system. Anarchy and disorder are unnatural conditions. In fact, they are so contrary to human nature that even an injust system is preferable to them.........this confidence (that a group will be able to harmonize a disintegrated system and integrate it into a united whole) can be reposed in such a group only as has actually formed a political government and has such control and discipline within the confines of its authority that the group can be termed as *al-Jamaah* (the state). Until a group attains this position it may strive (by religiously allowable means) to become *al-Jama'ah-* and that endeavor would be its *jihad* for that time-but it does not have the right to wage an 'armed' *jihad.*

"The second reason is that the import of power which a group engaged in war acquires over the life and property of human beings is so great that the sanction to wield this power can not be given to a group the control of whose leader is based merely on his spiritual and religious influence, there is not sufficient guarantee that the leader will be able to stop his followers from *fasad fi al-ard* (creating disorder in the society). Therefore a religious leader does not have a right to allow his followers to take out their swords (that is to wage an armed struggle merely on the basis of his spiritual influence over them, for once the sword is unsheathed there is great danger that it will not care for right and wrong and those who drew it will end up doing all (the wrong which) they had sought to end. Such radical groups as desire revolution and the object of whom is nothing more than disruption of the existing system and the deposition of the ruling party to seize power for themselves play such games – and they can, for in their eyes disruption of a system is no calamity nor is cruelty of any kind an evil. Every thing is right to them (as long as it serves their purpose). However the leaders of a just and righteous party must see whether they are in a position to provide people with a system better than the one they seek to change and whether they will be able to stop their followers from doing such wrong as they themselves had sought to root out. If they are not in that position, then they do not have the right to play games with the life and property of people on the basis of their confidence in mere chances and to create great disorder than the one they had sought to end.[29]

On this classical approach to Islamic justifications of waging war against the combatants is the unanimity of all the scholars in the Islamic history. "There is no example in the Quran, the hadith and in the model of the holy companions that might have justified the suicide even for the noble cause. The worst situations had confronted with the Muslims; the entire populations were some times burnt; males were massacred and females were mass-raped. The women in some crucial times thought better to suicide but none dared to call these the martyrdom" as some scholars clearly denounced.[30]

Shaykh Qaradhawi's justification for victimizing and targeting the non combatants – the civilians, innocent children and women – though mistakenly and his declaring it as "unavoidables of war" opens the back door for violence and terrorism unconditional. This approach is dangerous and is also opposed to the Islamic standards maintained strictly in the Quran and Sunnah. Islamic standards do not allow even in the war to kill the non-combatants, destruct the common and civil properties and to destroy the crops. The holy Quran defines these activities as *fasad* (mischief) and bannes them publicly:

> When he lurns his back,
> His aim every where
> Is to spread mischief
> Through the earth and destroy
> Crops and cattle.
> But God loves not mischief.[31]

> We sent Shuaib one
> Of their own brethren: he said:
> "O my people! Worship God;
> You have no other God
> But Him. Now has come
> Unto you a clear (sign)
> From your Lord! Give just
> Measure and weight, nor withhold
> From the people the things
> That are their due; and do

No mischief on the earth
After it has been set
In order: that will be best
For you, if you have Faith.[32]

The Islamic standards were clearly explained by Abu Bakr, the first caliph of Islam. When he dispatched the Islamic army to Syria he ordered its commander-in-chief Yazid bin Abu Sufyan unambiguously:

> "I instruct you to maintain ten points: Do not kill any child, any woman or any old-aged man; do not cut any tree fruiting; do not destroy any land cultivative; do not set a fire to the bees, nor make them dispersed; do not cheat in the affairs of booty and do not show cowardice in the battle."[33]

Deterrence Theory

Some Muslims, due to heavy political and strategic pressures laid on them, express their support to offensive violence and terrorism and title it as 'preventive strike' that also was denounced by the prominent scholar of Islamic economics Dr. Nijatullah Siddiqui on certain grounds. Dr. Siddiqui has discussed the issue in Indian perspective providing an Islamic guide line for the Muslims in minority. "The theory of 'deterrence' is not justified because it is incorrect to attack Hindus either in advance on the same target or on their targets in order to prevent any Hindu aggression; also is wrong to respond violently against any other target or other group and; is also unacceptable to hit any Hindu individual or group in retaliation with the aggressions committed against them." This deterrence is against the teachings of Islam," Dr. Siddiqui further asserts, because the innocent can not be targeted. Being a citizen of a democratic country like India also, we are bound not to do so; the clear violation of the law of the land in this context is also against the Islamic teachings. The principles and ethics of war to be implemented in between the two sovereign states can not be applied upon the communal tensions of a country. In response to an aggressive group, any non-combatant pacifist group can not be attacked in pre-or-post tragedy."[34]

Maulana Ateequr Rahman Sanbhali, addressing to those Muslim youth influenced with the approach of Umar Bakri, Abu Hamzah and the like, refers a unique Quranic verse that seems very useful in understanding the Islamic view of terrorism. The verse reads:

> Those who believed,
> And adopted exile,
> And fought for the Faith,
> With their property
> And their persons
> In the cause of God
> As well as those
> Who gave (them) asylum
> And aid, - these are (all)
> Friends and protectors,
> One of another.
> As to those who believed
> But came not into exile
> You owe no duty
> Of protection to them
> Until they come into exile;
> But if they seek
> Your aid in religion,
> It is your duty
> To help them,
> Except against a people
> With whom you have
> A treaty of mutual alliance.
> And remember God
> Sees all that you do.[35]

Maulana Sanbhali says that the ending part of the above-quoted verse which reads: Except against a people with whom you have a treaty of mutual alliance" throws complete light on our present situation. The verse provides a guide line: If some Muslims are residing in a non-Muslim populace (non-Muslim sate) and they there face such a problem that may be resolved only through the interference of Muslim power or state. It is incumbent upon the Muslim power to help such helpless Muslims for the sake of Faith. However if there is a friendly and peaceful pact between that non-Muslim state and the Muslim power, then it is not lawful (even for the Apostle of Allah) to rush to assist these oppressed Muslims who are the seekers of help for the sake of the Faith (not for worldly affair), Maulana Sanbhali explains.

In order to clarify his point, Maulana Sanbhali offers his own example: "Suppose this non-Muslim state is Britain and I have officially acquired its citizenship. If Britain has waged a war unfortunately against any Muslim country; how it becomes legal and justified for me in Islam to fight against Britain while possessing its citizenship? Such an action is called treachery in Islamic Shariah.[36] "Beware!" Says Maulana, "Forbidding treachery is described in the midst of the dealings with the enemies like the Jews; it is not allowed with them also." [37]

Ghazwa's Call for Jihad

How the extremists explain the holy institution of Jihad in order to serve their own interests or how they are confused and misinterpreting it, it may be seen in their statements and speeches. After several bombings in New Delhi on 29th October, 2005 Indian media necessitated highlighting afresh the theory, practice and ideology of Lashkar Taibah allegedly involved in these blasts. In one of such writings Praveen Swami fully analyses the theoretical and ideological expositions of the *Lashkar*. According to that writeup just last month (October, 2005) the Lashkar served public notice of its intentions. In its September 23 issue, the *Lashkar* affiliated magazine *Ghazwa* editorially called for a renewal of Pakistani state support of the jihad in Jammu and Kashmir. India, it claimed, was working to divide Pakistani society "cunningly using the slogan of friendship", while at once supporting forces hostile to it in Baluchistan and Afghanistan. *Ghazwa* demanded the President Musharraf admit that the detente process had given Pakistan nothing and work instead "to fortify the Jihad."

Of arguments that continued support for Jihad imposed unacceptable costs upon Pakistan, *Ghazwa* was dismissive, elaborated Praveen Swami. "Now is the right time for Pakistan to support the *Jihad* in Kashmir,"*Gazwa* said, "Because America has entangled herself in the wars of Iraq, and Afghanistan· and in addition is suffering from severe afflictions like Katrina and Rita." "Pakistan should remember," the magazine asserted, "that even so-called super-power like the United States has been badly worn at the hands of the *Mujahideen*. Remember what happened to the Union of Soviet Socialist Republics and think about India: how can it resist the Jihad?"

Understanding the Lashkar position, argues Praveen Swami, requires an engagements with its core position: that the *jihad* in Jammu and Kashmir is not a battle over territory, but a part of an irreducible conflict between Islam and unbelief. Committed to the eventual creation of a caliphate that would rule over all the world's Muslims, the Lashkar asserts that a jihad – without – end must continue "until Islam, as a way of life, dominates the whole world and until Allah's law is enforced every where in the world."

The writer has quoted Yoginder Sikand, who has "perceptively" pointed out, "the Lashkar's vision of Islam is one that leads it to represent the Quran itself as a manifesto for jihad." Indian rule in Jammu and Kashmir is, in this construction, analyses the writer Praween Swami, necessarily evil and oppressive, because "the Hindus have no compassion in their religion." "In fact," Hafiz Mohammad Saeed, who heads *Markaz Dawah wa al-Irshad,* a seminary which turns a massive network of charitable and educational institutions in Pakistan, had declared some years ago, "the Hindu is a mean enemy and the proper way to deal with him is the one adopted by our forefathers, who crushed them by force." India is, in turn, part of just a global system of oppression that must be overthrown by force. As the Lashkar spokesperson Nazir Ahmad bluntly stated: "through the jihad that the *Mujahideen* have launched in Kashmir, Islam will become dominant all over the world."[38]

This confusing and misleading perception of *jihad* and Islamic domination is not confined to Lashkar-e-Taibah and its contemporaries in the subcontinent. The line of violence and terrorism taken in the last 20 years by few Muslim groups against their own Muslim governments or against America, Russia, Britain, France or other occupying foreign power in response to their oppressive policies or violent aggressions, pleaded the same arguments and their own theorization of jihad. The responding and retaliative violence allegedly committed by some Muslim groups across the world violated the Islamic standards of jihad and the Quranic criteria of using the violence if unavoidable.[39]

Yes. Jihad-without-end is the Islamic concept. But what does it mean? Whether the word *jihad* necessarily implies the actual fighting in all the cases? Then why another term of the Quran, *qital* that is exclusely for actual fighting and violence, was used frequently? And what does convey the Quranic verse, *wa jahidhum bihi jihadan Kabeera*[40] that reads: And strive (do jihad) against them with the utmost strenuousness with the (Quran)? These serious questions are to be responded in Islamic perspective by the *Lashkar* and its spokesmen.

What is the problem with Yoginder Sikand and the like? Why do they not accept the Quran as "a manifesto for jihad?" The holy Quran is of course a book of jihad that teaches how to fight evil, corruption, aggression and occupation. It is not advocating a passive, isolated, subjugated, oppressed and targeted life. It insists upon combating all the wrong. It justifies the use of violence but in the given situation and accompanying with certain standards. This Quranic jihad is all-pervading, multi-dimensional and conclusive. It calls the Muslims to stand for the establishment of justice, peace, security and universal human rights. It insists for ordering the good and forbidding the wrong. The misperceived and mispropagated jihad is of course out of the deliberation.

The *lashkar* and the like minded perhaps know that the classical jurists had divided the entire world into various categories of *dar al-Islam* (abode of Islam), *dar al-harb* (abode of war), *dar-al-kufr* (abode of paganism) and *dar al-amn* (abode of peace) correctly and suitably with their times. Now the situation is entirely changed. All the states have eagerly accepted the membership of United Nations and are now living in a plural culture and global environment. This now requires a new strategy and a new Islamic discourse.[41]

The *Lashkar* and other extremists perhaps are not capable to appreciate it and respond accordingly. This is the reason why Shaykh Yousuf al-Qaradhawi, the famous Islamic scholar and preacher has coined a new term *dar al-Dawah* (abode of preaching) that necessitates a cordial, co-operative, interacting and peace loving world. The Shaykh has cited from the Prophet's life the model of Mulim migrants to Ethiopia as the most suited to the contemporary plural world.[42]

Jihadist Islamic History

Some western scholars have studied the entire Islamic history from the Prophet till date in the jihadist/violent perspective and thus have projected the history as the most inspiring and motivating force to pursue the terrorist attacks in the modern world. I wondered to see the response of the columnist on *al-Jazeerah* net, Soumaya Ghannoushi that, "How political Islam develops is in the hands of the West".[43]

In this context, to have portrayed a 'jihadist history' seems a conspiracy plotted by the West against Islam and the Muslims. This jihadi's orientation of history was well designed and executed by John L. Esposito, the famous orientalist in one of his recent writings entitled "*Unholy War : Terror in the Name of Islam* though composed in post-9/11 scenario but equally important in its contents, spirit and way of arguments in the post- 7/7 London bombings. Esposito declares without any hesitation that:

> "The history of the Muslim Community from Muhammad to the present can be read within the frame work of what the Quran teaches about jihad".[44]

> "What are we to make out of this sweeping generalization," comments on it the famous Islamic scholar Ibrahim M Abu Rabi of Hartford Seminary, Connecticut, "except to say that the history of the Muslim world from the seventh century to the present has been subject to all sorts of political, social and economic factors and can not simply be explained by the impact of one text, however sacred it is, or one idea from that text. The history of the Muslim world in the past century or so has been subject to a myriad of fundamental forces such as nationalism, colonialism, westernization, globalization and religious fundamentalism, none of which has been monolithic in nature."[45]

Esposito is prompted by the events of September 11 to condemn the terror committed in the name of Islam. However, what was behind this horrible event in recent human history? Is it the "Islamic movement," or the Islamic notion of jihad, or the effort on the part of the disgruntled people who were left to their fates after the withdrawal of the Soviet Union from Afghanistan? Esposito is tentative in his approach to this question. He seems to have chosen the most comfortable, which is to yet again a survey of central Islamic theological concepts, such as jihad, and treat the position of Islam in the most general terms. However the main question is to be addressed is the method. Do we treat Islamism as a phenomenon or do we approach it through the writings of a few select individuals?

To gain an adequate understanding of Islamism, it seems to me, says further Prof. Abu Rabi, that one needs to state the following:

(1) Far from monolithic, Islamism (or fundamentalism) is a multi-layered phenomenon in the Muslim world. It is not a purely religious phenomenon.

(2) It is possible to delineate several phases of Islamism: precolonial, colonial and post-colonial.

(3) Islamism is the product of the major factors affecting the Muslim world in the past two centuries or so.

(4) Islamism in large measure is the product of modern European colonialism in the Muslim world and the failure of the modern nation-state to accommodate protest movements in their political systems.

(5) The relationship between Islamism and the state in the Muslim world has been complex. In the case of Wahhabism, Islamism and the state have been at odds. The state in the modern Muslim world is a nineteenth century creation prompted by European colonialism.

(6) As such, Islamism has never been a static phenomenon. It has invented a powerful religious discourse to legitimize itself in the eyes of the masses and gain political and economic support.

(7) Islamism has been in crisis for the last four decades for many complex reasons: first because the whole of Muslim tradition has been in crisis and second, because the new guard of Islamism is not satisfied with the achievements or lack there of on the part of the old

guard. This is true in the case of Wahhabism, and bin Laden is an example.

Therefore one must analyse Islamism or any other social or political movement in the Muslim world, or the Third World for that matter, in the context of the relationship between the Muslim world and the West since the dawn of colonialism, argues the writer. This context is the more important when one investigates the post-World War II climate in the world, the decline of traditional European colonial powers, the rise of the United States to a new colonial reality, and the rise of independent movements in the Third World. It is interesting to note, argues Prof. Abu Rabi, that overall since the 1940s, the United States has not favoured in any financial or political sense any truly democratic regime or any regime trying to chart an independent nationalist course. To the contrary, the United States fought against many democratically elected regimes in the last half century. The collapse of the Soviet system and the American intervention in the Gulf in 1990 did not change the picture. For a while, the United States has supported authoritarian regimes across the globe. Many of the political elite in the Muslim world, who found their anchor in American support to their decadent regimes, have diligently served American interests. That is why *jihad* is the last thing on the minds of these political elite. In addition in its drive toward globalization, the United States has cared less about the increasing number of the poor and more about its national interests in the Arab and Muslim worlds. Esposito does not think that globalization has been a major factor in American politics and economy.[46]

Esposito's main flaw, as Abu Rabi criticises, is that he assumes that Islamism is the product of ideas, most specifically, the idea of *jihad*. That is why he gives us a long detour into fourteen centuries of Islamic history to convince us that the terrorist attacks against the United States on September 11, 2001 were the product of the jihad ideology and the theology of Islam itself. To prove his point, Esposito goes on to analyse the worldview of Osama bin Laden, whom he calls "master or global terrorist."[47] The essential point here is that bin Laden is consumed by *jihad* and though this concept is moved by all sorts of external factors, jihad is a self-propelling philosophy.[48]

Prof. Abu Rabi insists on the point that it is always crucial to investigate the historical, social and political factors that lead to the rise of such an important phenomenon as "Islamist *jihad*" in Afghanistan, the Egyptian *jihad* movement or any other movements. Theology alone can not explain these phenomena, even if we helieve that the brand of theology these movements espouse is the "normative" or "true" one. That is why Esposito's drawn-out explanation of Islamic history to interpret the rise of *jihad* worldview in the modern era is a big waste of the readers' time.

Esposito notes, perhaps correctly, that "Bin Laden played to the Muslim sense of historic oppression, occupation and injustice at the hands of the West."[49] If this assessment was true before September 11, it is now more true than even, Abu Rabi goes on arguing : Yes, educated Muslims and Arabs feel that they are governed by oppressive regimes, most of which they say as allies of the West, especially the United States. "It is true that the U.S. is seen as treating the Arab world with a double standard as in the case of Arab-Israeli conflict. This is all true. But what is also real is the fact that the conditions that produced people like bin Laden or Ayman al-Zawahiri and other extremists in the Muslim world still exist, and may be more fertile than ever."[50]

A Shia Legacy

Christoph Reuter, who spent eight years to study in deep the phenomenon of suicide bombing in different countries of the world he, for an ideology of suicide refers Hassan bin Sabah and his followers in the second half of the 11th century. In western writings they are called the *Assassins* and in Muslim literature *Batiniyun.* They were the radical offshoot of Shia Ismailies. Their motive was to disrupt and destroy the Sunni ruling *Abbasids* (749-1258 AD). Bin Sabah took refuge in the inaccessible Elburz mountains in today's northern Iran. Here he conquered the fortress of Alamur in 1090 and laid the foundations of the *Fidais'* (self-sacrificer). In 1092 an Assassin under the guise of a sufi killed Nizamul Mulk. According to the author, this was the beginning of a 170-year-long series of targeted murders which turned a tiny sect in to the dreaded opponent of the great powers. 'They stabbed to death princes, generals, governors, two caliphs, even theologians and Franconian crusader lords, but never attempted to flee... The Assassins saw themselves as the avant-grade in the struggle against the oppressors and betrayers of true Islam, offering the most extreme proof of their strength of faith by their willingness to die. Their opponents, by contrast, saw them as a brand of deluded fanatics and murderers and painted the blackest possible picture them.[51] However the Assassins had no realistic plan for what to do the enemy be seriously weakened without actually being defeated. Later they lost much of their appeal and totally doomed in the Mongolian campaigns of conquest. The set disappeared without any trace, leaving behind no tradition, no religious heritage.

According to Christoph Reuter, notwithstanding the pretence of traditional religion in which their actions are typically clocked, suicide bombers are quintessentially modern interpretation of religion, whereas in all monotheistic religions-Judaism, Christianity and Islam-there is a ban on killing oneself. Because, the power over human life, including the right to take it away, belongs exclusively to God. But suicide bombers take their lives, and therefore their deaths, in to their own hands. The author further elaborates that murder by suicide began its modern-day renaissance at the start of 1980s, on the battlefields of the Iran-Iraq war.[52]

On September 22, 1980, the then Iraqi President Saddam Hussain invaded Iran on a 400-mile-wide front. Imam Khomaini declared *jihad* against Iraq. In this war, according to the author, even children were not spared. The mobilization of children was to be one of the state's prime objectives. Without seeking the parents' consent they were persuaded to join this war. 'In order to find stocks of human canon-fodder for the waves of attacks, recruiters trawled through the schools. They told the children the heroic epic of *Karbala* like a fairytale adventure, a grandiose stage on which they themselves were summoned to appear as heroes, as martyrs.'[53]

On some days, entire classes were taken directly to the barracks of Revolutionary Guards. The females were given only a short message that their sons had volunteered to go to war. After two-week training, the children had to go to the front. They hung the title "Key to paradise" around their necks. According to Reuter, from 1981 onwards, they sent 10,000 children in to the line of fire and across minefields. They were sent in order that their bodies would explode all the mines and thus clear the way for the soldiers that were following them. The author sums up many of the deaths were celebrated with a traditon that would find favour many years later with Sunni Palestinian suicide bombers in their homes in Gaza. In Iran, Bahisht-e-Zahra, became a big visiting place. Martyr's photo would be placed on the head stone of every grave.

In October 1983, the U.S Marines headquarters in Beirut was exploded by suicide bombers killing 141 American troops. A second bomb destroyed two six-storey quarters of the French parachutes killing soldiers. (58) They were forced to withdraw from Lebanon. The author claims the attacks were made by a group of Shiite radicals, then they ruled the western Beirut. Radical Lebanese Shiite group, Hizbullah, which officially appeared in 1985, but its cadres had been working years before, adopted the policy of suicide bombing. They were not unanimous in the beginning. The question was: under what circumstances could a human bomb be justified theologically? This was especially urgent in the light of the fact that, Shaikh Fadlallah, the highest religious authority in the region, initially refused to issue a *fatwa* to sanction the assassins, instead referring to the historically attested Islamic ban on suicide. Hizbullah leaders sought their justification directly from Iran. Shaikh Naim Qassem the Hizbullah 'number two' also justified it that these attacks had nothing to do with suicide – a fighter just "chooses the manner of method in which he will die," otherwise the time of death is fixed by God. Little by little an entire culture of martyrdom arose among the radical Shiites of Lebanon. However later, Hizbullah employed this method very selectively and joined and adopted the democratic method.

Outside the above world, *Hamas (Harakah al-muqawamah al-Islamiyah)* was the first to employ this method. Hamas was established in 1988 just one year after the *Intifada*. Palestinian Islamists; who neither wanted to place themselves under the Arafat-dominated united command that had quickly taken hold of the uprising, nor stand on the side lines as passive observers, formed *Hamas*, which divided its functions between a political civil arm and a military one the Ezzuddin al-Qassam Brigade, named after the *mujahid* (died in 1935) who built up an armed organization in Haifa in the 1920s. This Brigade started suicide attacks on Israeli soldiers in 1989, with the aim of fuming Gaza in to a living hell for the Israeli occupiers. When in December 1992, Isreal expelled 415 leading cadres of *Hamas Islamic Jihad* to southern Lebanese hills for a year, their direct interaction with Hizbullah started, and according to Reuter, they learned both the techniques of suicide attacks and religious justification.[54]

This brief survey of the origin and development of the ideology of suicide bombing in Shia tradition also reveals no justification on the firm ground. The logic of Shaikh Naim Qassem that these attackes have no concern with the suicide prohibited in Shariah and that a fighter just "chooses the method in which he will die," is basically an insult to be differentiated. Then what would be meant by the term suicide? The decision of a man to put himself in to death or to choose the method of his death has essentially no distinction in between the two. This was the reason perhaps why Shaikh Fadlallah did not approve it. In Shia tradition also there was no legal and religious sanction to this ideology in the pre-Khomaini history.

If there is no Islamic justification to the suicide bombing, what made the young Muslims, raised in this society, do this? Bush, Blair and their fellow warlords have a pre-conceived answer. Muslims are "in the grip of a dangerous cult" of the "poisonous misinterpretation of Islam." But a thorough study of 7/7 blasts and the multi-dimensional factors responsible for that tragedy and of the evangelicalism[55] of the West reveal, as Mr. Abdullah Jan has observed "It is not some kind of inspiration due to misinterpretation of Islam, but depression and desperation as a result of the lies and double standards of those who have exploited freedom and democracy to the extent of turning it into some thing worse than a death cult."[56]

The problem with the West in general and U.S. and U.K. in particular is that they cannot afford to accept an urgent need to revise their policies towards Islam and the Muslims and are therefore too anxious to highlight anti-western and pro-Islamic political opinion as the key that explains the bombings. In this campaign against what Tony Blair called "extremist ideology" they include not only political activism inspired by Sayyid Qutb, Sayyid Maududi and others but also the fundamentals of Islam. The most hitted figure among the modern Islamic thinkers is of course Sayyid Qutb – the ideologue of the Islamic movement in *Egypt-al-Ikhwan al-Muslimun,* now banned by Hosni Mubarak government but still survived as the most influential, deeply-rooted, moderate movement not only in its birth place but in the entire Arab world. Simply because he advocated a resurgent, politically active and dynamic Islam, and fought against the western-supported authoritative Egyptian government and criticized severely the morally bankrupt and politically exploiting and occupying West, Qutb can not be declared as the "champion of terrorism."

Resistance to occupation, as well remarked by Haifa Zangana, the Iraqi-born novelist and former prisoner of Saddam Hussain's regime, is a basic human right as well as a moral responsibility[57]. That was the case during the Algerian war of independence, the Vietnamese war of independence, and it is the case now in Iraq, Palestine and every where.

Notes and References

1. See Seumas Milne, Insult to deny Iraq link to London attacks The Guardian, July 14, 2005, also visit: **s-milne@guardian.com.UK**. On November 10, 2005, a day after American forces called off their assault on Husaybiyah, a town along the Iraq –Syria border they said was an Al-Qaeda stronghold, a suicide bomber blew himself up in a restaurant in Baghdad. At least 30 persons were killed and 19 wounded in the strike on Thursday. Iraqi police forces have been known to frequent the restaurant in Baghdad. At least 30 persons were killed and 19 wounded in the strike on Thursday. Iraqi Police forces have been known to frequent the restaurant. Witnesses said the explosion in the city centre was so powerful it could be heard several kilometers away. The attack came after the Iraqi wing of Al-Qaeda claimed in an online statement that it avenged the attack by the United States on Husaybiyah. For five days an estimated 30000 Iraqi and US troops backed by aerial support had pounded the town. The US claimed Husaybiyah was the nerve centre for smuggling in weapons and Islamist militants across the border from Syria.

   On the same day and for the first time since the US invasion of Iraq, a spate of bombings has rocked Jordan's capital Amman. Serial blasts shook three American-owned hotels, causing massive casualties. It is estimated that 57 people have been killed in the near-simultaneous explosions at the Grant Hayqat, Radisoon and Days Inn hotels. Nearly 300 people, mostly Jordanians, were injured. Al-Qaeda in Iraq, led by Jordon-born Abu Musab al-Zarqawi, has claimed responsibility for the attack, "A group of four best lions launched a new attack on some dens.... After casing the targets, some hotels were chosen which the Jordanian despot turned into a backyard for the enemies of the faith, Jews and Crusaders", the statement on a Website, usually used by the group, said, "Let the tyrant of Amman know that his protection.... for the Jews has become a target for the Mujahideen and their attacks, and let him expect the Worst", it added.

Mr. Atul Aneja says that the targeting of Jordan has not come as a surprise. Amman has been the chief ally of US in the region in its occupation of Iraq. US present including private "security contractors" transit through Amman in order to travel to Iraq. The UN also has a strong presence in Amman ever since Al-Qaeda demolished its Canal hotel headquarters in Baghdad in August 2003. This country has been known to provide the occupation forces with intelligence... Britain has been training Jordanian Special Forces since 1997. Another reason for resentment is that Jordan, along with Egypt, is the only other Arab nation that has signed a peace treaty with neighbouring Israel. It's security situation becomes all the more wobbly as a majority of its population is of Palestinian origin. Atul Aneja is of the view that two-and-a half years of US rule has converted Iraq into an Al-Qaeda hub, which has now begun to radiate violence and extremism in the region. Inspite of all these realities the West-supported Jordanian king remains a severe victim of "official otherworldliness" and is not ready like his western counterparts to read the writings on the wall. See, Atul Aneja, American occupation and the Rise of Al-Qaeda, *The Hindu*, November 11, 2005.

2. *Radiance*, Vol. XL, No. 12, 31 July – 6Aug. 05, p. 19.

3. The holy Quran, al-Maidah: 35. The verse basially refers to Israel but is equally applied to others. Israel rebelled against God, slew and insulted righteous men who did them no harm but on the contrary came in all humility. When God withdrew His favour from Israel because of its sins and bestowed it on a brother nation, the jealousy of Israel plunged it deeper in to sin. To kill or seek to kill an individual is to kill the whole mankind. What could be stronger condemnation of individual assassination and revenge?

4. *Radiance*, 31 July – 6Aug. 05, p. 19.

5. Editorial, *Crescent International*, vol., 34, No.6, August 2005, p. 3-4.

6. Ziauddin Sardar, *Desperately Seeking Paradise: Journeys of A Sceptical Muslim*, Granta Publications, London, 2004, 354 pages.

7. Quoted in Jawed Ali, A Questioning Muslim in Search of Paradise, (a review on Sardar's above –quoted book), *Radiance* viewsweekly, Vol. XL, No. 12, 31 July – 6 August 2005, p. 25.

8. Interview with Maulana Maududi in *Nawai Waqt, Lahore,* November 11, 1963, p. 4. See for more references, Fahad, Obaidullah, Jihad: Violent or *non-Violent, Studies on Islam.* Delhi, Vol.1, No.1, 2004, pp. 78-99.

9. Shaykh Yousuf al-Qaradhawi, Filistin al-Muslimah, London, Rabi al-Thani, 1417 AH/ September 1996, pp. 51-52, Urdu translation and Summary by Prof. Masudur Rahman Khan Nadvi, *Zindagi* Nau, Delhi, March 1997, pp. 18-20.

10. Hafiz Ibn Kathir narrates this tradition having ascribed to Abu Dawud, Tirmidhi, Nasai, Abu Yala, Ibn Hibban and al-Hakim and declares it authentic (*sahih*) according to the recquisites mentioned by Bukhari and Muslim. See *Tafsir al-Quran al-Azeem*. Halbi Publications, Vol. 1, pp. 228-229.

11. The Holy Qruan, 9:111.

12. The Holy Quran, 3:169.

13. The Holy Quran, 2: 207.

14. The Holy Quran, 31:17.

15. Imam Hakim has narrated this hadith through Jabir and has declared it *sahih* (authentic). Imam Dhahabi has criticized its' authenticity while Albani has accepted it aunthentic as per narration from Khatib in *Tarikh Baghdad*, which reads: "the chief of the martyrs is Hamzah and the man who stood against an oppressing leader; checked him; ordered him (for right) and forbad him (from wrong) and was slained.

16. This is quoted by Abu Dawud, Tirmidhi and Ibn Majah; Tirmidhi has categorized it as *hasan ghareeb*. According to al-Mundhiri, Imam Nasai has narrated it through the true channel of Tariq bin Shihab al-Muntaqua (hadith no. 1364).

17. Abu Dawud, *Kitab al-Sunan*, No. 2511, Ahmad bin Hanbal, *al-Musnad*, No. 7997. Shaykh Shakir has accepted the hadith true (*sahih*). Ibn Hibban has also narrated it in His *Sahih*.

18. Abu Bakr Jassas, *Ahkam al-Quran*, vol. 1, pp. 262-263.

19. Muhammad bin Ahmad al-Qurtubi, *Al-Jami li Ahkam al-Quran (Tafsir al-Qurtubi)*, Dar al-Kutub al-Misriyah, Vol. 2, p. 363.
20. Fakhruddin Razi, *Mafatih al-Ghayb* (Tafsir Kabeer or Tafsir Razi) Vol. 2, p. 148.
21. The Holy Quran 4:84.
22. Ibn Kathir, *Tafsir al-Quran al-Karim* (Tafsir Ibn Kathir), Halbi Publications, Vol. I p. 229.
23. Ibn Jarir Tabari, *Jami al-Bayan fi, Tafsir al-Quran*, ed. Mahmud Muhammad Shakir, Dar al-Maarif, Egypt, Vol. 3, pp. 588-589.
24. Who were the makers of the pit of fire (referred to in the holy Quran, chapter al-*Buruj*) in which they burnt people of their Faith? The words of the Quran are perfectly general, and one needs not search for particular names except by way of illustration. In ancient history, and in Medieval Europe, many lives are sacrificed at the stake, because the victims did not conform to the established religion. In Arab tradition there is the story of Abraham: Nimrud tries to burn him to death, but on account of Abraham's Faith, the fire became " a means of safety" (The Quran, 21:66). Another case cited is that of Zu Nuwas, the last Himayarite king of Yemen, by religion a Jew, who persecuted the Christians of Najran and is said to have burnt them at the stake. He seems to have lived in the later half of the sixth Christian century, in the generation immediately preceding the Propeht's birth in the 570AD. While the words in the Quran are quite general, a reference is suggested to the persecution to which the early Muslims were subjected by the Pagan Quraish. Among other cruelties, they were stripped, and their skins were exposed to the burning rays of the Arabian summer sun. Abdullah Yusuf Ali, *The Holy Quran – Text, Translation and Commentary*. Amana Corp. 1983, p. 1714 footnote No. 655.
25. Ibn Taimiyah, *Majmu Fatawa Shaykh al-Islam*, Vo. 28, p. 540.
26. Muhammad bin Ali Shawkani, *Fath al-Qadaeer*, Dar al-Wafa publications, Egypt, Vol. 1, p. 262.
27. Muhammad Rashid Rida, *Tafsir al-Manar*, Egypt, vol. 2. p. 213.
28. Shaykh Yousuf al-Qaradhawi, *Zindagi Nau*, op.cit., pp. 21-30. It infers from the translator's notes added in the beginning of the article that Prof. Nadvi, the learned translator is fully convinced with the opinion and arguments of Shaykh Qaradhwai.

29. Amin Ahsan Islahi, *Dawat-e-Din Awr Uska Tariq-e-Kar*, (Preaching of the Religion and Its Methodology), Delhi, pp. 241-242. (translated by Asif Iftikhar) courstesy: *The Milli Gazette*, vol. 6, No. 5, 1-15 August 2005, p. 29.

30. Prof. Dr. Khalid Hamidi, (editor) *Allah Ki Pukar* Monthly, N. Delhi vol. 14, No. 87, October 2005, p. 115. The editor has unambiguously called Shayk Qaradhawi "the chief of modern Khawarij" (vol. 14, No. 85, August 2005, p. 81) and repeatedly defended his own stand (vol. 14, No. 87, October, 2005, 116). One may agree or disagree with the views of Shaykh Qaradhawi but none is "advisable" to defame his personality and challenge his respectability in the Muslim community. Accusation and labelling does not suit the serious scholarship.

31. The Holy Quran, 2: 205.

32. The Holy Quran, 7: 85.

33. Malik bin Anas, *Kitab al-Muatta*, the Chapter on, Ahkam al-Khilafah, bab al-Nahy an al-ghulul Wa al-ghadar.

34. Dr. Muhammad Nijatullah Siddiqui, Tashaddud Awr Musalman (Violence and the Muslims) *Zindagi Nau*, N. Delhi, Vol. 30, No.3, March, 2004, pp. 35-36.

35. The Holy Quran, 8:72.

36. The Holy Quran, 8:58. The immediate occasion was the repeated treachery of the Banu Quraiza after their treaties with the Muslims. But the general lesson remains obligatory, as noted in the verser (56-58). Treachery in war is doubly wrong, for it endangers so many lives. Such treachery should be punished in such a way that it gets no chance again. Not only the actual perpetrators but those who follow their standard should be rendered powerless. And the broken treaty should be denounced so that the innocent party can at least fight on equal terms. Abdullah Yusuf Ali, op.cit., p. 429, foot note No. 1224.

37. Ateequr Rahman Sanbhali, Hamara Din Din-e-Wafa hai! (Our Religion is the religion of truthfulness!) *Al-Furqan*, Lucknow, Vol. 73, No. 11, November 2005/Shawwal 1426AH/pp. 9-17.

38. Praveen Swami, The Lashkar-e-Taiba, in Theory and Practice, *The Hindu* November 3, 2005. the writer has tried the best to prove the involvement of the Lashkar in the Delhi serial

bombing on October 29, 2005. To the writer, others to have demonstrated both the intent and capability needed to strike across India in the past. Bilal Beig's Jammu and Kashmir Islamic Front, which allegedly bombed Delhi's Lajpat Nagar in 1996, has been showing signs of revival. Both the *Jaish-e-Mohammad* and the *Hizb-ul-Mujahidden* have suspectedly carried out operations outside the valley in the past. Yet the author argues, given the strength of Lashkar's infrastructure and its deep links with Pakistan's military establishment, it is without doubt the principal terrorist threat to India today.

39. Dr. Muhammad Nijatullah Siddiqui, op.cit., p. 33.

40. The Holy Quran, 25:52. The verse clearly categorises another method – as opposed to the western image – of jihad that is intellectual and argumentative one.

41. Professor Khurshid Ahmad, *Amrika – Muslim Duniya Ki Be Itminani* (America – The Muslim world dissatisfied with), Manshuraat, Lahore (ed. Saleem Mansur Khalid), 2002, p. 284.

42. Quoted in, *Ibid*, pp. 284-285.

43. Soumaya Ghannoushi, Many Faces of Islam, *The Hindu*, October 6, 2005.

44. John L. Esposito, *Unholy War: Terror in the Name of Islam*, Oxford University Press, New York, 2002, p. 27.

45. Ibrahim, M. Abu Rabi, *The Muslim world*, Vol. 92, Fall, 2002, p. 498.

46. Esposito, Op.cit., p. 153.

47. Ibid., p. 07.

48. Ibid., p. 11.

49. Ibid., p. 22.

50. Abu Rabi, op.cit.,pp. 494-500.

51. Christoph Reuter, *My Life Is A Weapon: A Modern History of Suicide Bombing,* Manas Publications, New Delhi, 2005, p.25.

52. Ibid., p. 11.

53. Ibid., p. 44.

54. See for a critique of Christoph Reuter, Jawed Ali, Suicide Bombing: A Shia Legacy? Radiance views weekly, Vol. XL, No. 16, 28 August-3 September 2005, pp. 26-27. This discussion on Shia Legacy is basically derived from this source.

55. MSNBC's reporter Alex Johnson writers how Bush, for example, undergoes conversion to evangelicalism, which is called the 'born again experience described in John 3:3, when a sinner undergoes an intense conversion during a personal interaction with the Holy Spirit, often Jesus Himself. "Bush" has often said he was pointed on the earth to God after a discussion with evangelist Billy Graham in 1985". In Bush's words over the course of that weekend, Reverend Graham planted a mustard seed my soul, a seed that grew over the next year. He led me to the path, and I began walking. It was the beginning of the change in my life. I had always been a "religious" person, had regularly attented church, even taught Sunday school and served as an altar boy. But that weekend my faith took on a new meaning.It was the beginning of a new walk where I would commit my heart Jesus Christ". The secret of this story is in that conversion to extremist Christianity – and so is part of the crisis in the U.S.,U.K. and other contries.

56. Abidullah Jan, The Death Cult or Super Fascism, *Radiance* Views weekly. Vol. XL, No. 12, 31 July-6 August 2005, p. 17.

57. Haifa Zangana, Iraq now worse than under Saddam. *The Guardian*, January 4, 2007.

7

RESISTANCE Vs.TERRORISM

Godfather of Resistance

Sayyid Qutb(1906-1966) is perhaps the most accused, misunderstood and misinterpreted Islamic figure in the modern world. John L. Esposito in one of his recent books has described him as the "godfather of Muslim extremist movements"[1] without delving in any real sense into his worldview and the conditions surrounding his life.

Esposito has portrayed Qutb as a writer and thinker who transformed the ideology of Hassan al-Banna and Maududi into a "rejectionist revolutionary call to arms", and whose interpretations of jihad were linked by Osama bin Laden or the leaders of other terrorist groups to their "militant jihadist worldview"[2]. He bluntly claims that the Wahhabi name is primarily designated to Saudi Arab's ultra conservative Islam, while its second and overtly political meaning is "Islamic extremism, radicalism, and terrorism with a direct connection to the Taliban and bin Laden". The blanket use of Wahhabi to describe militant jihad groups "obscures more than it enlightens. Organizations and movements are branded as Wahhabi because they possess common "family resemblances" such as "ultraconservative, literalist, puritanical and exclusivist religious doctrines'. However, many of these movements, as well as Osama bin

Laden, actually owe more to the "militant ideology" of Sayyid Qutb or Egyptian radical groups.[3]

Following the same line, Britain-based Pakistani writer Ziauddin Sardar charges the allegations of violence and terrorism on *al-Ikhwan al-Muslimun* in general and Sayyid Qutb in particular having based his arguments entirely on military junta's statements. Sardar normally exposes himself as a Muslim who questions and criticizes the Shariah but in this case he does not use his faculty of reasoning and evaluation and believes blindly in the dictators of Egypt. He unambiguously says that during the mid-1940s its members were implicated in terrorist activities inside Egypt; in December 1948 the Egyptian Prime Minister, Mahmud Fahmi Nokrashi was assassinated by a member of the organization, in retaliation Hassan al-Banna himself was killed by government's agents in Cairo in February 1949.' He again writes that on October 24, 1954 a member of the Organization attempted to assassinate Nasser as he spoke before an immense crowd in Alexandria. Nasser responded by summarily executing six conspirators and arresting over a thousand activists of the Brotherhood including Qutb, who was sentenced to 15 years' imprisonment. He was released in 1964 only to be arrested on charges of sedition. The prosecution's case was built largely on the inflammatory passages contained in Qtub's *Milestones* published in 1964. He was sentenced to death and hanged on August 29, 1966'.[4]

A French scholar trying his best to revive Refa'ah al-Tahtawi's thought in the current discourse of enlightenment in the Arab and Muslim countries predicts the trend represented in the 'puritan Islam' might have led to extremism and violence as an enlightening and emancipating Islam was initiated in the nineteenth century Egypt by the prominent thinker al-Tahtawi. The "progressive Muslims" in the modern age have been counting themselves as the 'children of Tahtawi', as the both writer and his publisher claim; they are obstinate to their faith and culture and supportive to the spirit of enlightenment as well as are resistant openly to the religious extremism. The French writer advocates a sound tie with these natural allies of the West in the Arab world. He interviewed with these 'children of Tahtawi' from across the Arab world and the Muslim countries like Turkey. Iran, Indonesia and Bangladesh probably post 11 September 2001.

According to the French analyst who is primarily concerned with the peace and security of the West, Egypt is the source of the disease and its remedy simultaneously since it has the tremendous affect on the religious and cultural dimensions of the Arab and Muslim world. He ascribes the puritanism, violence and extremism in Islam largely to Sayyid Qutb and assumes on his own line of thinking bin Laden as the follower of Qutb and claims that this ideology is a novel in Islam and is rooted in the clash with the western modernization, and is nourished in the failures of attempts made in the previous century in order to follow the West and compromise with the modernization. The writer says that this ideology (of Islamism) as is practiced in Afghanistan, Iran and Sudan is harmful to the West and is tarnishing the image of Muslims.[5]

How a man who has deep knowledge of the situation and an insight in the ideologies of Ikhwan and its ideologue Sayyid Qutb, can accept these allegations. Very interesting is the fact that non-Muslim scholars like Esposito and others usually talk in terms of "the repressive Egyptian state",[6] "moral decadence of the West"[7] , "Anti-Arab, pro-Jewish coverage in the newspapers, and movies" [8] of the United States, "ten years of imprisonment in the equipment of a concentration camp," and "repressive, anti-Islamic governments and societies"[9] and other factors responsible for the radicalization of Qutb. The ultra-secularists like Sardar are not ready to accept any such causes and to give any microscopic concession to Muslim Brotherhood and Qutb. Sayyid Maududi used to say in his life repeatedly:

"The Muslim governments and their dictators sentence the death against those activities and reasons that are normally counted in a non-Muslim government as one responsible for the punishment of imprisonment. The Muslim dictators, nevertheless, would be remembered as champion and conqueror *(ghazi)* in the life and as 'God-blessed' (*rahmatullah alaih)* after the death". This applies to extremely secularist Muslims also.

These scholars and journalists do not distinguish between the Muslim thinkers and revivalists claiming for the resurgence of Islam through political process and those activists striving for armed revolution. They are also confused about the fighters against the foreign occupation and those who – just contradictory to the first group – are involved in violent activities against the civilians. The West in its campaign of 'war on terror' has gradually initiated the fighting against Islamic teachings of resistance. Those Muslim writers, thinkers and activists who discuss the West as morally decadent, condemn Israel or talk in terms of the superiority of Islam over other religions are also criticized and targeted. "The key question" says Iqbal N. Siddiqui, "is how we understand Islam. The West would like us to see it in purely personal "religious" terms, but for most Muslims Islam is far more than that; it includes principles for collective social morality, and demands that we enjoin good in the broadest possible sense. That is why Muslims all over the world see Islam as central to their politics ... That is why Muslims criticize Western societies – for many of the same ills that Westerners themselves highlight – in Islamic terms, and that is why Islam is envoked whenever and wherever Muslims fight against aggression and oppression; which usually means, in the modern world, against western governments or their allies, or both. This broader, more complete understanding of Islam what the West is more definitely at war with; both because westerners are at war with any thing that stands in the way of their hegemony and interests, and because of the deep-seated and irrational hatred for Islam that many secular westerners harbour".[10]

Take the case of Sayyid Qutb, the pioneer of Islamic resistance in the Arab and Muslim world. The very excerpts cited by Esposito reveal a resurgent, dynamic and politically dominant Islam. These quotations from Qutb advocate a legitimate jihad against all kinds of occupations and oppressions.

Modern *Jahiliyah*

Sayyid Qutb's main emphasis has been on creating a society similar to that established by the Prophet of Islam on the foundations of sovereignty of God. The models for education and training of this society would be the first unique generation of Muslims whose instructions came solely from one pure source, the Quran. "From it we must also derive our concepts of life, our principles of government, politics, economics, and all other aspects of life"[11] because "our foremost objective is to change the practices of this society ... to change the *jahili* system at its very roots – this system which is fundamentally at variance with Islam and which, with the help of force and oppression is keeping us from living the sort of life which is demanded by our Creator."[12]

Qutb used the classical designation for the pre-Islamic Arabian society, *Jahiliyah* – a period of ignorance – to paint and condemn the modern societies based on violation of God's rules as un-Islamic and anti-Islamic:

> "We must free ourselves from the clutches of *jahili* society, *jahili* concepts, *jahili* traditions and *jahili* leadership. Our mission is not to compromise ... nor can we be loyal to it... We will not change our values and concepts ... to make a bargain with this *jahili* society. Never! We and it are on different roads, and if we take even one step

> in its company, we will lose our goal entirely and lose our way as well".[13]

Sayyid Qutb theorized the 'modern ignorance' and outlined its basic features so much so that he could be considered the exponent of *jahiliyah par excellence*. He, unlike his brother Mohammad Qutb who could not declare the total disappearance of Islam from the society, be it socially or politically,[14] advanced a rigorous classification of all the modern societies:

> "*Jahiliyah* has the same characteristics, irrespective of time and place. Whenever people's hearts are devoid of a divine doctrine that governs their thought, and concomitant legal rules to regulate their lives, *jahiliyah* is bound to rear its head in one form or another.... The one in which contemporary societies wallow is not different in its nature from that of ancient Arabia before the rise of Islam..... Humanity is today living in a large brothel! One has only to take a glance at its press, films, fashion shows, beauty contests, ballrooms, wine bars, and broadcasting stations! Or observe its mad lust for naked flesh, provocative postures, and sick suggestive statements in literature, the arts, and the mass media! And add to all this, the system of usury which fuels man's voracity for money and engenders vile methods for its accumulation and investments, in addition to fraud trickery, and blackmail dressed up in the garb of law."[15]

Qutb explains the Islamic movements in the Muslim world must be actively engaged to establish the Islamic society because the present governments and societies are repressive and anti-Islamic:

> "It is necessary to revive that Muslim community. ... which is crushed under the weight of those false laws and customs which are not even remotely related to the Islamic teachings, and which inspite of all this, calls itself the "world of Islam".[16]

Jahiliyah, as an Islamic concept, was first articulated by the Indian scholar Sayyid Abul Ala Maududi in 1939. for Maududi, modernity was "the new barbarity", incorporating values, lifestyles, political theories, and systems of government that were, in his view, fundamentally incompatible with Islam.[17] In 1950 another Indian scholar Syed Abul Hasan Ali al-Nadwi the then Rector of Darul Uloom Nadwatul Ulama Lucknow, published a book in Arabic entitled *What has the World lost by the Decline of the Muslims*? It immediately became a best-seller and was warmly received by a great number of Muslim men of letters, particularly in Egypt where it was first printed, before its translation in to Urdu in 1954. As its title indicates, the book primarily seeks to explain the decline of Islam by offering a historical account of its rise, expansion and gradual regression.[18] The authors' depiction of Muslim decadence, which is seen to have taken place under the Ottomans, is followed by a grim description of "the genealogy of western civilization', embracing the Greeks, the Romans, Christianity, materialism, the theory of evolution, nationalism and scientific progress. His verdict is unambiguous: 'Christian Europe' has become in its entire civilization 'pagan and materialistic' (*jahiliyah madaniyah*). The Muslims have been forced to join in this mad pursuit of materialism, turning in to 'mere passengers' in a train driven by European nations. Nevertheless, al-Nadwi asserts, the Muslims are essentially immune to outright 'pagan materialism since their spiritual heritage is 'still preserved in its pristine purity.'[19]

Maududi's writings on the theme served to highten the exclusive nature of Islam. He branded modern political ideologies with the stigma of paganism, along with certain politicians, intellectuals and misguided individuals in the Islamic world. Muslims in general were still considered worthy of carrying the name of their religion once its principles were fully explained to them. Hence, although *jahiliyah* reared its head during the reign of the third caliph Uthman (644-56) and gradually overwhelmed the community under the Umayyads (661-750) and the Abbasids (750-1258) "it would be wrong to say that Islam at any time was wholly routed and completely overpowered by this onslaught of *jahiliyah*".[20]

Qutb theorized this exclusive nature of Islam. To his writings, nationalism, secularism, socialism, capitalism, communism and democracy constitute one single entity which has developed in the West in direct opposition to the message of original Islam. He explicitly defines:

> "......the callers to Islam should not have any superficial doubts in their hearts concerning the nature of *Jahiliyah* and the nature of Islam and the characteristics of *dar al-harb* and of *dar al-Islam* for through these doubts many are led to confusion. Indeed there is no Islam in a land where Islam is not dominant and where its Shariah is not established; and that place is not *dar al-Islam* where Islam's way of life and its laws are not practised."[21]

Americanised Islam

In June 1952, Sayyid Qutb coined a term 'Americanised Islam' – Islam as portrayed in the American and pro-American literature – to condemn the American vested interests in the Middle East. The Americans and their allies were taking keen interests in the studies of Islam because of their emergent need of survival against the communism, though they were combating Islam since nine centuries or more. They need Islam today just as-not more than-they need Germany, Japan and Italy targeted and destroyed in the last world war, in order to fight the ghost of communism, Qutb says.[22]

This Americanised Islam to be implanted in the Middle East neighter fights against colonialism nor occupation and oppression; it fights against communism only. They desire no government of Islam nor can tolerate it. Because when Islam will dominate, it will educate and train the nations to acquire power and defeat colonial forces since both the colonialism and communism are two sides of a coin – the enmity and hostility against Islam, Qutb argues.[23]

That was the reason, to Qutb, why the Egyptian media revolved around Islamic issues. The journals and periodicals that had no knowledge of nor any commitment with Islam earlier, were now full of the Islamic debates. The "professional theologians" had now gained name and fame, status and dignity and financial resources. Now they organized essay competitions on "Islam and communism" with the pronouncements of heavy prizes and prestigious awards, but the original Islam that combats colonialism and communism as well, none talks about that. The Islam that governs the life and dictates the true orientation is explained by none. "Islamic view of family planning may be traditionally discussed, joining the parliament by an woman may be ascertained in Islam. But the view of Islam of our economic, financial or social problems can not be traced back. Our political and national issues and our relations with the colonialism can never be examined in Islamic perspective. 'Islam and democracy', 'Islam and good conduct', Islam and justice are the topics that may cover the scope of essays, more interestingly a fully fledged book may be prepared, but 'Islamic system of government' 'Legislation and Islam' the Domination of Islam" are the topics on which no one needs to opine or to make them under discussion".[24]

"The Americanised Islam", bitterly says Qutb, "was informed of something like Zakah if implemented again in Middle East, the growing communist trend might be combated. Consequently the "Circle of Social Studies" established only last year in Egypt started taking keen interest in the themes like the system of Islamic social security and Zakah, and initiated a series of debates on the topics like this. Since the motivating factor was from America none on the part of Egyptian authority and administration opposed it. They had severely condemned the scheme of implementing Zakah at the time when Abdul Hamid Abdul Haq, the then Minister of Social Welfare planned the same. These authoritative people may oppose when ordered by Allah. They have no option except to surrender willingly when instructed by the Americans".[25]

But what is satisfying is the active presence and dynamic leadership of the faithfuls like those, says firmly Qutb, "who fight against colonialism, aggression as well as communism; who know very well that Islam should reign in order to produce its entire fruits; who may not be deceived by the crusaders' friendship imported in Islam since they are fully aware of nine centuries' enmity and hostility of the crusaders with Islam". These champions of Islam, says the writer indicating clearly the Ikhwan *mujahids*, "do not wish any benevolence for their sake; they rather demand the complete social justice. They do not exploit their services and commitments to gain from colonial forces; they are desirous of justice, dignity and self-respect. They do not use their sacrifices for any propaganda campaign; they instead make them a shield in their struggle for truth".[26]

Islamic Vanguard

Sayyid Qutb in early 1960 published a book entitled *al-Islam wa Mushkilat al-Hadharah* (Islam and the Problems of Civilization) in which he advocated for the first time in his career the necessity of organizing 'a body of believers ' (*usbah muminah*) to be existed by the faith of one man.[27] This new corps would be confined to the 'chosen elite' (*al-safwah al-mukhtārah*), the vanguard of professional revolutionaries who dedicate their whole life to one purpose. Well disciplined, highly-organized and imbued with the spirit of a new era in the long march of Islam, they can not fail to win.[28]

This compact group is, moreover, directly modeled on the physical and political structures of its enemy. As contemporary paganism Qutb argues, is not simply a theoretical formula, but a dynamic movement in command of a society, which constitutes an organic whole, Islam itself must be embodied in a dynamic association of its own, surpassing its rivals ideologically and structurally. This is the only way to possess the capability of obliterating a new cycle of *jahiliyah*. Being dynamic like a living organism, the vanguard has to demarcate its own spatial boundaries by asserting its unequivocal independence. It can not, therefore, allow political expediencies to impinge on its ultimate aim – the seizure of political power. All other issues – parliamentary elections, amending the constitution or expounding the details of an exhaustive programme – become futile exercises in casuistry. Exclusively built on doctrinal allegiances, the vanguard shuns the lower forms of earthly loyalties.[29]

Thus the battle lines are clearly drawn: two antagonistic forces face each other in a life and death fight. The inevitability of a violent encounter between two irreconcilable entities necessitates an immediate dissociation and separation from the battleground of the enemy. Each side is then instantly recognized by its organization and leadership, titles and labels, ideology, loyalty and way of life. This declaration of war entails at the practical level the withdrawal into a new society which rejects all the laws of the old one. However, it is an internal withdrawal within one's own country, and takes place as a policy of non-co-operation at the political, educational and administrative levels. This idea of migration from the land of unbelief to settle in that of belief is creatively reinterpreted so that only the form is modified.[30]

Jihad is then the continuation of God's politics. It is an obligation that becomes incumbent on the believers whenever the tenets and rules of Islam are violated or neglected. In this sense jihad is a form of political struggle designed, as Qutb argues, to disarm the enemy so that Islam is allowed to apply its *Shariah* unhindered by the oppressive power of idolatrous tyrannies. By the mere removal of the political obstacles, the central aim of revolutionary struggle is accomplished, a fact which refutes the charge of forcible conversion. This is, for example, the correct meaning of the Quranic statement: 'there is no compulsion in religion'. This Quranic verse presupposes the hegemony of Islam in society, thereby freeing individuals from the political domination of non-Muslim rulers. Once political power is in the hands of the new Islamic elite, and its divine laws are firmly established, the subjects of the state are given the choice either to embrace Islam or persist in practicing their inherited religions and beliefs. However, this tolerance is a conditional agreement concluded between a victorious party and vanquished subjects.[31]

Qutb viewed that the jihad against non-Islamic oppressive forces would be actualized through the emergence of a corps of believers to which he attached a new term of (*taliah)* vanguard. In the light of its crucial importance, the vanguard should be provided with 'signposts' to guide it along the tortuous road towards the ultimate destination. These signposts spell out the exact nature of the struggle, delineate its initial and final stages, and clarify the functions of this brave vanguard.[32]

Qutb has firmly established that the whole world is living in a state of religious ignorance (*jahiliyah*) and wallowing in a sink of iniquity. This is an essential fact that has to be grasped and kept in mind at each interval of the journey. A true believer can not fail to see that all societies are governed by persons who devise their own laws, and in this way transgress God's legislative authority, His most exclusive attribute and prerogative. This universal transgression is the underlying reason for moral degeneration, and which manifests itself in psychological dilemmas, personal misery and spiritual viciousness. One has only to survey the available statistics in Western societies in divorce, illicit sexual relationships, illegitimate children, homosexuality, promiscuity, drunkenness, gambling and suicide, to appreciate the depraved nature of such a civilization. As a result, it is destined to a grim fate. A true Islamic society is, by contrast, a superior haven to moral values and clean healthy relationships.[33]

No Forced Islamization

All the modern main-stream scholars of Islam[34] including Qutb, have differentiated between political injustice and religious disbelief in course of waging a war. They did not sanction jihad merely on grounds of difference in belief. They have distinguished disbelief from persecution or injustice and held that unbelief alone is not sufficient condition for waging war. Sayyid Qutb too is no exception in this regard. He has explicitly rejected the idea of any forced conversion. The people will choose the conversion provided jihad is successfully launched and Islamic state is established in its true sense:

> "It is not the intention of Islam to force its beliefs on people, but Islam is not merely "belief"... Islam is a declaration of the freedom

> of man from servitude to other men. Thus it strives... to abolish all those systems and governments which are based on the rule of man over men and the servitude to one human being to another. When Islam releases people from this political pressure and presents to them its spiritual message, appealing to their reason, it gives them complete freedom to accept or not to accept its beliefs. However, this freedom does not mean that they can make their desires their gods or that they can choose to remain in the servitude of other human beings, making some men lords over others.[35]

Explaining the oft-quoted verse no 253 of the Quranic chapter *al-Baqarah* Sayyid Qutb elaborates explicitly that the variety in nature, the difference in the opinions and thoughts do not go against the will of God; it is rather in accordance with His regulated laws and redesigned will. The difference of nature, feeling and thinking accompanying the unity of origin is included in the laws of the Creator. The diversity in the universe is a part of divine scheme. God never desired to create the unified people so as they are printed by the carbon papers. This diversity is designed for the sake of variation and integrative perfectness. If the diversity is operated on this pattern it will be resulted in to positive and fruitful conclusions.[36]

While elaborating the verse no. 256 of the same Quranic chapter *al-Baqarah*, Qutb firmly believes in the freedom of religion assigned by Allah. In explaining this magnificent principle, the author asserts, Allah has demonstrated the human dignity, respect for his free thought and action and the entire responsibility owing to his deeds good or bad. The freedom of religion is the most fundamental right of the human being. Islam preceded all the movements and campaigns in the process of emancipating the human conscience and proclaiming the human rights. The Quranic style of expression, Qutb argues, negates the very compulsion. The force and violence itself is condemned, as the holy Quran felicitates the negation and rejection of violence with all its forms and shapes. It expresses this condemnation as there exists no force and no violence in the matter of faith. The existence of force in the faith is entirely rejected because both the belief and unbelief are clear; let a man decide his own way, his own faith and let him exercise his will and power of judgement.[37]

The religion of Islam, as Qutb explains, was revealed in order to abolish all injustice from the earth, to bring people to the worship of God alone and to bring them out of servitude to servants in to the service of the Lord of servants. He says:

> "Islam does not force people to accept its belief, but, it wants to provide a free environment in which they will have the choice of beliefs. What it wants to abolish those oppressive political systems under which people are prevented from expressing their freedom to choose whatever beliefs they want, and after that it gives them complete freedom to decide whether they accept Islam or not.[38]

How to Establish the Religion

The religion in its entirety may be established only through a fully-fledged movement of *jihad*, as Qutb says. He quotes in his favour Ibn Qayyim's *Zad al-Maåd*. This movement owes several distinguished features. First is its practicability and its realism. This treats people as they actually are and uses resources which are in accordance with practical conditions. Since this movement comes in to conflict with the *jahiliyah* which prevails over ideas and beliefs, and which has a practical system of life and a political and temporal authority behind it, the Islamic movement had to produce parallel resources to confront this *jahiliyah.* This movement uses the methods of preaching and persuasion for reforming ideals and beliefs; and it uses physical power and jihad for abolishing the organizations and authorities of the *jahili* system which prevent people from reforming their ideas and beliefs but forces them to obey their aberrant ways and makes them serve human lords instead of Almighty God.

The second feature of the jihad movement is that it is a practical movement which progresses stage by stage, and at every stage it provides resources according to the practical needs of the situation and prepares the ground for the next one. It does not face practical problems with abstract theories, nor does it confront various stages with unchangeable means.

The third feature of this movement is that the new resource or methods which it uses during its progressive stages, do not take it away from its fundamental principles and aims. From the very first day, whether the Prophet addressed his near relatives or the Quraysh, or the Arabs, or the entire world, his call was one and the same: submission to one God and rejection of the lordship of other men.

The fourth feature is that it provides a legal basis for the relationship of the Muslim community with other groups. This legal formation is based on the principle that Islam is a universal message which the whole of mankind should accept or make peace with. No political system or temporal power should put hindrances in the way of preaching Islam. It should leave every individual free to accept or reject it.[39]

The way to establish the religion on the earth, says Qutb, is not that some consecrated people-the priests-be given the authority to rule, as was the case with the rule of the Church, nor that some spokesmen of God become rulers, as is the case in a theocracy. To establish God's rule means that his laws be enforced and that the final decision in all affairs be according to these laws. This can not be achieved through preaching only. The oppressors and tyrants would not give up their authority merely through mobilization. This Islamic proclamation is not merely a theoretical philosophical and passive proclamation. It is a positive, practical and dynamic message with a view to bringing about the implementation of the *Shariah* of God and actually freeing people from their servitude to bring them into the service of God, the One without associates. This can not be attained unless both 'preaching' and 'the movement' are used. This is so because appropriate means are needed to meet any and every practical situation.

If through preaching, beliefs and ideas are confronted through the movement material obstacles are tackled, explains Sayyid Qutb. Foremost among these is the political power which rests on a complex yet interrelated ideological, racial, class, social and economic support. Thus these two-preaching and the movement-unitedly confront 'the human situation' with all the necessary methods. These two methods, according to Qutb, should work side by side.[40]

Islamism not terrorism

Adam Crutis, the British analyst has well evaluated the "Islamist phantoms" created by the West in the post -7/7 situations. He has distinguished the Islamic movements over the globe from the tiny minority of terrorist advocates, grouped initially around Osama bin Laden and Ayman Zawahiri in the late 1990s and turned to attacking the West. To Crutis, "we must be aware of this distinction so as to avoid a witch-hunt against the whole Islamist movement". He further argues:

> "We may not agree with its reactionary vision of the political use of Islam and pessimistic, anti-progressive beliefs that lie at the heart of Qutb's teachings, but it is

> essential to realize that there is no inherent link between these ideas and terrorism. There are worrying signs that journalists are confusing the murderous beliefs of a genuinely destructive minority with the political ideas of a much wider movement. By lumping Islamism into a freighting, violent, anti-western movement led by the "preachers of hate", they risk exaggerating and distorting the threat yet again".[41]

Voice of resistance and liberation

Since the acts of violence and terrorism grab the headlines and the activities of the Islamic movements-very constitutional, democratic and political-are not distinguished from the first, the West knows a lot of the "preachers of hate", of the "advocates of the violence and terrorism" so much so that any difference between the two groups- the mainstream resistant Islam and the tiny minority of "jihadist militant" Islam- is almost missing in the western media and intelligentia as well. The fact is that huge majority of Muslim intellectuals are working toward a dynamic, resistant, asserting and identity-based Islam. Today, Islam's encounter with the West and the need for Islamic identity and civilizational dialogue are being addressed by Islamically oriented intellectuals, religious scholars and Islamist academicians and activists all in the perspective of creating a new Muslim *ummah* capable of reconstruction, rehabilitation and reassessment of both the internal and external world. They are trying their best to reformulate the Islamic agenda for 21st century in order to cope with the contemporary challenges and to resist all the aggressions and occupations through the methods of both the Islamization and modernization simultaneously. The mainstream Islamists, by their nature and method as well as by their concepts and ideologies, are constitutional and democratic. They openly and publicly struggle for Islamic domination and believe in the process of mass-mobilization. The problem with the West is that it is not convinced ever with the moderate and democratic Islamists and mostly follows Samuel P. Huntington's theory of "clash of civilization".

Huntington published his controversial theorization first in a shape of article in 1993 in *Foreign Affairs* and warned that a "clash of civilization will dominate global politics".[42] The attacks of September 11, 2001 and the global threat of Osama bin Laden and Al-Qaeda, as over propagated by the West, resurrected a knee-jerk response of this theory for an easy answer to the question, why do they hate us? Esposito argues.[43]

Huntington played into old stereotype by characterizing Islam and the West as age old enemies-"conflict along the fault line between western and Islamic civilizations has been going on for 1300 years"- and by citing Islam's resistance to secular western models as necessarily hostile to human rights and progress-"western ideas of individualism, liberalism, constitutionalism, human rights, equality, liberty, the rule of law, democracy, free markets, the separation of church and state, often have little resonance in Islamic (and other)...cultures.[44]

In his 1997 follow-up book, Huntington concluded that "Islam's borders are bloody and so are its innards".[45] His blanket condemnation went beyond "Islamic fundamentalism" to Islam itself: "the underlying problem for the West is not Islamic fundamentalism. It is Islam, a different civilization whose people are convinced of the superiority of their culture, and are abscessed with the inferiority of their power."[46]

The civilization-clash mentality was updated and significantly refined by Tony Blair who after 7/7 attacks in London made the "evil ideology" solely responsible for all the terrorist activities in the world. Not only Bush but most of the academicians and journalists of the West found it more expedient to fall back on convenient stereotype of a monolithic Islam and historic clash of civilization rather than to root out this cancer. They are not serious to understand the psychology, argument and methodology applied by the main-stream Islamists who are struggling for the survival of Islam within the political and constitutional boundaries. Shaykh al-Qaradhawi is a clear case in this context.

Yousuf al-Qaradhawi

Al-Qaradhawi is the most authentic and respectable scholar of the contemporary world. Regarded as *mufti al-jihad*, his *fatawa* and religious pronouncements have a say not only in the Islamic movements across the world but even in the violent jihhadist groups because of his sound scholarship and uncompromising leading personality. He has been closely associated with *al-Ikhwan al-Muslimun* in Egypt, Syria and the Arab world and is constantly advocating all the resistance movements against the colonial powers. His religious speeches especially the Friday sermons are extremely popular in the Arab world. Being a sincere moderate preacher he is often invited by all other religious associations and groups through out the Muslim world. His line of Islamic renaissance is marked between the official western-based rejection and the Islamic extremism. He in his book *al-Sahwah al-Islamiyah Bain al-Juhud wa al-Tatarruf* (Islamic Awakening between Rejection and Extremism) accused the Muslim governments and those in power and authority of denying Islamic Shariah and implementing the western model of society and state. He on the other side is not in favour of using any violence and operating any terrorist activity in order to Islamize the society. All kinds of extremism and fanaticism are in violation of Islamic law. Religious extremism is the antithesis of *dawah* and therefore should not exist in normal conditions. Although it is in part a reaction against oppression, it has also resulted from a deficient or distorted knowledge of the basic source of Islam, a subject Shaykh al-Qaradhawi has discussed with great skill and insight. For historical reasons, the cessation of *ijtihad* resulted in the rise and eventual domination of *taqlid* (blind following and imitation), a very damaging and negative development which still afflicts vast areas of the *ummah* in our own days. The Muslims' adherence to *taqlid* has led to a distortion of Islam's mission, to stagnation of thought and as a result of this, to lack the approaches to the Quran and the Sunnah which do not take into account changes coming about due to the passage of time and evolving social conditions.

It is in such a situation that the eternal validity of the Quran for all peoples is blocked: opinions, interpretations and decisions made on a particular issue, in a particular circumstance, at a particular time are strongly adhered to and considered the solution *par excellence* for similar issues in our time. Such an intellectual discrepancy brings about shunning of *ijtihad*, a concentration on minor issues at the expense of major one's and breeds divisions and strife. Focusing on non-issues deprives Islam of its claim being a viable and global alternative way of life, thus depreciating its real dimension in the eyes of humanity and engendering increased hostility towards Islam and Muslims world wide.[47]

Religious Extremism

It was this intellectual deficiency and these mistaken attitudes which al-Qaradhawi's book sought to address when it was first published in the early 1980s in *al-Ummah* magazine in the form of two-part article. On the request of *al-Arabi* magazine to discuss the subject of "religious extremism" the author wrote a series of articles in 1982. He discussed "the phenomenon of Excessive *Takfir*" in *al-Muslim al-Muasir* also. The issue was too sensitive and complicated. To attempt to do so in the case of Islam was an almost hazardous task-at least one fraught with likely traps. Shaykh al-Qaradhawi was well aware of this sensitiveness for he admitted in his introduction that he hesitated to open a dialogue on religious extremism "for fear that what I may write, especially these days, could be misinterpreted or even deliberately explained to serve something contrary to my intentions..."[48] Unfortunately, his caution was well founded.

In this book al-Qaradhawi called for adherence to straightforward path (*al-Sirat al-Mustaqim*) and rejected and oppsed all kinds of extremism: *ghuluw* (excessiveness), *tanattu* (transgressing; meticulous religiosity) and *tashdid* (strictness; austerity). He has quoted the following traditions in this regard.

1. "Beware of excessiveness in religion. People before you have perished as a result of such excessiveness".[49]

The people referred to in this hadith are the people of the other religions, especially *ahl al-Kitab*; Jews and Christians and mainly the Christians. The Quran addresses these people:

> *Say*: O people of the book! Exceed not in your religion the bounds (of what is proper), trespassing beyond the truth, nor follow the vain desires of people who went wrong in times gone by who misled many, and stayed (themselves) from the even way.[50]

2. "Ruined were those who indulged in *tanattu*".[51] and the Prophet repeated this thrice. Imam Nawawi said that the people referred to here as 'those indulging in *tanattu*' meant those who went beyond the limit in their utterance as well as in their action.

3. The Prophet used to say: "Do not over-burden yourselves, lest you perish. People (before) over-burdened themselves and were perished. Their remains are found in hermitages and monasteries."[52]

Citing the Quranic verses (7: 31-32: 5:86-88) al-Qaradhawi argues that all the things good and pure (*tayyibat*) are to be enjoyed and all the excessiveness found in the religion are to be resisted. Islam disapproves and rejects the tendency to prohibit *tayyibat* and beautification (*zinah*) which Allah has provided for the human beings.[53]

Then what is religious extremism? Says al-Qaradhawi: we should not condemn the practice of any Muslim or accuse him of extremism" if he adopts a hard-line opinion based on juristic judgment through which he seeks Allah's pleasure. We have no right to force him to abandon his opinion or ask him to follow a line of behaviours which is contrary to his convictions."[54] There are four basic manifestations of extremism, as al-Qaradhawi elaborates:

1. First indication includes bigotry and intolerance which make a person obstinately devoted to his own opinions and prejudices as well as rigidity, which deprives him of clarity of vision regarding the interests of other human beings, the objectives of *Shariah* or the circumstances of the age.

2. The second characteristic manifests itself in a perpetual commitment to excessiveness, and in attempts to force others to do likewise, despite the existence of good reasons for facilitation and the fact that Allah has not ordained it.

3. The third characteristic is the out-of-time and out-of-place religious excessiveness and overburdening of other, i.e when applying Islamic principles to people in non-Muslim countries or to people who have only recently converted to Islam, as well as to newly committed Muslims.

4. The fourth one manifests itself in harshness in the treatment of people, roughness in the manner of approach and crudeness in calling people to Islam, all

of which are contrary to the teachings of the Quran and Sunnah.[55]

While speaking of the factors and causes of extremism, Shaykh al-Qaradhawi declares it a complex phenomenon with numerous interrelated causes, some of which are direct, others indirect; some found in the distant past, others in the present. Consequently, one may not focus on one cause and totally ignore the others, as do people who advocate some schools of thought.

The main cause, however, may be traced in "the extremist himself, in his relationship with the members of his family, or-if deeply analysed- may be found in his society and all its contradictions between faith and behaviour, ideals and reality, religion and politics, words and actions, aspirations and achievements, the secular and the divine." It may also be initiated by "the corruption of regimes, i.e. the despotism of rulers, their egoistic pursuits, their adherence to the views of corrupt counsellors and advisors as well as various foreign enemies of the *Ummah* and their total disregard for the rights of their people."[56]

Shaykh al-Qaradhawi, however, traces and evaluates in detail the following internal factors responsible for religious extremism:

1. Intellectual shallowness and lack of religious insight also manifest themselves in an interest in marginal issues at the expense of major ones- those which could affect the existence, identity and destiny of the whole *Ummah.* Such contradictory behavior once outraged Abdullah bin Umar when a man from Iraq asked him-following the murder of the great Muslim martyr al-Husayn bin Ali-whether it was *halal* or *haram* to kill a mosquito. Imam Ahmad has related in his *Musnad*: As I was sitting with *Ibn Umar* a man came and asked him about the blood of a mosquito. (In another version of the hadith, the man asked about a pilgrim killing a

mosquito). Ibn Umar asked the man: "where are you from." The man answered. "From Iraq. "Then Ibn Umar said: "Look at this man! He is asking me about the blood of mosquitoes while they (the Iraqis) had already killed the Prophet's grandson (i.e al-Husayn Ibn Ali). I heard the prophet saying: "they (al-Hasan and al-Husayn) are my two sweetest –smelling flowers of this world."[57]

2. Lack of thorough Knowledge of Islamic jurisprudence reflects in making things difficult through an invalid extension of prohibitions. The Prophet's companions as well as the early righteous forebears never prohibited any thing unless they were sure that it was categorically so. Extremists, however hastily prohibit without reservation, out of piety and cautiousness, if we take them to be well-meaning, or possibly out of other motives known only to Allah.

3. Misconceptions about the fundamentals of Islam as the concepts of *Islam, Iman, Ihsan, Kufr, nifaq, jahiliyah, irtidad* etc. the complexities of language, the difference between figurative or metaphoric and the literal meanings, the categorization and grading of faith and un-faith and other expertized knowledge is missing and causes dangerous consequences.

4. Overemphasis on allegorical texts and disregard of categorical ones has been a root cause of extremism. This cannot be attitude of those with knowledge and insight, but of those who cherish deviation in their hearts.[58]

5. The extremists never listen to people who hold different views, never accept any dialogue with them, and never imagine that their own views could be tested in the light of others and be either contradicted or refuted. They have not been taught by reliable Ulama specialized in the field.

6. Lack of insight in to history, reality and the natural laws of Allah, has sometimes reflected in a seek or demand of the impossible and unavailable. The illusory means and imaginary methods are then used bypassing the natural laws of God or the essence of Shariah. To realize the unrealistic objective, extraordinary courage, daring and sacrifice is showed by the extremists.

7. The hasty enthusiasm usually overlooks two important *sunnahs* of Allah i.e gradation and that achieving goals requires the allowance of due time. For this reason, the Prophet used to advise his companions to be patient and not to expect victory before its appointed time.[59]

8. Lack of adherence to the teachings of Islam in Muslim countries where perversion, corruption and falsehood are rampant, is perhaps the most alarming and unbearable factor for any religious extremism to evolve. This can basically be attributed to the imposition on Muslim societies of secularism-"an alien trend which is at odds with all that is Islamic."

9. The impediments imposed on the collective system of preaching in most Muslim countries are the main causes to generate extremism. The censorship of freedom to call people to Islam as a *din* and as a system of beliefs and a way of life, and the intimidation of the preachers and those who call for the application of Shariah, the establishment of the Islamic state, the unity of the *Ummah*, the liberation of the Muslim land, and the support of Islamic causes. Quite logically the youth meet force by force and violence by violence. This situation should not be allowed to continue. The gravest mistake of the authorities is resorting to violence, physical as well as psychological torture in prisons and concentration camps, where humans are treated as animals. Extremism and *takfir* were born in these notorious prisons. Shaykh al-Qaradhawi finally concedes: "the observable fact is that violence not only

breeds violence but also contaminates clear thinking; suppression inevitably causes revolt."[60]

Shaykh al-Qaradhawi in his concluding chapter emphasized on two points:

1. This resurgence sgnifies a natural, healthy phenomenon which is clearly indicative of a return to *fitrah,* to the roots.

2. The rigidity and extremism of the youth can not be rectified by violence, threats or allegations which will be counter productive and may lead to more severity and stubbornness. It requires a patient intellectual dialogue.

The author advised the young Muslims to respect specialization in Islamic learning; and to eschew excessiveness and extremism and to commit themselves to temperance and facilitation. Highlighting the ethics of preaching the religion and conducting a dialogue, al-Qaradhawi emphasized on the following points:

1. Parental and kinship rights must be observed.

2. Islamic equality does not negate the age difference and the show of politeness and respect.

3. The people of rich experiences and very active in the field of *dawah* must be given the due consideration.

4. The day dreams and unrealistic idealism must be abandoned.

5. The youth must liberate themselves from fetters of pessimism and despair and assume innocence and goodness in fellow Muslims with certain prerequisites.[61]

Flexible Fatawa

Active as modern enlightened *mufti,* Shaykh al-Qaradhawi-as opposed to the Western image-criticizes both the westernized scholars and orthodox Ulama. Most of the researchers and writers about Islam, argues al-Qaradhawi, are "blinded by the glamour of Western civilization; overawed by this great idol, they worship it, approach it imploringly, and stand before it humbly with downcast eyes, accepting Western principles and customs as unassailable and proven beyond doubt. Accordingly, if some aspect of Islam agrees with these principles and customs, they praise and extol it, while if some aspect opposes them, they try to find similarities and agreements, offer excuses and apologies, or resort to farfetched explanations and distortions, as if Islam had no choice except to surrender to the philosophy and customs of the Western civilization."[62]

The second group of scholars, to al-Qaradhawi, is frozen in its fixed opinions concerning questions about the *halal* and *haram*, following a statement in a text which they assume to be Islam. "They do not budge a hair's breath from their position, nor do they try to weigh their opinion against the arguments of others, and to arrive at the truth after a comparison and critical evaluation of all opinions."[63]

Shaykh al-Qaradhawi is not ready to be in either of those two groups. He has not compromised his religion by 'taking the West as his god' nor has he compromised his intellect by "following one particular school of jurisprudence in all its judgements, whether right or wrong", suspending his own faculty of reasoning and discernment. He quotes Ibn al-Jawzi saying: "A blind follower does not have any trust in what he follows. To imitate is to suspend the use of the intellect, whereas the intellect is created for thinking and reasoning. It is stupidity when a person is given a light to show him the way, he should extinguish it and walk in darkness."[64]

Al-Qaradhawi, therefore, did not confine himself to any of the several schools of jurisprudence, because the truth is not the monopoly of any one school. It is not worthy of a Muslim scholar who is capable of comparing and choosing the better to tie himself to a single school of jurisprudence or to submit to the opinion of a particular jurist; he must give weight to arguments and proofs.[65]

The author has applied in this marvellous book the following principles of jurisprudence:

1. The basic principle is the permissibility of things.
2. To make lawful and to prohibit is the right of Allah alone.
3. Prohibiting the *halal* and permitting the *haram* is similar to committing *shirk.*
4. The prohibition of things is due to their impurity and harmfulness.
5. What is *halal* is sufficient, while what is *haram* is superfluous.
6. Whatever is conducive to the *haram* is itself *haram.*
7. Falsely representing the *haram* as *halal* is prohibited.
8. Good intentions do not make the *haram* acceptable.
9. Doubtful things are to be avoided.
10. The *haram* is prohibited to everyone alike.
11. Necessity dictates exceptions.[66]

Lawfulness of Singing and Music

In the process of appling these principles of jurisprudence to the confronting issues, Shaykh al-Qaradhawi exposes himself as the most liberal, reforming and accomodating *mufti* who provides the maximum relaxations, conveniences and comforts to the masses within Islamic paradigm. His flexible approach, for example, declares the permissibility of singing and music under the condition that "it not be in any way obscene or harmful to Islamic morals. There is no harm in its being accompanied by music which is not exciting." In order to create an atmosphere of joy and happiness singing is recommended on festive occasions such as the days of Eid, weddings and wedding feasts, births, *aqiqah* (the celebration of the birth of a baby by the slaughter of sheep), and on the return of a traveler. Al-Qaradhawi has quoted several *ahadith* as reported by Bukhari, Muslim and Ibn Majah in his favour. He has cited al-*Ghazali's Ihya Uloom al-Din* also. All the traditions being reported against singing are "weak and have shown by the researchers to be unsound" Qadi Abu Bakr Ibn al-Arabi says: 'No sound hadith is available concerning the prohibition of singing". While Ibn Hazm has said: "All that is reported on this subject is false and fabricated."[67]

This flexible individual opinion provocated even Indian admirer (and translator of the book into Urdu) Shams Peerzadah a great commentator of the Quran, to add a footnote disagreeing with Shaykh al-Qaradhawi. The learned translator as being pressurized by the local environment, declared the conditions of the author very strict and the songs prevalent consequently *ultra vires*, provocative, illegal and prohibited one because Islam is too sensitive in the matters of morality and ethics and does not even tolerate in the case of woman to be too complaisant of speech lest one in whose heart is disease should be moved with desire".[68] Such kinds of songs are therefore clearly prohibited to Peerzadah.[69]

Moderate Islamic Culture

Dealing with the non-Muslims individually or collectively, Shaykh al-Qaradhawi is very clear and unambiguous. He advocates for a cordial relations with the non-Muslims and treats the holy verses of the Quran preaching otherwise as those addressing the combatants. The verses like *al-Maidah : 54-55 , 51, 52; Aal Imran :* 118-119; *al-Mumtahinah* :01 and others basically deal with those people who were hostile to Islam and made war compulsory upon the Muslims.[70] Inspite of this situation, the Quran did not dismiss the hope that some day there might be reconciliation; it did not declare utter disappointment in them but encouraged the Muslims to entertain the hope of better circumstances and improved relationships, for in the same *surah al-Mumtahinah* Allah says:

> It may be that Allah will bring about affection between you and those who are your enemies from among them. And Allah is All-Powerful, and Allah is Forgiving and Merciful.[71]

This Quranic statement gives the assurance that this bitter hostility and deep hatred will pass away as it is also stated in the *hadith* :

"Hate your enemy mildly; he may become your friend one day."[72]

Shaykh al-Qaradhawi is firm in his stand that Islam respects a human being because he is human; how much the more then, if he is a Christian or Jew (the people of the Book) and still more if he is a *dhimmi* , says the author.[73]

This is the reason why Shaykh al-Qaradhawi did not accept the classical division of the world into *dar al-Islam* , *dar al-harb* , *dar al- kufr* and coined a new term for the entire world *dar al-dawah* that denotes a normal and cordial relationship with the entire humanity. Muslim attitude toward Ethiopia during the Prophet period was declared by al-Qaradhawi as the model for today's Muslims. The Muslims sought help and shelter to the Ethiopian King, joined the social and economic activities of the country as partners and maintained law order along with their Islamic identity at any cost.[74]

In the post 9/11 situation while dilevering a lecture in a seminar at Kuwait on Shawwl 10, 1422/December 10, 2001, Shaykh al-Qaradhawi emphasized again on the moderate and balanced view of Islamic culture. He advocated "to opt an accomodative approach without any suspicion and fear. There is no harm to accept from outside any thing that may be exploited in the process of reformation and reconstruction. Some scholars are very much reluctant in this regard. It is incorrect. They think every thing from the past as sacrosanct and therefore unchangeable."[75]

Al-Qaradhawi criticized those orthodox scholars who do not tolerate any modernization or reformation, or even difference in the religion. He quoted the case of Shaykh Abu Zahra the leading orthodox jurist of Egypt. Shaykh Abu Zahra while speaking on Islamic law in a seminar at Madinah al-Baydha Libya in 1972 said that: "Brothers in Islam! I wish to express my individual opinion that I had been hiding since last twenty years. Before I breath my last I desire to utter it" And when he completed his talk, the scholars from all the corners started condemning him. Consequently he never expressed any novel opinion at any issue after that. Shaykh Abu Zahra was traditional jurist and used to defend all the conventional lines. He was, even then, not allowed to differ from the norms. Al-Qaradhawi says that this attitude endangers the Muslim community. Renovation and reconstruction of this *Ummah* is impossible unless its jurisprudence and its thought is overhauled.[76]

No Violent Jihad

Islamic culture aims at creating a community of a construction-loving people who are the champion of civilization and who stand as witness to the mankind (The Quran 2: 143). It is feasible only "when we properly deal with our culture; we preach comfort instead of hardship and inconvenience, we believe in hopes and love instead of frustration and hatred and we stand for convenience and relaxation instead of extremism and alienation."[77]

Shaykh al-Qaradhawi rejected the idea of initiative jihad. "Now it is confined within defensive jihad. Muslims fought violently against Romans and Iranians in the history because these governments created hurdles in the way of preaching Islam......Now you may convey the message of Islam to the entire world through modern resources; internet, T.V. channels and magazines in different languages. Whether we have exhausted all these resources and whether jihad is left the only method? We did not use what is in our access and are anxious of what is not in our jurisdiction. I told some of my friends: Alas! if we demand such people from among the Muslims who are ready to die in the way of Allah, the dozens and hundreds will probably welcome us. But if you need a group fully convinced with living in the way of Allah and remaining alive for the cause of Islam, only few will be rarely available."[78]

Shaykh al-Qaradhawi insisted on the usefulness of only those people "who live for the cause of religion; who firmly believe in Islam as the only way to God; who emphasize on the fundamentals, not the subsidiaries; who preach the spirit not the structure; who propagate the common teachings not the controversial; who advocate construction not demolition and teach unity and love not hatred and enmity. We today need the preachers of such talents; the activists of such nature and characteristics.....It is quite possible that Islamic resurgence may overcome. But some diseases have certainly affected it; some mistakes have crept in it and some deviations have penetrated it. I think this resurgence must be oriented in the right alongwith the firm faith, practical wisdom and sound argument." [79]

Some Westerners accuse the Mulsims to train their youth and new generation in such a way they start hating the others, critises al-Qaradhawi. No Muslim thinks in this term. None claims that those who do not embrace Islam are their enemies. It is wrong. The holy Quran declares clearly:

> God forbids you not with regard to those who fight you not for (your) Faith nor drive you out of your homes, from dealing kindly and justify with them: For God loves those who are just.[80]

A peace-loving pagan who is not rampant and out to destroy us and our Faith, deserves our kind and equitable treatment. Shaykh al- Qaradhawi convincingly argues that the Quran has used in this verse two terms: *birr* and *qist.* The last connotes a just dealing; the first term qualifies a greater degree of piety. The term *birr* means excellence and may be equated with *Ihsan.* Paying whatever is due is entitled as *qist* and the payment of more than due is *birr. Qist* demands to receive one's right while the *birr* requires the withdrawal from one's right. Allah has never forbidden Muslims to deal kindly with the non-Muslims. The Prophet of Islam, the holy companions and the Muslim community of early history do practice the same dealing of *qist* and *birr*. Then why do we not prevail this culture over ?[81]

Sayyid Qutb and Shaykh Yousuf al-Qaradhawi are but two of main stream voices of Islamic reform and resistance. They demonstrate that there is no extremist or terrorist Islam or Muslim society. All the Islamists advocate Islam as a culture, a way of life, a political system, a civilized society that confronts all kinds of aggressions and occupations and teaches its followers to liberate themselves from all alien concepts and ideologies. This Islam appreciates and encourages the dialogue and the cooperation and seeks to develop new paradigms and new approaches within the broader and enlightened framework of Islamic Shariah.

That was the reason why the mayor of London Ken Livingstone threatened to take the British government to court if it banned Shaykh Yousuf al-Qaradhawi from entering the country under the new controversial terror guidelines implemented in the post-7/7 Britain. 'If no body else takes the government to the courts if they banned Dr. al-Qaradhawi, I would'. Livingstone told BBC radio on August 24, ' I do not think he should be banned. He has opposed all acts of terrorism by Al-Qaeda around the world. He urged Arabs to donate blood after September 11, added Livingstone.[82]

Notes and References

1. John L. Esposito, *Unholy War – Teror in the Name of Islam*, op.cit., p. 56.
2. *Ibid.*, p. 28.
3. *Ibid.*, p. 111.
4. For a detailed study see Ziauddin Sardar's book, *Desperately Seeking Paradise*: *Journeys of A Sceptical Muslim*, op.cit.
5. Ghey Surman, Abna Rifaah al-Tahtawi-Muslimun wa Hadathiyun, translated in Arabic by Maram al Misri, the review article by Mazin Hijazi, Al- Majallah, London, No. 1322, 12-18, june 2005, p.20.
6. Esposito, op.cit., p. 56.
7. *Ibid.*, p. 57.
8. *Ibid.*
9. *Ibid.*, p. 58.
10. Iqbal N. Siddiqui, *Crescent International*, Vol. 34, No.7, Rajab-Shaban, 1426/September, 2005, p. 04.
11. Sayyid Qutb, *Milestones*, Stuttgart, Ennst Klett Printers, 1978, pp. 32-33.
12. *Ibid.*, p. 34.
13. *Ibid.*,
14. Qutb, Muhamamd, *Jahiliyah fi al-Qarn al-'Ishrin,* Maktabah Wahabah, Cairo, 1964, p. 11.
15. Sayyid Qutb, *Fi Zilal al-Quran,* 1981, Vol. 1, pp. 510-511.
16. *Milestones*, p. 12.
17. Elfanor Abdella Doumato, in: John L.Esposito, (ed.). *The Oxford Encyclopedia of the Mdoern Islamic World*, Oxford University Press, 1995, Vol. 2, p. 353.
18. Youssef M. Choueiri, *Islamic Fundamentalism*, CBS Publishers and Distributors, N. Delhi, 1991, pp. 94-95.
19. Abul Hasan Ali Nadvi, *Madha Khasira al-Alam bi Inhitat al-Muslimin,* Dar al-Ansar, Cairo, 1977, p. 279-85.

20. Maududi, S. Abul Ala, *A Short History of the Revivalist Movement in Ilsam*, Islamic Publciations, Lahore, 1979, pp. 31-32
21. Sayyid Qutb, *Milestones*, p. 239.
22. Sayyid Qutb, *Dirasat Islamiyah* Urdu trans. Dr. Muhammad Raziul Islam Nadwi, *Islam Aur Maghrib Ki Kashmakash,* Markazi Maktaba Islami, Delhi, 1996, p. 126.
23. *Ibid.*, p. 127.
24. *Ibid.*, p. 128.
25. *Ibid.*, pp. 128-129.
26. *Ibid.*, p. 130
27. Sayyid Qutb, *al-Islam wa Mushkilat al-Hadharah*, Dar al-Shuruq, Beirut and Cairo, 1980/1400, 6th ed., p. 193.
28. Sayyid Qutb, *Fi Zilal al-Quran, Dar al-Shuruq, Beirut and Cairo, revised edition, 1981, Vol. 1, pp. 2036-37.*
29. *Ibid.*, pp. 216-17; Vol. III, pp. 1556-62: Vo.l IV, p. 1946.
30. *Ibid.*, Vol. IV, pp. 1947. 2101-2, 2438.
31. Sayyid Qutb, *Milestones*. Op.cit., pp. 71-75.
32. *Ibid.* 11-13
33. Sayyid Qutb, *al-Islam wa Muskilat al-Hadharah*, op.cit., pp. 120-62.
34. Dr. Abdul Hamid Abu Sulayman, Sayyid M. al-Naquib al-Attas, Sayyid Abul Ala Maududi, Abdul Karim Pareekh, Sayyid Jalaluddin Umari, Mohammad Faruq Khan, Dr. Anis Ahmad, Shaykh Mahmud Shaltut, all the scholars have nullified any type of force to be used for conversion. See the author's article: Jihad: Violent or Non-violent, *Studies on Islam*, Vol.1, No.1, 2004, pp. 78-99.
35. *Milestones*, op.cit., pp. 109-10.
36. Sayyid Qutb, *Fi Zilal al-Quran*, explanatory note on the verse No. 253 of Chapter al-Baqarah.
37. *Ibid.*, verse No. 256
38. *Milestones*, op.cit., p. 100.
39. *Ibid.*, pp. 98-101.

40. *Ibid.*, pp. 104-106.

41. Adam Crutis, *The Hindu*, August 31, 2005. The author suggests that the real danger lies in suppressing Islamism and thus making its ideas more attractive to already marginalized young men.

42. Samuel P. Huntington, *The Clash of civilizations and the Remaking of World Order*, New York, Simon and Schuster, 1997.

43. Esposito, Op.cit., pp. 126-127.

44. Huntington, *The Clash of Civilizations*, Foreign Affairs, 1993, 22: 40.

45. Huntington, 1997, p. 258.

46. *Ibid.*, p. 217.

47. Preface to Yousuf *al-Qaradhawi*, *Islamic Awakening between Rejection and Extremism*, Eng. Trans. A.S. al-Shaikh Ali & Mohammed B.E. Wasfy. Herndon, 1416 AH/1995, pp. 5-6.

48. *Ibid.*, p. 13.

49. Reported by Ahmad, al-Nasai, and Ibn Majah in their *Sunan.*

50. The Holy Quran 5:77.

51. Reported by Muslim. Al-Suyuti attributed this hadith to both Ahmad and Abu Dawud.

52. Reported by Abu Yala in his *Musnad* on the authority of Anas bin Malik. Cited by Ibn Kathir in his interpretation of Quran 57:27 namely: "but the monasticism which they themselves invented, we did not prescribe for them".

53. *Islamic Awakening between Rejection and Extremisn*, Op.cit., pp. 21-24.

54. *Ibid.*, p. 32.

55. *Ibid.*, pp. 33-38.

56. *Ibid.*, p. 49-50.

57. Reported by Ahmad bin Hanbal. Shaykh Ahamd Shakir confirms that its *isnad* is authentic.

58. The Holy Quran declares: "He it is who has sent don to you (Muhammad) the Book: in it are verse basic or fundamental (of established meaning); they are the foundation of the Book;

others are allegorical. But those in whose hearts is perversity follow the part there of that is allegorical, seeking discord, and searching for hidden meanings, but no one knows its true meanings exept Allah. And those who are firmly grounded in knowledge say: We believe in the Book; the whole of it is from our Lord" and none will grasp the message except men of understanding" (3:7).

59. Al-Qaradhawi has quoted a hadith reported by *Al-Bukhari* in this regard. When Khabbab bin al-Arat complained to the Prophet of the great suffering which he encountered for the sake of Islam and asked him to invoke Allah for help, the Prophet was so angry that his face became red and he said: "A believer before you used to be cut off with iron cutting tools so that nothing of his flesh or nerves remained beyond his bones, and another used to be sawed (alive) into two parts, but neither would abandon his religion. By Allah, He will surely make Islam prevail so that a traveler from San'ā (in the Yemen) to Hadramawt (in Oman) will not fear (during his journey) anything except Allah, and the wolf for his sheep But you are (always) impatient".

60. *Islamic Awakening between Rejection and Extremism,* Op.cit., pp. 56-95.

61. *Ibid.*, pp. 149-167.

62. Yousuf al-Qarahdawi, *Al-Halal wa al-Haram fi al-Islam, The Lawful and Prohibited in Islam*, Eng trans, Kamal El-Helbawy, M. Moinuddin Siddiqui and Syed Shukry, Noida. Distributed by Muslim Welfare Scoiety Jammu and Kashmir, p. 2.

63. *Ibid.*, p. 3.

64. Ibn al-Jawzi, *Talbis Iblis,* p. 81

65. Al-Qaradhawi, op. cit., p. 4.

66. For a detailed study of these *usul al-figh* see, *Ibid.*, pp. 11-37.

67. *Ibid.*, pp. 300-303. The learned scholar, however has imposed certain limitations to be observed: (a) the subject matter of songs should not be against the teachings of Islam; (b) the manner of singing should not include any *haram* act as if accompanied by suggestive sexual movement; (c) excessive involvement with singing like anything is prohibited; (d) it should not arouse one's passions leading him to sin and (e) it should not be performed in conjunction with *haram* activities for example at a drinking party.

68. The Holy Quran, 33: 32.
69. *Islam Mein Halal o Haram*, Urdu trans. Shams Peerzadah, Mumbai, 1976, p. 383, footnote No.1.
70. *The Lawful and Prohibited in Islam,* op.cit., p. 340.
71. The Holy Quran 60:7.
72. Reported by al-Tirmidhi. Al-Bayhaqi reported it in his *Shuab al-Iman* from Abu Hurairah. Al Suyuti called it "good" transmitting the first part as "Love your friend mildly; he may become your enemy one day".
73. *The Lawful and the Prohibited in Islam*, op.cit., p. 343.
74. Cited by Khushid Ahmad, *Amrika – Muslim Duniya Ki Be Itmenani,* op.cit., p. 284.
75. Yousuf al-Qaradhawi, *Islami Thaqafat mein Ietidal Awr Miyanahrawi*, (Balance and Moderation in Islamic Culture) Urdu trans. Dr. Mohamamd Raziul Islam Nadvi, *Zindagi Nau,* N. Delhi, vol. 29, No. 8, August 2003, p. 16.
76. *Ibid.*, pp. 19-20.
77. *Ibid.*, p. 22.
78. *Ibid.*, p. 24.
79. *Ibid.*, p. 26.
80. *The Holy Quran*, 60:8.
81. Yousuf al-Qaradhawi, *Zindagi Nau*, op.cit., pp. 23-24.
82. *Radiance* views weekly, vol. XL, No. 17, 4-10 September, 2005, p. 32.

GLOSSARY

akhirah	Day of resurrection
Americanised Islam	Islam serving the American interests; a term used by Sayyid Qutb originally in Arabic as *Islam Amrikani.*
Anthrax	a serious disease of sheep and cattle, able to be transmitted to humans.
apartheid	the official system of segregation or discrimination on racial grounds formerly in force in South Africa.
apostate	a person who abandons a belief or principle.
aqiqah	celebrating the birth of a baby by the slaughter of a sheep/ goat.
Ashāb al-Ukhdud	Referred to in the Quran 85:4, meant the "makers of the pit (of fire)". Who were the makers of the pit of fire in which they burnt people for their faith? The words of the Quran are perfectly general, and we need not search for particular names, except by way of illustration. In ancient history, and in Medieval Europe many lives were sacrificed at the stake because the victims did not conform to the established. In Arab tradition there is story of Abraham: Nimrud tries to burn him to death, but on account of

	Abraham's Faith the fire became "a means of safety for Abraham": xxi, 69. Another case cited is that of Zu Nuwās, the last Himyarite King of Yemen, by religion a Jew, who persecuted the Christians of Najran, and is said to have burnt them at the stake. He seems to have lived in the latter half of the sixth Christian century, in the generation immediately preceding the Prophet's birth in 570AD. See A. Yusuf Ali, The Holy Quran, Text, Translation and Commentary, 1983, p.1714 footnote no 6055.
Ashariyyah	main stream sunni sect founded by Abdul Hasan al-Ashari (873-935) in order to bridge a gap between a literal interpretation of Islam and the one based on reason. His ideas and those of his followers had a major influence on Sunni Islam for many centuries.
Assassin	derived from Arabic *hashshashin*: hashish eaters; a person who undertakes to assassinate somebody; especially (history) any of a band of Nizari Ismaili Muslim fanatics in the time of Crusades who were allegedly sent on murder errands by the Old Man of the Mountains or by later leaders. The name was given to them by their enemies refers to their supposed use of the drugs hashish as part of their violent activities. The Assassins were active from about the 1090s to the mid 1200s. Historically in 1094, Nizar, eldest son and the chosen successor of the Fatimid calip, was

	captured by political enemies and imprisoned. The Ismailis who remained loyal to Nizar became the Nizari Ismailis. A missinary named Hassan bin Sabbah became leader of the Nizari Ismailis. Hasan's impressive religious scholarship and strong personality helped him amass a fiercely devoted following which came to be known as the Assassins.
atavism	the idea of return to something ancient or inherit from a remote ancestor.
axis	an imaginary line through a body, about which it rotates; an imaginary line about which a regular figure is symmetrically arranged.
Basque	A member of a people living in the Western Pyrenees in France and Spain.
bellicose	aggressive and ready to fight
Berlin Wall	a fortified and heavily guarded wall built in 1961 by the communist authorities on the boundary between East and West Berlin. it was opened in 1989 after the collapse of the communist regime in East Germany and later dismantled.
black hole	a region of space having gravitational field so intense that no matter or radiation can escape.
CIA	abbrev. Central Intelligence Agency.
cluster-bomb	an anti-personnel bomb spraying pullets on impact.
conservative	opposed to change and holding traditional values.
cynical	believing that people always act from selfish motives. a person who raises doubts about something.
dar al-dawah	the land of propagation; applied to the

	whole world since Islam addresses the whole mankind, and is therefore advocate of maintaining peace and justice at any cost.
dar al-harb	areas of land that are out of Muslim control, enemy/ hostile land and territory.
dar al-Islam	the Islamic land governed by Muslims and its inhabitants; Islamic territory
dar al-kufr	territory of paganism
dawah	call to Islam
debauch	corrupt morally
Dhahiriyah	a sunni school of law which never gained a significance and was founded by Dawud al- Dhahiri (204-241/809-855) who rejected completely the *qiyās* (analogy) in Islamic law and the opinion of any but the closest of the companions and insisted upon a strictly literal interpretation of the Quran and the Sunnah.
dhimmi	non-Muslim citizen residing in an Islamic state, is granted full protection and citizenship rights.
Draconian	(of laws) excessively harsh; named after the ancient Athenian legislator Draco.
dud	a thing that fails to work properly
ETA	a Basque separatist movement in Spain, which since 1959 has waged a terrorist campaign for an independent Basque state.
Ethnocentris-m	evaluating other races and cultures by criteria specific to one's own.
euphemism	a less direct word used instead of one that is harsh or blunt when referring to something unpleasant or embarrassing.
evangelical	of or according to the teaching of the

	gospel or the Christian religion; of a branch of Protestant Christianity emphasizing the authority of Scripture, person conversion, and the doctrine of salvation by faith in the Atonement.
fatwa	pl. *fatawa* an advisory opinion issued by a recognized authority on Islamic law and tradition in answer to a specific question raised by any ordinary man in a written form known as *Istifta*; the authority responding to it is known as *mufti*.
FBI	abbrev. (in the U.S.) Federal Bureau of Investigation.
fetish	an object worshipped for its supposed magical powers
fitrah	nature
Franconian	adjective and noun from Franconia; of or pertaining to (the inhabitants of) Franconia, a region of Germany, formerly a duchy, bordering the River Main; a group of Medival West Germanic dialects, combining features of low and high German; the group of modern German of dialects of Franconia.
G-8	Group of Eight
ghuluw (*fi al-din*)	excessiveness in the religion; forbidden in Islam. It applies to all forms of beliefs, worship and transaction, as clearly defined by the *ahadith*.
halal	that which God has explicitly permitted.
hanafid	a Muslim following Abu Hanifah's juristic school.
harām	that which God has explicitly

	forbidden to do and for which he specified a penalty.
heathen	a person who does not belong to a widely held religion, as seen by those who do.
Holloween	the night of 31 October, the eve of All Saint's Day.
homicidal	murderous
Ibadhis	or Ibadhiyah, a moderate Muslim sect being traced in the Khariji division of early Muslims is ascribed to Abdullah Ibn Ibad. A few decades later (c.715CE) the sect conducted a process of training missionaries and dispatched them to the Maghrib and Oman. The Ibadi state of Tahirt established by Ibn Rustam lasted from 776 to 909. The sect took strongest root in Oman, where it has existed continuing exfluence on the state. They in contrast to Kharijites, accept co-existence with other Islamic groups and sects.
Ihsān	Literally means excellence, and doing what is beautiful a divine and human quality about which the Quran says a good deal, mentioning in particular those who possess it. In the famous hadith of Gabriel, the Prophet describes *Ihsan* as the inner most dimension of religion, after *Islam*. It is a deepened understanding and experience that, in the words of that hadith, allows one "to worship God as if you see him".
ijtihad	in general usage the Arabic word denotes the utmost effort physical or mental, expended in a particular

	activity. In its legal connotation, it denoted the thorough creative exertion of the jurist's mental faculty in finding a solution for the case of law from the legitimate sources.
imam	the religious man leading the daily prayers of the Muslims in the mosque.
Intifada	derived from Arabic, literally means shaking off, An uprising by Arabs; espec. that begun by Palestinians in December 1987 against Israel in the West Bank and Gaza Strip. Israel occupied these lands following its victory in the six-day war in 1967. After 20 years of discrimination, the imprisonment of tens of thousands of Palestinians, and the building of Jewish settlement in the heart of Arab towns and cities, Palestinians decided to initiate the uprising. In September 2000, a second *Intifada* erupted.
IRA	abbrev. Irish Republican Army
irtidād	apostasy, abjuration of allegiance to God as well as to the Islamic state of which one is a citizen.
Islamophobia	portraying Islam as extremely dangerous or irrational.
Jafariyah	the Shia school of law founded by Jafar Sadiq (80-148AH) is based on the traditions reported by *Ahl bait*. After the Quran, the traditions of *ahl bait* and sayings of imams (the innocents) are main sources. Al-Kulayni (d. 329 AH), Al- Qummi (d. 381 AH), Tusi (d. 460 Ah) and Al-Hilli (d. 676 AH) are main jurists of the sect.
Jahiliyah	Pre-Islamic Arab society ignorant of

	Islam.
Jahiliyah (jadeedah)/ Jahiliyah madaniyah	The theory was developed in the late 1940s by Sayyid Qutb to connote a state signified by the domination of man over man rather than the submission of man to God. The theory denotes any government system based on manmade values and institutions, such as democracy, monarchy, or dictatorship. *Jihiliyah* is also materialism, communism or any other philosophical system in which there is no central place for God. According to Qutb, a total rejection of Western values was needed to combat the new *jahiliyah*.
Kharijite	one of the oldest Muslim sects that rebelled against Ali and later on Muawiyah also; both of whom had accepted the principle of arbitration amidst the battle of Siffin (37AH / 657AD). The sect organized itself later on into a militant socio-religious movement against the main stream Muslims.
kufr	disbelief, the act of declaring solemnly disbelief.
libel	the crime of publishing a false statement that harms a person's reputation.
madrasa	Islamic seminary of higher learning
malevolent	wishing evil to others
malikid	a Muslim following Malik bin Anas in his juristic issues.
maniac	a person who behaves in an extremely wild or violent way; a person with an extreme enthusiasm for something.
Mc Carthyism	(esp. in the U.S.) the policy of hunting

	out suspected or known communists and removing them esp. from government and departments; named after J.R. Mc Carthy, US senator (d. 1957), who instigated the policy in 1950 claiming to know of many communists in the State Department.
Miller	Arthur(b.1915), American dramatist. His plays include *Death of a Salesman* and *The Crucible*, which used the Salem with trials of 1962 as an allegory for McCarthyism in America.
misogynist	a man who hates women
mufti al-jihad	the religiously committed scholar issuing the legal verdict in favour of violent fighting against the enemies of Islam.
nasihah	moral advice
nifãq	hypocricy; contradiction between claims and deeds.
niqab	veil
obtuse	annoyingly slow to understand.
OKC	Oklahoma City
opprobrium	harsh criticism, public disgrace as a result of bad behavior
ostensible	apparently true, but necessarily not so.
ostracized	excluded from a society or group
pacifist	one who believes that disputes should be settled peacefully and that war and violence are always wrong.
Palvo	Ivan (Petrovich) (1849-1936), Russian physiologist. He is best known for his studies on conditioned reflexes in dogs showing how the secretion of saliva can be stimulated not only by food but also by the sound of a bell associated with the presentation of food.
perfidious	(literary) deceitful and disloyal.

phantom	a ghost, a figment of the imagination.
pliant	easily bent, easily influenced or persuaded.
polemicist	one who attacks a theory strongly in written or verbal; who is engaged in fierce discussion.
rahmatullah alaih	May God bless with him!
reactionary	opposing political or social progress or reform.
Reich	Steve (b. 1936; full name Stephen Michael Reich), American minimalist composer. His work is influenced by Balinese and West African music and includes *The Desert Music* for chorus and orchestra.
Reichstag	The diet or parliament of the North German Confederation (1867-71), of the German Empire (1871-1918), and of post imperial Germany until 1945.
relativism	the idea that knowledge, truth and morality exist in relation to culture, society or historical context, and are not always the same.
retrogressive	adj. returning to an earlier and worse state.
seismic	having to do with earthquakes, very great in size or effect.
shafiite	a Muslim following Shafii's school of law.
shirk	association of other beings with God; opposite of *Tawhid.*
sifwah mukhtarah	the chosen elite working as the vanguard of Islam, as advocated by Sayyid Qutb.
Silicon Valley	an area in California south of San Francisco, noted for its computing and electronics industries.

spurious	false or fake; of a line of reasoning apparently but not actually correct
tahlukah	self-destruction; suicide.
Takfir	Literally means to declare a person guilty of announcing his/ her disbelief (*kufr*). *Jama`at al-takfir wa al-Hijrah* in modern Egypt readily branded as *kāfir* any body who committed a sin and did not immediately repent; more condemned in its view are the rulers who do not apply Shariah. Still more sinful are those Ulama who do not openly condemn them as pagans, as well as those who reject the *jamā`at's* belief and submit to the laws elaborated by the four great jurists of Islam on the basis of *ijma*, *qiyas*, *masalih mursalah* or *istihsān*.
tali'ah	the vanguard of Islam
tanattu'	the term used in hadith as quoted by Muslim in his *al-Sahih*, signifies to go beyond the limits in the utterance as well as action; strictly prohibited in Islam.
taqlid	following or imitation of a legal expert by a non-expert; is generally viewed negatively and is opposed to *ijtihad*.
tashdid	being equated with modern *tatarruf* (in Arabic),it qualifies the strictness, austerity and extremism in the religion; clearly declared by the Prophet as unlawful in Islam, because Islam recommends moderation and balance in all the walks of life including religious one.
tayyibāt	all things good and pure.
Ummah	the community as identified by its ideology, law, religion, its group

	consciousness, ethics and mores, culture and art.
unadulterated	not mixed with any different or inferior substances
'usbah muminah	a body of true believers
Westminster	an inner London borough which contains the houses of parliament. Full name City of Westminster.
witch-hunt	a campaign directed against a person or group seen as abnormal or a threat to society.
WTC	World Trade Centre
Zaidiyah	The shia school of law as ascribed to Zayd bin Ali (80-122AH) tilts to some extent to hanafid school in the principles of deduction, individual reasning, ijitihad and in issuing fatwa as Abu Zahra of Egypt has claimed.
zinah	thing or act of ornamentation, beautification taken as source of enjoyment.

INDEX

13/12 (Delhi), 113
9/11 (event) 61, 66, 69, 80, 97, 98, 113, 117, 118, 122, 137, 142, 152, 155, 192, 193, 194, 198
(al) safwah (al) mukhtārah (the chosen elite), 260
(al)Sirat (al) Mustaqim, 271
7/7 see also July 7 attacks/London bombings/ July bombings, 1,22, 29, 30, 31, 32, 42, 43, 47, 111, 112, 113, 117, 131, 136, 147, 148, 154, 194, 195, 198, 212, 241, 268
9/11 Commission, 120, 121, 122

A

Abbasids, 241, 257, 260
Abdul Haq, Abdul Hamid, 259,
Abdul Malik, 222, 225
Abdullah (Jordan's King), 6, 81, 208, 209
Abortive bombings, 160
Abraham, 246
Abu al-Ghait, Ahmad, 6
Abu al-Hayyah, Abdur Raziq, 63
Abu Bakr, 227
Abu Gharib, 48, 121, 139, 195, 199, 204
Abu Hurayrah, 225
Abu Imran, 219
Abu Khadeejah, 25, 26
Abu Marzouq, 7
Abu Rabi, M. 234, 236, 237
Abu Zahra (Shaykh), 281
ACPO (Association of Chief Police Officers), 190
advocates of terrorism, 267
Afghan jihad , 188, 192
Afghan Mujahidin, 199
African National Congress, 175
Ahl al-Kitab, 271
Ahmad, Nazir, 231
AIMMM (All India Muslim Majlis Mushawarat), 210
akhirah, 219
Akhtar, Jawed, 141
Akram (Munir), 18, 19

Al-Abadi, Abdul Salam, 208
Al-Azhar, 7, 8, 212, 213
Albright (Madeleine), 133
Alec Station, 57
Al-Fatiha, 171
Al-Fāyda, 120
Algerian war of independence, 242, 246
Ali, Tariq, 132, 133
Aligarh Muslim University, 153
All India Muslim Personal Law Board, 140.141. 144
all-embracing ideology, 159
all-white Britain, 134
Al-Muhajiroon, 15,67, 145, 182
Al-Qaeda phenomenon, 20, 23
Al-Qaeda, 2, 10, 12, 14, 16, 19, 20, 21, 23, 24, 27, 39, 40, 45, 47, 48, 49, 53, 54, 58, 59, 60, 63, 66, 67, 68, 69, 70, 71, 73, 75, 77, 78, 83, 91, 93, 94, 97, 99, 100, 101, 102, 105, 110, 115, 121, 122, 123, 125, 126, 127, 132, 150, 190, 211, 215, 216, 247, 248, 272, 289
American intervention in the Gulf (1990), 49-51
Americanised Islam, 261, 262
Amorin, Celso, 16
Aneja, Atul, 244
Anglo-American war, 102, 166, 169
animal-rights activists, 178
Annan, Kofi, 4, 110,114
Ansari (Abdul Haq Dr.) 201
Ansari, Abu Ayyub, 219
Ansari, Al-Bara bin Adhib, 222
antagonist (Muslims), 199
anti-Americanism, 135, 138
Anti-Islamism-Anti-Communism, 120
anti-Muslim riots, 194
anti-progressive beliefs, 55, 271
anti-semitism, 188
Anwar, Jawed, 192, 194, 195, 196, 197, 198, 212
apartheid regime, 179
apocalyptic terrorist, 121
aqiqah, 279, 283
Aqsa, Masjid al, 205
Arab League, 6
Arab pop singers, 82
Arab-Israel conflict, 237, 241
Arafat, Yasser, 138
Arafat-dominated (command), 240
Armageddon, 121
Asad Bashar al, 5
Ashariyyah, 213
Aslam (Ejaz Ahmad), 190
Assasins, 237, 238, 239
asserting Islam, 267
Aswat, 30, 31, 56, 58, 66, 67, 68, 69
Ata, Mohammad, 45
Ateyah, Abdur Rahman bin Hamad al, 6
axis of evil (North Korea and Iran), 73
Ayyubi (Salahuddin), 205, 206
Azhar, Masud (Maulana), 45
Aznar (Maria Jose), 65, 200

B

Babri Masjid - Ramjanambhumi, 128

Backlash (anti-Muslim), 146, 186
Badat, Sajid, 60
Badawi (Abdullah Ahmad), 143
Bahisht-e-Zahra, 243
Bai, Abdullah, 94
Bakri, Umar, 228
balance of terror, 122
Balasingham, 111
Bali bombings, 200
Bangash (Zafar, 173, 174, 175, 176
Banna, Hassan al, 250, 251
barbaric attacks, 4, 108
Baroud, (Ramzy), 163, 164, 165, 166
Barroso, Jose Manuel, 4
Basque separatists, 68,102
Bathist Iraq, 48,
Batiniyun, 237, 241
BBC accusing Islam, 185
bearded Mullahs, 171
Beaver, Paul, 27
behaviour (unacceptable), 182
Benedict XVI (The Pope) 201, 202, 203,
Benjamin, Daniel, 121
Benn, Hilary, 19
Bergen, Peter, 45, 54
Berlin Wall, 92
Berlusconi, Silvio, 199
Beslan (terrorism), 139
Bhutto, Benazir, 116
Bibi, Safia, 141
Bibi, Zafran, 142
bin Kathir, Al-Hafiz Ismail, 222
Bin Laden, 57, 65, 71, 121, 123, 124, 125, 126, 127, 176, 241
Bin Laden's Foreign Policy, 121
bin Sabah, Hassan, 237
Binnori Town madrasa, 47
birr, 283
Blair (Tony), 2, 4, 5, 8, 12, 14, 18, 26, 33, 39, 44, 59, 107, 112, 117, 135, 151, 165, 174, 183, 241, 268
bloody stalemate, 82
Bloomberg, Michael, 29
Blum (William), 74, 75, 76
Blumenthal, Sidney, 49, 50, 51
Blunkett, David, 161
BNP (British National Party), 112, 131,
Bonn Conference, 52
Bouey, Kate, 31
brain-washed bombers, 169
Brezezinski, 96
Brezhnew, 199
British racists, 178
British Raj, 194
Bronson, Rachel, 28
Bruk, Jason, 122
brutal invasion, 122
Buddha (Siddartha Gautama), 155
Bukhari, Imam, 224, 279
Bunting, Madeleine, 42, 43
Bush (George W.), 5, 38, 47, 50, 75, 117, 174
Bush Senior, 175
Bush-Blair world-view, 135

C

Calrymple, William 43, 44, 45, 46.
Carlos the Jackal, 204
Carter (Jimmy), 96
Champion of terrorism, 241

Chatillon, 209
Chaudhary, Asaf, 24
Chirac (Jacques), 5
Christ (Jesus) 155
Christan Europe (pagan amd materialisitc) 256,
Christian terrorist- 192,
Christians-only continent (Europe), 205
Churchill (Sir Winston), 95
CIA Asset, 68
CIA Counter-Terrorism Centre, 120, 124, 128
Civilizational problem vs. police problem, 80
Civilizational dialogue, 267
civilizational fall out, 83
civilization-clash mentality, 273
Clancy, Tom, 138,
Clarke (Peter), 61
Clarke, Charles, 11, 183.
Clash between civilization and non-civlization, 200
clash of civilizations, 48 137,268,269
clash of ideas, 199
clergy domination, 65
Clinton (Bill) 49, 196, 200.
Cluster bomb, 164
cluster-bombing civilians, 64
Co-existance (peaceful), 177
cold-blooded murder, 109
Collecctive shame, 147
collective guilt, 112, 115, 176
colour of Allah, 200
conservative Islam, 143,146, 253
Constructive dialogue, 201
Cook, Robin 39, 40, 41, 113
Cooley, John, 96
Corsican terrorism, 102
criminalize the community, 187, 207
Cross-Islam ophobia, 192
Crusaders (Present-day) 119,173, 201, 202
Crutis, Adam 51, 52, 53, 54, 266
cynical propagandist, 175

D

dar al-amn, 236,280
dar al-dawah, 233, 280, 285
dar al-harb, 236, 257, 260, 280, 285
dar al-Islam, 236, 257, 260, 280, 285
dar al-kufr, 233
dawah, 274, 280, 281, 285
Dearlove, Richard (Sir), 49
decontextualizing events, 173
deep-seated hatred, 180
defensive jihad, 286
dehumanize the bombers, 62
de-Islamization of Muslims, 203
dejected jihadists, 82
Delta Force, 58
democratic Islamists, 268
Democratising at the barrel of gun, 135, 166
demonstrative attacks, 24
depoliticised (Muslim) leadership, 196
depraved civilization, 262
destructive minority, 56, 271
deterrance theory, 228
Dhahiriyah, 209
dhimmi, 280, 285
Dobbins (James), 50,51
draconian measures, 61
Dud bombers, 66

E

Eagleburger, Lawrence, 137
Egyptian *jihad* movement, 240
Elizabeth II, 27, 28
Elnashar (Magdy), 13
Engineer (Asghar Ali) 153, 154, 155
Esposito (John L.) 233, 234, 236, 237
ETA (Spain), 64, 66
Ethiopian King (during the Prophet period), 281
ethnic cleansing, 197
ethnocentrism, 167
Euro-Jehadis, 88, 91
European colonialism, 238
European Convention of Human Rights, 107
Evangelical Muslims, 148
evangelicalism of West 241,
evil ideology, 9, 39, 40, 53, 55, 174, 175, 178, 179, 184, 185, 188, 212, 268, 273
evil masters, 62
exclusivist religious (call) 251,
exit strategy, 79
extremist ideology, 179, 183, 241, 245
extremism (the causes), 273-286
extremist minority, 14

F

Fadlallah, Shaikh' 239, 240
Faisal, Saud al, 207
Falluja, 48, 77, 88, 134, 135, 168
Farah, Joseph, 55
Faris, Iyman, 69
far-right extremists, 134
fasad, 194, 226, 227
Fatwa culture, 146
fatwa, 10, 144, 146, 151, 170, 187, 207, 209, 210, 239, 269
Fayda, 118, 119, 120
Fidais, 237, 241
Field, Frank, 46
finger-pointing exercise, 173,
fitrah, 276, 280
Flat Earth Society, 168, 171
Forced Islamization, 262, 266
forced liberalism, 82
forcible conversion, 262, 265
FOSIS (Federation of Students Islamic Society, Britain) 215.
Franconian crusader lords, 241
Free Speech Zoning, 72
Friedman (Thomas L.) 77-81, 121,

G

G-8 (Summit), 2, 4, 5, 41, 110, 111, 132,
Galderoli, Reberto, 199
Galloway, George, 37, 211,
Gandhi (Mahatma), 153, 155, 156
Ganguly (Swagato), 95, 96
Gannoushi, Somaya, 233
Gardner, Frank, 38, 212
Gazali al, (Abu Hamid) 279
GCC (Gulf Cooperation Council), 6
Germail, Lindsey, 12, 32
Ghazi, 253
Ghazy, Prince, 209
ghuluw (excessiveness), 271, 275

GIA (Algerian Islamic Armed Group), 102
Global citizens, 94,98
Global struggle against violent extremism. See also GSAVE, 91
global terrorist, 236, 240
globalisation of democracy, 88
globalisation of terrorism, 92
glorifying (terrorist violence), 77, 107, 181
Glover (Jonathan) 61, 62.
godfather of resistance, 250
godfather of terrorism, 250
God's legislative authority, 262
Goss (Porter) 56,
Graham, Billy 246.
Greenaway, Peter 45,
GSAVE, 91, 94
Gujarat riots, 92, 95
Gulf sheikhdoms,200, 201.
Gurdwara 9, 153.
GWOT (global war on terror) 49, 50, 51, 90, 91,

H

Haddad, Nabil, 209
halal, 185, 273, 277, 278
Hamas.Islamic Jihad, 240, 244
Hamas, see also *Harakah al-muqawamah al-Islamiya*, 6, 7, 68, 240
Hamdi, Issac, 23
Hamzah (bin Abdul Muttalib), 221
Harakah al-muqawamah al-Islamiyah, see also Hamas 240.
haram, 197, 213, 273, 277, 278
harmonious co-existence, 181
Hartford Seminary, 234, 237
Harvard of Jehad, 81, 91
Hasan (bin Ali) al, 274.
hate material, 15, 115

hate material, 15, 115

haumane Islam, 140
Hekmatyar (Gulbadin) 96
Henshall (Ian) 64, 65, 66
heretical innovation, 174
Hewitt, Thomas (Bishop), 8
hijab 179, 185
Hindu aggression, 288
Hindu India, 96
Hindustwa, 83,
Hiro (Dilip), 97, 98, 99.
Hitler (Adolf) 95
Hizb al-Tahrir (Britain), 10, 15, 183, 184
Hizbullah, 239, 240, 243, 244
holocaust, 193
holy warriors, 188, 192
homicidal maniac, 60
Hottinger (Arnold) 204, 205,
Hudood Ordinance (Pakistan) 141, 142
Human Rights Act (India, 1993), 109
humane Islam, 140
humanize (the bombers), 58
Huntington (Samuel P.) 58, 268
Husain, Hasib 11, 43,94
Husayn bin Ali, 274, 278
Hussain, Osama, 23
Hussain, Zakir, 160
hypocrite rulers, 123

I

Ibadhis, 213
Ibn Abbas. Abdullah, 221

Ibn Abdul Wahhab (Muhammad) 169, 172
Ibn al-Arabi, Qadi Abu Bakr, 279.
Ibn al-Jawzi, 282, 293
Ibn Hazm, 284
Ibn Khaldun, 147
Ibn Khuwaz Mandad, 225
Ibn Majah, 279
Ibn Qayyim, 264, 268
Ibn Taymiyah/Taimiyah 172, 223.
Ibn Umar (Abdullah) 273, 274.
Ibrahim, Mukhtar Said, 23
ICG (International Crisis Group) 116, 117
identity-based Islam, 267
ideology of compassion, 133
ideology of terrorism, 109
IHF (International Helsenki Federation for Human Rights) 209.
IHRC (Islamic Human Rights Commission), 183, 186.
Ihsan, 274, 283.
ijtihad, 274
Ikhwan al-Muslimun al, see also Muslim Brotherhood/ Brotherhood, 241, 251, 259, 269.
Ikramah, 225
Illegitimate children, 262
Illegitimate targets, 214
imaginary Islam, 101,
iman, 278, 294
imperialist Europe, 101
Informed dialogue, 174, 178
Ingram, Adam 37, 164, 211.
initiative jihad, 286
insurgency attacks, 128.
intellectual terrorism, 171
inter-community debate, 194
Internal plot (9/11), 194
international terrorism, 53, 102
Intifada, 240, 244
intolerant Islam, 187
invasion of kuwait (1990), 133
Iqbal, Allama, 20
Iran-Iraq war, 101, 242
Iraq-terror link, 136
Irish nationalists, 103,182
Irish Republic Army/IRA, 59, 65, 132
irrational hatred for Islam, 180
irtidad, 274
ISI (Interservices Intelligence of Pakistan), 96
Islahi (Amin Ahsan), 225
Islam Hadhari, 146, 147
Islam, Sahara Akhtar ,147
Islamic ban on suicide, 244
Islamic caliphate, 62, 63, 65, 66
Islamic Commission of Spain, 207, 211
Islamic empires, 25
Islamic extremism, 10, 250, 253, 269, 273
Islamic Flat Earth-er, 171
Islamic Foundation, 183
Islamic fundamentalism, 160, 272
Islamic paradigm 156.
Islamic renaissance, 273
Islamic standards, 156.
islamic Terrorism 45, 106
Islamic Websites, 201.
Islamic-Christian Alliance, 207, 209, 212, 213
Islamism as a phenomenon, 238
Islamist extremists, 38, 39, 216
Islamist fanaticism, 144
Islamist militants, 14, 247

Islamist phantoms, 53, 87, 266, 270
Islamist radicals, 135, 151.
Islamo-anarchists, 135
Islamophobic witch hunt, 181, 185, 209.
Islamophobic, 96, 182, 185, 189, 210
Islam's War on Terror, 24
Israeli occupiers, 240, 244
Issac Fati, 23.

J

Jafariyah, 213
jahili, 257, 258, 269
Jahiliyah Jadeedah, see also Jahiliyah madaniyah, 255.
Jahiliyah madaniyah, see also *Jahiliyah Jadeedah*, 171, 256.
Jahiliyah, 257, 258, 259, 260, 262, 290
Jain, Mahavir, 155.
Jaish-e-Muhammad, 47
Jamaat Ahl al-Sunnah, 187, 206
Jamat Islami, see also JI, 190, 201, 216.
Jan, Abdullah, 241
Jassas (Abu Bakr), 219, 220.
Jehad/Jihad (and Terrorism), 7
Jelloun, Tahar Ben, 105
Jenin (massacre), 134,165
Jew terrorist, 192
JI see also Jamaat Islami, 117.
jihadist bombers, 82
jihadist death cult, 83
Jihadist ideology, 188, 189.
jihadist playground, 48
Jihadist worldview 250.
Jihad-without-end, 235
Johnson, Alex, 249
JUI (Pakistan)/Jamiat Ulama-e-Islam, 117
July bombings, see also 7/7/London Bombings, 22, 176, 177, 178, 183, 206
Juma'ah al, 225.
Juma'ah, Sheikh Ali, 208, 209

K

Kaczynskis, Ted ,192.
Kafir, 148.
Karbala, 238, 242
Karzai, Hamid 15, 44, 48, 50, 195.
Kennedy, Charles, 37.
Kepel(Gilles), 45
Kerry (John), 122
Key to paradise, 239
Khalid Sheikh Mohammad, 16, 71
Khan, Ayyub, 216
Khan, Gaffar Khan, 156
Khan, Mohammad Siddique 11, 17, 19,31,43,54, 57, 94, 130
Khan, Syed Ahmad 153, 160
Khan, Zafarul Islam, 186, 187
Kharijites, 171, 172, 175
Khilafah 179, 183, 251
Khomaini, 238, 242, 245
Khudri, Abu Said, 221
khwaja, Maruf, 162
Kosovo crisis, 67, 193
Kreker (Mullah), 102
Kufr, 274, 278

L

Laskhar 117, 153, 230, 231, 232, 233.

legitimate jihad, 254.
Leiken, Robers S, 100
Lesbian intellectual, 168
Lewthwaite, Samantha, 32
Libelous falsity, 171
Liberal Islam Network, 159
Liberation Tigers of Tamil Elam, see also LTTE, 108.
literalist interpretation of Islam, 81
Livingstone (Ken) 2,37,41, 109, 135, 163, 284
Lloyd (Richard), 164
Loftus (John), 67
London bombings see also 7/7, 13, 49, 51, 61, 79, 88, 108, 133, 160, 170, 195, 233
Lone, Salim, 133, 134
LTTE, 108, 111

M

mad mulla, 148
madrasa, 19, 21, 43, 44, 32, 45, 47, 86, 87, 107, 115, 119, 120
Madrid (terror attacks) 105, 153.
Mahfouz Naguib, 77.
MAK, 99
Make Poverty History, 110.
Makkah Declaration, 210
Maktab al-Khidmat/MAK, 96,
malevolent atavism, 174
Malik, Shahid, 12,130
Malik, Taqiuddin, 166
Mandela, Nelson, 175
Manji, Irshad, 168
marfu, 225
marginalization of Muslims, 41, 54
Markaz Dawah wa al-Irshad (Pakistan), 231
Marr, Andrew, 38, 212
martyrs not suiciders, 218
Masjid al-Aqsa, 209
Masood, Ahmad Shah, 96
Masood, Ehsan, 162
Masri Brigades, Abu Hafs al, 10,
Masri, Abu Hamza al, 24,30, 57, 63, 68, 228
Masri, Muhammad al, 182.
Maududi (Sayyid Abul Ala), 179, 215, 216, 241, 250, 253, 256, 257.
MCB (Muslim Council of Britain) 11, 137,150,152,179,185.
McCarthyism, 176, 180, 183
McCracken, Ivan, 29, 30
medieval barbarism, 174
Meinhof, Baader, 199.
Menezes de, 16,17,58,59,108.
MET (Metropolitan Police in London) 190.
militant ideology, 251
militant Islam, 41, 59, 62
militarization of terrorism, 51
Miller, Arthur, 171
Milne, Seumas, 37,38,39,211,212
Mina,Jehan, 141.
misperceived jihad, 232
Mladic, General, 40
MMA (Pakistan), 14, 15, 115, 116.
moderate Islam, 159.
moderate Muslims, 147, 153, 154
Modi (Narender), 83.
Modood, Tariq, 160.

Mohammad (SAW), 138, 142, 144, 146, 155.
Mohammad VI, King, 142
Mohammad, Omar Bakri, 182
Mohammadiyah, 159
Mohellavi, Losiane, 30.
monolithic Islam, 269
monotheistic religions, 242
moral degeneration, 262
moral relativism, 167,170
morally bankrupt West, 241
morally decadent (west), 252, 253
mortally wounded credibility, 171
Morticia, 60
mosques largely tribal, 189
Moudawana (Indonesia) 142,143.
Moussa, Amr, 6
Moussaoui, Zaccharias, 68
MSD (Muslims for Secular Democracy, India), 141
Mubarak (Hosni), 200, 241
mufti al-jihad, 273
mujahid/mujahidin 40, 101, 117, 122, 134, 215, 218, 219, 223, 231, 240, 259
Multiculturalism, 42, 113, 155, 160, 161, 162, 177.
Mumbai blasts (1993), 128
murderous beliefs, 56, 267, 271
Musa, Ahmad, 181
Musharraf Perwez 13, 15, 20, 21, 22, 56, 96, 106, 115, 116, 138, 142, 200
Muslim apologists, 130, 156.
Muslim Brotherhood, see also Ikhwan al, 172, 251, 253.
Muslim Flat Earth-ers, 171
Muslim Parliament, 187
Muslim Rosa Parks, 171
Muttahidah Majlis-e-Amal, see also MMA 14. 15, 115.
mutual suspicion, 176
Myers, Richard B, 199
mythical enemy, 75

N

Nadwatul Ulama, 259
Nadwi al, (Abul Hasan Ali), 256.
Naheed, Uzma, 141.
Nahyan, Sheikh Hammad bin Zayed al,6,
Naidoo, Kumi, 111,
NAM, 87, 88
nasihah, 201, 217
Nasser, Gamal Abdel, 251
national embrassment, 57
National Intelligence Council, 49, 51
Natta, Don Van, 56.
Navy Seals, 58
Nawawi, Imam, 271.
Nazi (tyranny), 95.
Nazir, Osama, 18.
negotiating with terrorists, 123.
Nehru, jawahar Lal, 87.100.
nerve-centre of Islam, 203
New Age Islam, 169.
new barbarity, 259
New Labour, 123
nifaq, 274.
Nimrud, 246
niqab, 185.
Nizami curricula, 47
Nizamul Mulk, 241
Nokrashi Mohmud Fahmi, 251.
non-fanatical 'insiders' (orthodox) 152.

November 17 terrorism in Greece, 103

O

Objectives of *Hizb al-Tahrir*, 184
Occupational terror, 192.
Occuping West, 241
Occupying Jews 224.
official otherworldliness, 39, 216, 217, 244, 248
OIC (Organisation of Islamic Conference) 207.
OKC (bombing) 66,
Olympic Games, see also Olympics, 39
Olympics, see also Olympic Games 1, 64
one-sided dialogue, 64
onslaught against political Islam, 179
opium poppy cultivation, 119, 199
Oregon case, 60
Oreikat, Saeb 6,
Osama bin Laden 14,31,40,46, 48, 53, 54, 58, 74, 80, 90, 96, 118, 145, 250, 251, 266, 268
Ottoman Empire, 205, 256.
Over-dramatic prose (of Z. Sardar), 170

P

Pacifist *fatwas*, 176
pacifist religion, 213
Pakistani Briton, 14
Palestinian bomber, 239
Palestinian resistance, 66
PAS (*Partai Islam Se-Malaysia), 143*
Pashtun violence, 51
Patriot Act, 72
Pavlovian reaction to morality, 171
Pearl, Daniel, 45, 93
Peerzadah (Shams), 279
Pentagon, 50, 52, 99, 102, 139, 142
perfect sleepers, 109
perfidious attacks, 5
Perira, Alex Alves, 17
perpetrators of evil, 24, 25
perverted faith, 3
perverted reading of Quran, 12, 148
pessimistic, anti-progressive beliefs, 55, 270
Pfaff, William, 161
Phillips, Trevor, 161
pliant *imam*, 179
pluralism (religious), 78, 79, 144
poisonous misinterpretation (of religion), 241
political Islam, 184, 188, 233, 237, 241
political war against Islam, 181
Pope Urban II, 209
popular Islamic movements, 214
post-Westphalia Europe, 100
Powell, Colin, 44
preachers of hate, 56, 267, 271
pre-emptive war, 191
Prevention of Terrorism Act, 61, 135
professional theologians, 261
progressive Islam, 146
progressive Muslims, 251, 255
pro-living vs. pro-suicide, 79

pseduo (intellectuals/scholars), 167, 168
Puniyani Ram, 117, 119
puritan Islam, 251

Q

Qaddafi/Gaddafi (Mu'ammar Muhamamd al,), 67, 90, 200
Qadri, Muhammad Gul Rahman (Mufti), 206
Qardhawi (Yousuf) al, 217-225, 233, 269-284
Qasim bin Fuhaymarah al, 222
Qasim bin Muhammad al, 222
Qassam Brigade, Ezzuddin al, 240
Qassem, Shaikh Naim, 239, 240
qist. 283
qital, 232
Quaid-e-Azam, 20
Qurtubi (Muhammad bin Ahmad), 222
Qutb (Sayyid), 53, 100, 172, 241, 250, 251,252,253, 254, 257, 258,260,261, 262, 263, 264, 266, 283
Qutb, Mohammad, 255

R

radical *imams*, 44
radical polemicist, 49
radical preaching, 182, 186
radicalization (of Qutb), 252
Rai(Milon), 120, 123
Rajghatta, Chidanand, 56, 128
Ram, Vidya, 111, 112
Ramadan (Tariq), 189, 190
Ramda (Rachid), 102
Ras Shiran (terrorism), 200
Rashmee (Roshan Lal), 92, 93, 94
Rawi, Bisher al, 67
Razi (Fakhruddin), 222
Red Army, 122
Red Brigade (Italy), 199
Reddy (Muralidharan), 115, 116, 117
Reese (Charley), 72, 73, 74
reformulating Shariah, 140
Regan, Ronald, 117
Reichstag Fire, 68
Reid (Richard), 93, 94
rejectionist call of Islam, 250
religious excessiveness, 272
religious extremism, 32, 45, 212, 255, 252, 275, 276, 278, 279
Renaissance, 187
renegades from Islam, 172, 175
repressed intellectuals, 167
repressive Egyptian state, 252
repressive rulers, 120, 175
resistance Vs terrorism, 175
resistant Islam, 267, 271
retrogressive thinking, 20
Reuter (Christoph), 237, 238, 239
Revolutionary Guards, 243
Ribentrop, Joachim Von, 95
Rice (Condoleezza), 133
Richard (The Leonheart), 206
Rida, Rashid, 223
right-wing Islamists, 119, 120
rogue states, 142
Roosevelt (Theodore), 95
rooting out cancer, 80
Rowley (Coleen), 68
Roy, Olivier 101,
Roy, Ranjan, 100, 101

Royal Institute of International Affairs, 49
Rudolphs, Eric, 192
Rum, Maulana, 155
Rumsfeld, Donald, 44, 51, 76, 98, 199
Rushdie, Salman, 141, 146, 150, 151, 160, 176

S

"shoddy perversion (of Islam), 112
Sachs, Jeffrey, 110
Sacraine, Iqbal (Sir), 11, 150, 151, 152
Saddam (Hussain/Hussein), 25, 90, 98, 99, 198, 238, 241
Saeed, Hafiz Mohammad, 231
Sageman (Marc), 94
Sajid, Mohammad, 162
Salafi, Jihadis, 44, 46, 188
salafist/wahabist teachings, 192
Salam, Ziyaus, 97
Sanbhali (Ateequr Rahman), 228, 229, 230
Sangh Pariwar, 159
Sardar (Ziauddin), 135, 137, 139, 144, 149, 170, 171, 172, 173, 215, 251, 252
Sarkozy, Nicolas, 103
Satanic Verses, 150, 154,176, 177, 180, 181
Saudi dissident, 186
Scheuer (Michael), 55, 120, 121, 122, 123
Schroeder, Gerhard, 5
secretive extremism, 44
secular "outsiders", 152
self-criticising (process), 173
self-fulfilling prophecy, 51
self-loathing, 173
self-observed rhetoric, 165
self-proclaimed Islamic state, 145
self-propelling philosophy of Jihad, 236
self-righteous aggressively, 171
self-serving reading of Quran, 150
self-styled traditionalists, 171
self-sustaining democracy, 82
Sen, Anita, 89
separatist violence, 128
September 11 (event) see also **9/11**, 2, 8, 54, 59, 145, 165, 167, 284
Shadjareh, Massoud, 186
Shahabuddin, Syed, 210
shared dialogue, 193
Sharif, Nawaz, 116
Sharm al-Shaikh, 20, 22, 190, 200,
Sharma (Rajesh), 102, 103, 104, 105
Sharon, Ariel, 65, 66, 191
Shawkani al, 223
Shaybani al, 220, 222
Shayler, David, 67
Sheikh, Omar, 45, 93
shirk, 278, 282
shoe-bomber, 97
short-termism", 152
Siddiqui, Gayasuddin, 187
Siddiqui, Iqbal N., 176, 213, 214, 215, 253
Siddiqui, Nijatullah, 227
Sikand, Yoginder, 231
Silicon Valley, 46
Simon, Steve, 121
Simons, Lewis, M., 126, 127

simplistic assertions, 174
Singh, Manmohan, 125
Sipah-e-Sahabah, 120
Sistani, Ayatollah Ali, 208, 209
Sonnessa, Antonietta, 23
soul-searching, 44
spiritual viciousness, 262
Srebrenica (massacre), 40
Stalin (Joseph), 95
state terrorism, 202
status quists, 153
Stock (Raymond), 77
Straw, Jack, 5, 16
suffocating atmosphre (in the mosques), 189
suicide bomber, 11, 13, 16, 19, 25, 27, 31, 40, 56, 78, 79, 81, 82, 91, 92, 105, 110, 115, 133, 138, 141, 157, 191, 192, 215, 223, 242, 243, 247
suicide bombing, 25, 32, 79, 84, 191, 192, 194, 201, 217, 221, 228, 241, 243, 244, 245
suicider and *mujahid* (difference), 218
sunnahs of Allah, 275, 279
Sunni Bathists (Iraq), 79
Sunni Council (*fatwa* against terrorism), 206
Sunni-traditionalist-jihadists, 81
Suraiya, Jug, 91, 92
Suroor, Hasan, 146, 147, 148, 149
Swami, Praveen, 230, 231

T

Taba (tragedy), 200
Tabari (Ibn Jarir), 223
tahlukah, 223, 226, 227, 228
Tahtawi (Refa'ah), 251
Takfir, 270, 275
talaq, 143, 144
tali'ah (the vanguard of Islam), 261
Taliban, 14, 45, 46, 51, 60, 81, 93, 99, 149, 188, 253
Talibani, Jalal al, 6
tanattu' (meticulous religosity) 271
Tantawi (Mohammad Sayyed), 7,8, 169, 208, 209
Tanweer, Shehzad, 11, 17, 19, 31, 43, 94
taqlid, 274
tashdid, 271, 275
Taylor (Richard Norton), 47, 48, 49
Taylor, Steve, 29,
tayyibat, 272
terrorism (government-sponsored), 195
terrorist training school, 45, 70
Tharoor (Shashi), 113, 114
Thatcher, Margaret, 132, 175
Truman (Harry S.), 95
Twin Terror, 91
Twin Towers (U.S.), 66, 90, 194

U

UAE (United Arab Emirates), 6
Ujaama (James), 57, 58
UK Terrorism Act, 108
Ukhdud, Ashab al, 223
ultra-conservative, 46
ultra-conservative Islam, 250
ultra-militant, 47

ultra-secularist (Muslims), 252
Umayyads, 257, 260
unadulterated evil, 57
unavoidables of war, 227, 230
United Nations Commission on Human Rights, 209
Urban-II (The Pope), 205
usbah muminah (a body of believers), 260
US- invasion of Kuwait (1990), 133
US-leading terrorist state, 124
US-war in Iraq and Vietnam, 126-128
Uthman (the Caliph), 257

V

Veighs, Timothy Mc, 192
Vietnamese war of independence, 242
violent jihad, 47, 260, 282

W

Wahhabi bomber, 172
Wahhabi misogynist, 172
Wahhabis/Wahabis, 169, 170, 172, 250
Wahhabism, 46, 169, 170, 172, 173, 174, 175, 239
Walia, Shelley, 110, 111
war ethics of Quran, 196
war on Islam, 85, 180, 184
war within Islam, 80
Wasfi (Ausaf Saied), 198-201
Watson (Steve), 66, 68
Watson, Joseph Paul, 69, 72
Western modernisation, 252
Western values, 78, 107
Western-backed dictatorships, 40
Wilkinson, Paul, 47
Win, Thin Lei, 31
WMD (weapons of mass destruction), 52, 99, 165
Wolf, Martin, 161
WOT (War on Terror), 118, 164, 167, 190, 191, 192
Wright, Robert, 68
Wright, Tony, 38
WTC (World Trade Centre), 66, 100, 133, 134, 139

Y

you vote-you die, 80
Younge (Gary), 58, 59, 60
Yusuf, Ramzi, 100

Z

Zaidiyah, 213
Zain, Abdullah Mohd., 143, 144
Zakah, 259
Zangana, Haifa, 241
Zarqawi (Abu Musab) al, 63, 78
Zawahiri al, (Ayman), 45, 53, 63, 237, 266
Zero Tolerance, 106
Zia ul-Haq, Muhammad, 141, 158
zinah, 272
Zionist Crusaders, 46
Zionist Israel, 178
Zu Nuwas, 246
Zubaida, Sami, 162